Node.js for PHP Developers

Daniel Howard

O'REILLY®

Beijing · Cambridge · Farnham · Köln · Sebastopol · Tokyo

Node.js for PHP Developers

by Daniel Howard

Published by O'Reilly Media, Inc., 1005 Gravenstein Highway North, Sebastopol, CA 95472.

O'Reilly books may be purchased for educational, business, or sales promotional use. Online editions are also available for most titles (*http://my.safaribooksonline.com*). For more information, contact our corporate/institutional sales department: 800-998-9938 or *corporate@oreilly.com*.

Editors: Simon St. Laurent and Meghan Blanchette	**Proofreader:** Kara Ebrahim
Production Editor: Kara Ebrahim	**Indexer:** Potomac Indexing, LLC
Copyeditor: Jasmine Kwityn	**Cover Designer:** Karen Montgomery
	Interior Designer: David Futato
	Illustrator: Rebecca Demarest

December 2012:   First Edition

Revision History for the First Edition:

2012-11-28   First release

See *http://oreilly.com/catalog/errata.csp?isbn=9781449333607* for release details.

ISBN: 978-1-449-33360-7

[LSI]

Table of Contents

Preface

Why bother with this book?

PHP is an old language, as Internet languages go, invented in 1995. Node.js is new, very new, invented in 2009. Looking at PHP side by side with Node.js gives you a bird's eye view of where web servers started, how far they have come, and what's changed. But, more importantly, it shows what hasn't changed—what the industry as a whole has agreed are good practices—and a little bit of what the future holds.

The biggest difference between PHP and Node.js is that PHP is a blocking language, relying on APIs that don't return until they are done, and Node.js is a nonblocking language, relying on APIs that use events and callbacks when they are done. But, except for that, they are surprisingly similar. Both use the curly bracket notation ({ and }) for blocks of code, just like the C programming language. Both have the function keyword, which serves the exact same purpose and has the exact same syntax in both languages. If Node.js shows that blocking APIs are the past, it also shows that a pretty specific variation of the C programming language is the past, present, and future. Callbacks may be an evolution, but syntax is almost frozen.

But beyond just, "oh, isn't that interesting," why bother with this book?

PHP is supported by a zillion cPanel website hosting services. If you develop a web application and want to give it to other people to run, they can install it almost anywhere if it is written in PHP. They can buy web hosting for $10 per month, install your PHP web application, and be on their way.

Node.js is not supported by a zillion cPanel website hosting services. In fact, I don't know even one web hosting service that supports it. But I know that a lot of developers are interested in it and are writing Node.js code. By writing Node.js code, you make your web application code interesting and useful to a lot of developers. If you develop a web application and want to give it to other developers to improve and reuse, they can get your Node.js web application from GitHub or wherever else the source code is hosted.

In a perfect world, you could appeal to both sets of people.

Ours isn't a perfect world, but you can still achieve this goal by porting your PHP code to Node.js code and simultaneously having and developing two working codebases in two different languages.

The Mission

The mission of this book—and when I write "mission," I mean it in the "I really, really, really, really want you to do it" kind of mission—is to convince you to convert some of your PHP code to Node.js code. I don't want you to just read this book. I want you to actually sit down at a computer and take some of your most tired, annoying PHP 4 code and convert it to Node.js using this book as a guide. I want you to see for yourself that PHP and Node.js are not that different. I want you to see for yourself that your PHP code does not need to be thrown away and rewritten in Node.js from scratch. I want you to see for yourself that you don't have to surrender to just living with your PHP code, being a prisoner of the past.

As you will see, converting your PHP code to Node.js code isn't just about Node.js. It is also about improving your PHP code. An important step throughout this book is refactoring and improving your PHP code such that it is easier to convert it to Node.js code. This book isn't just about making a new Node.js codebase. It is about improving your PHP codebase and creating a new Node.js codebase. It is about both codebases: your PHP codebase and your Node.js codebase. Converting your PHP codebase to Node.js can make you a better PHP developer.

If you are a PHP developer, this book is perfect for you because you can learn how to develop Node.js code by using your existing PHP knowledge. You can see how certain code works in PHP, such as reading a text file, and in the next few paragraphs, you can see how exactly the same thing is accomplished in Node.js. Unlike other Node.js books, this book does not describe file handling in general. It specifically compares it to PHP so you can see the nuts and bolts of what it looks like in the language that you know as well as in the language you are learning. You might even find a few corners of PHP you weren't previously aware of, because a few of those PHP corners are central concepts in Node.js.

If you are a Node.js developer already, you have a decent chance of learning PHP from this book. After all, if PHP developers can figure out Node.js by looking at PHP code side by side with Node.js, there is good reason to think that Node.js developers can figure out PHP by looking at the same code. Even better, by comparing Node.js to a specific different language, such as PHP, it will give you a good idea as to how much of Node.js is the same as PHP.

Comparing two languages or, even better, showing how to convert or port from one language to another, is a powerful way to become an expert in both languages. Other books, which deal with only one language, mostly read like step-by-step tutorials or encyclopedias. "This is this," they read, "that is that." They can describe concepts only as abstractions. Other books can't use the powerful explanation of an ongoing comparison of two languages that this book does.

Besides being more effective, a book such as this one can also be more interesting and focus on only the interesting topics. In a run-of-the-mill Node.js programming book, time is spent explaining what a statement is and why every Node.js statement ends in a semicolon (;). That's dull. But when a book is explaining how to program in Node.js in a vacuum without any point of reference (such as the PHP language), there is no alternative. With this book, I can assume that you already know what a PHP statement is and that a PHP statement ends in a semicolon (;). All that needs to be said is that Node.js is exactly the same way. With this book, I can assume that the reader has a specific background—PHP development—instead of needing to write more broadly for people who come with a Python or Microsoft Office macro background.

By proselytizing the conversion of PHP code to Node.js code, I am not saying that PHP code is bad. In fact, I think PHP is a very capable and pretty good language. I am not saying that you should convert your PHP code to Node.js code and then throw away the original PHP code. I am encouraging you to keep the original PHP code and improve it while, at the same time, becoming a skilled Node.js developer. PHP and Node.js are both important.

When first setting out to write this book, I made a very important decision early on: I was going to focus on real-life, practical, existing PHP code. PHP 5 is the current PHP version, but there is still a lot of PHP 4 code out there. This book has explicitly avoided the easy prescription: convert your PHP 4 code to PHP 5 code, then use this book to convert your PHP 5 code to Node.js. No, despite the fact that PHP 4 support is rapidly fading in favor of PHP 5 support, this book takes the much harder road of showing how PHP 4 code can be improved upon and converted to Node.js code without requiring PHP 5 features. Although this book does show how to convert PHP 5 code to Node.js, let me assure you that PHP 4 code is readily convertible to Node.js using this book.

Very soon after making the decision to embrace and address PHP 4 code, I made another decision related to this book: I was going to describe a system of conversion such that the PHP code and the Node.js code would be kept synchronized and working throughout the conversion process. At the end of the conversion process, both the PHP and Node.js codebases would be fully functional and, going forward, new features and bug fixes could be developed on both codebases simultaneously. This decision avoids a much easier approach, which would have been a "convert-and-discard" conversion process where the PHP codebase would be unsynchronized and possibly not working at the end of the conversion process and the developer's only option would be to proceed ahead with the Node.js codebase by itself. This would have made a much shorter book, but would have been a cheap trick—a way to make life easier for me, as the writer, and make the book less useful to you, as the reader.

These two decisions, one to support PHP 4 and the other to support two synchronized PHP and Node.js codebases as an end product, have made this book longer than it would otherwise be, but have also made it eminently practical. This is not a book that you will read once and put on the shelf as an "isn't that nice to know" book. This is a book that you can use for reference to quickly refresh yourself about important aspects of either PHP or Node.js.

By now, you might understand what the mission is and why it might be worthwhile. But maybe you are still doubtful.

Consider the following PHP code, which was taken from a real-world PHP web application that implemented instant message–style chatting:

```php
function roomlist() {
  $rooms = array();
  $room_list = mysql_query(
    'SELECT room FROM '.SQL_PREFIX.'chats GROUP BY room ORDER BY room ASC'
  );
  while ($row = mysql_fetch_assoc($room_list)) {
    $room = $row['room'];
    $rooms[] = $room;
  }
  print json_encode($r);
}
```

Now consider the equivalent code in Node.js:

```js
function roomlist() {
  var rooms = [ ];
  link.query(
    'SELECT room FROM '+SQL_PREFIX+'chats GROUP BY room ORDER BY room ASC',
    function(err, rows, fields) {
      for (var r=0; r < rows.length; ++r) {
        var row = rows[r];
        var room = row['room'];
        rooms.push(room);
      }
      res.writeHead(200, {'Content-Type': 'text/plain'});
      res.end(JSON.stringify(r));
    }
  });
};
```

Sure, the syntax is a bit different. To concatenate strings, PHP uses the dot (.) operator whereas JavaScript uses the plus (+) operator. PHP uses `array()` to initialize an array, but JavaScript uses square brackets ([and]). It's not identical.

But for heaven's sake, it's still pretty darn close. This isn't "fake" code, either: it uses arrays, accesses a MySQL database, uses JSON, and writes output.

The similarities and the possibility of converting PHP source code to Node.js, and consequently the writing of this book for O'Reilly Media, are a direct result of my experience with creating a Node.js implementation of my open source project.

Who I Am

I'm Daniel Howard, the founder and sole maintainer of ajaximrpg, a preeminent browser-based instant messaging (IM) and chat system. ajaximrpg is specifically geared toward playing tabletop role-playing games, such as Dungeons & Dragons, over the Internet, although the role-playing specific features can be stripped away to reveal a general-purpose client. ajaximrpg (*http://ajaximrpg.sourceforge.net/*) is completely open source and available via SourceForge with a full range of supporting services such as a Twitter feed, a Google Group, and a live demo.

ajaximrpg was originally written in PHP 4 with no inkling that it might someday be ported to Node.js JavaScript. But it works on PHP 5 and, now, on Node.js.

Starting in January 2012, it took me a single week to come up to speed on Node.js and do a proof of concept to have my client side JavaScript code detect the installation status of the server side running on Node.js. In a month, I had enough of a few thousand lines converted to enable users to log in and IM each other. It dawned on me that there were general principles at work here, and that these general principles could be laid out in a book to explain how to convert any PHP source code to Node.js and, using these principles, the reader of the book could apply them to his PHP source code much quicker and more accurately than just muddling along as I had.

I put aside my mostly working but not yet completed Node.js implementation and immediately set out to write this book that you now hold in your hands (or view on your screen).

This Book

This book consists of 12 chapters, starting out with the basics and moving on to more advanced topics.

Chapter 1, Node.js Basics

This chapter describes how to install Node.js and use the Node.js executables, node and npm. It also describes how to install the Eclipse PDT and configure it for use for a PHP to Node.js conversion.

Chapter 2, A Simple Node.js Framework

This chapter presents a simple Node.js framework such that individual PHP pages can be converted to Node.js files and the resulting Node.js files will be invoked when actions, such as visiting a URL, are taken against the Node.js web server.

Chapter 3, Simple Callbacks

This chapter explains how to refactor blocking PHP source code such that it can be easily converted to nonblocking Node.js source code that uses callbacks. It presents the concept of linearity as a simple way to analyze and improve PHP source code such that it can be placed in Node.js callbacks when converted to Node.js.

Chapter 4, Advanced Callbacks

This chapter presents a more sophisticated and generic way to refactor blocking PHP 4 source code to simulate anonymous functions, function variables, and closure. For PHP 5 source code, it explains how to use PHP 5 features to actually implement anonymous functions, function variables, and closure.

Chapter 5, HTTP Responses

This chapter explains how to convert PHP output, such as the `print` and `echo` keywords, into HTTP responses in Node.js.

Chapter 6, Syntax

This chapter explains how to convert PHP syntax, such as concatenating two strings, into Node.js syntax.

Chapter 7, Variables

This chapter explains how to convert PHP single and array variables into Node.js, as well as common operations, such as adding and deleting elements from array variables. It also describes how to convert PHP types to Node.js types.

Chapter 8, Classes

This chapter presents a way to implement PHP classes and class inheritance in Node.js with a step-by-step technique to perform the conversion.

Chapter 9, File Access

This chapter explains all the file reading and file writing APIs in both PHP and Node.js. It explains how to convert the PHP file handling APIs into their Node.js equivalents.

Chapter 10, MySQL Access

This chapter describes all the ways that a database, specifically a MySQL database, can be used in a web application. It provides a step-by-step procedure for converting database access code from the PHP MySQL APIs to use the `node-mysql` Node.js npm package.

Chapter 11, Plain Text, JSON, and XML

This chapter explains three data formats: plain text, JSON, and XML. It explains how to convert PHP source code that uses PHP JSON or XML APIs into Node.js source code that uses similar Node.js npm packages.

Chapter 12, Miscellaneous Functions

This chapter provides Node.js implementations for a large number of PHP API functions. These Node.js implementations can be used to speed along conversion and provide an interesting way to contrast PHP and Node.js.

Now let's get started with Node.js.

About This Book

This book is about how to take existing PHP source code and develop new Node.js source code from it. PHP and Node.js have many similarities, but of course, there are some significant differences. By leveraging the similarities and noting the differences, you can use your PHP experience to learn Node.js and, ultimately, create a Node.js web application that is a drop-in replacement for any existing PHP web application that you have.

This book assumes that you are a developer who understands the basics of development, such as creating and then implementing a design in working lines of programming code. It assumes that you are already familiar with classes, functions, and looping constructs. It also assumes that you are familiar with web development, including the basics of how web browsers and web servers interact to create a web application.

Furthermore, this book assumes that you have significant expertise in the PHP programming language. If you do not have a background in the PHP programming language, it is possible that you can use your background in another programming language (e.g., Python, Ruby, or C) and, by reading this book and examining the intersection between PHP, Node.js, and the programming language that is familiar to you, acquire a good understanding of both PHP and Node.js. Not necessarily easy, but possible.

This book can be read straight through as a Node.js tutorial, consulted as a reference to see how a specific PHP feature can be implemented in Node.js, or executed as a step-by-step recipe to convert an arbitrary PHP web application into a Node.js web application. The book was written to serve all these purposes.

No matter how you approach this book, as its author, I sincerely hope that it answers the questions you have about PHP and Node.js.

Conventions Used in This Book

The following typographical conventions are used in this book:

Italic
> Indicates new terms, URLs, email addresses, filenames, and file extensions.

`Constant width`
> Used for program listings, as well as within paragraphs to refer to program elements such as variable or function names, databases, data types, environment variables, statements, and keywords.

`Constant width bold`
> Shows commands or other text that should be typed literally by the user.

`Constant width italic`
> Shows text that should be replaced with user-supplied values or by values determined by context.

This icon signifies a tip, suggestion, or general note.

This icon indicates a warning or caution.

Using Code Examples

This book is here to help you get your job done. In general, you may use the code in this book in your programs and documentation. You do not need to contact us for permission unless you're reproducing a significant portion of the code. For example, writing a program that uses several chunks of code from this book does not require permission. Selling or distributing a CD-ROM of examples from O'Reilly books does require permission. Answering a question by citing this book and quoting example code does not require permission. Incorporating a significant amount of example code from this book into your product's documentation does require permission.

We appreciate, but do not require, attribution. An attribution usually includes the title, author, publisher, and ISBN. For example: "*Node.js for PHP Developers* by Daniel Howard (O'Reilly). Copyright 2013 Daniel Howard, 978-0-596-33360-7."

If you feel your use of code examples falls outside fair use or the permission given above, feel free to contact us at *permissions@oreilly.com*.

Safari® Books Online

Safari Books Online (*www.safaribooksonline.com*) is an on-demand digital library that delivers expert content in both book and video form from the world's leading authors in technology and business.

Technology professionals, software developers, web designers, and business and creative professionals use Safari Books Online as their primary resource for research, problem solving, learning, and certification training.

Safari Books Online offers a range of product mixes and pricing programs for organizations, government agencies, and individuals. Subscribers have access to thousands of books, training videos, and prepublication manuscripts in one fully searchable database from publishers like O'Reilly Media, Prentice Hall Professional, Addison-Wesley Professional, Microsoft Press, Sams, Que, Peachpit Press, Focal Press, Cisco Press, John Wiley & Sons, Syngress, Morgan Kaufmann, IBM Redbooks, Packt, Adobe Press, FT Press, Apress, Manning, New Riders, McGraw-Hill, Jones & Bartlett, Course Technology, and dozens more. For more information about Safari Books Online, visit us online.

How to Contact Us

Please address comments and questions concerning this book to the publisher:

O'Reilly Media, Inc.
1005 Gravenstein Highway North
Sebastopol, CA 95472
800-998-9938 (in the United States or Canada)
707-829-0515 (international or local)
707-829-0104 (fax)

We have a web page for this book, where we list errata, examples, and any additional information. You can access this page at *http://oreil.ly/nodejs-php*. To comment or ask technical questions about this book, send email to *bookquestions@oreilly.com*.

For more information about our books, courses, conferences, and news, see our website at *http://www.oreilly.com*.

Find us on Facebook: *http://facebook.com/oreilly*

Follow us on Twitter: *http://twitter.com/oreillymedia*

Watch us on YouTube: *http://www.youtube.com/oreillymedia*

Acknowledgments

This book is the product of many months of effort by me, of course, but also by several others.

I want to thank the editors at O'Reilly Media, Inc., specifically Simon St. Laurent and Meghan Blanchette, for their encouragement and feedback.

I want to thank Neha Utkur, the book's technical editor, for her enthusiasm and willingness to provide feedback on a whole range of areas that sorely needed her input. Her contribution has made this a much better book.

Finally, I want to thank Shelley Powers for lending a second pair of eyes to review the book for technical accuracy.

CHAPTER 1

Node.js Basics

Let's assume you have a significant PHP codebase that you have decided to convert to Node.js. You will provide both the PHP and Node.js codebases to your users for the foreseeable future, meaning that you will update and improve both codebases simultaneously. But you only know a little about Node.js; in fact, you have not really done any serious development with Node.js yet. Where do you start?

The first thing to do is to download Node.js (*http://nodejs.org/*) for your platform, probably Linux or Windows (yes, they have a Windows version now!). Since installation methods and installers vary from version to version and change over time, this book will not spend time on how to install the current version. Instead, if you need assistance with installation, you should use the online documentation (*http://nodejs.org/*) and, if that fails you, use Google or another search engine to find web pages and forum postings where others have come across the same installation issues you are having and have found solutions that you can use.

The node and npm Executables

Once installed, you will see that a Node.js installation is fairly simple and has two main parts: the main node executable and the npm executable.

The node executable is simple to use. Although it has other arguments, usually you will pass only one argument, the name of your main Node.js source file. For example:

```
node hello.js
```

The node executable will interpret the Node.js code within the source file (*hello.js* in this case), execute the code, and when it finishes, exit back to the shell or command line.

Notice that *hello.js* uses the *.js* extension. The *.js* extension stands for JavaScript. Unfortunately, files with the *.js* extension can contain either client-side JavaScript or server-side Node.js code. Even though they both use the JavaScript language, they have nothing else in common. Client-side JavaScript code needs to be served out to browsers, while server-side Node.js code needs to have the node executable run on it or otherwise needs to be accessible to the main Node.js code that is being run under the node executable. This is a serious and unnecessary cause of confusion.

In some Node.js projects, the client-side JavaScript files are put in one folder, such as a *client* folder, while the Node.js files are put in another folder named something like *server*. Separating client-side JavaScript files from Node.js files via a folder scheme helps, but is still problematic because many source code editors show only the filename but not the full path name in a title bar or tab.

Instead, I have adopted the *.njs* extension for Node.js files and reserved the *.js* extension for client-side JavaScript files in my own projects. Let me be clear, though: the *.njs* extension is not a standard! At least, not yet (and maybe not ever). I have diligently searched using Google, and it is common to use the *.js* extension for Node.js code. To avoid constant confusion between client-side and server-side JavaScript, I use the *.njs* extension for Node.js code, and in your own PHP to Node.js conversion, I suggest that you do the same.

So, instead of using the *hello.js* file given earlier, I would use *hello.njs*:

```
node hello.njs
```

The remainder of this book will use the *.njs* extension for Node.js files.

A simple *hello.njs* looks like:

```
console.log('Hello world!');
```

If you run node hello.njs on this source file, it prints "Hello world!" to the console and then exits.

To actually get a web server running, use the following *hellosvr.njs* source file:

```
var http = require('http');

http.createServer(function (req, res) {
  res.writeHead(200, {'Content-Type': 'text/plain'});
  res.end('Hello World!\n');
}).listen(1337, '127.0.0.1');
console.log('Server running at http://127.0.0.1:1337/');
```

If you run node hellosvr.njs, the command line will intentionally hang. The server must continue to run so it can wait for web page requests and respond to them.

If you start a browser such as Firefox or Chrome and type *http://127.0.0.1:1337/* into the address bar, you will see a simple web page that says, "Hello world!" In fact, if you go to *http://127.0.0.1:1337/index.html* or *http://127.0.0.1:1337/abc* or even *http://127.0.0.1:1337/abc/def/ghi*, you will always see the same simple web page that says "Hello world!" because the server responds to all web page requests in the same way.

For now, the important line in this source file is the first line that uses the Node.js `require()` global function. The `require()` function makes a Node.js module available for use. Node.js modules are what you might expect: a collection of data and functions that are bundled together, usually providing functionality in some particular area. In this case, the `http` Node.js module provides simple HTTP server functionality.

The `node` executable has a number of built-in modules: `http`, `https`, `fs`, `path`, `crypto`, `url`, `net`, `dgram`, `dns`, `tls`, and `child_process`. Expect these built-in modules and their functionality to vary from version to version.

By design, a module resides in a namespace. A namespace is an extra specification that is added to the front of a data or function reference; for example, `http` is the namespace that the `createServer()` function resides in. In Node.js, a namespace is just implemented as an object. When the `http` module is loaded, the `require()` function returns an object and that object is assigned to the `http` variable. The variable does not have to be called "http"; it could be called "xyzzybub" and, in that case, the server would be created by calling the `xyzzybub.createServer()` function.

Why have a namespace? Why not just put all the data and functions as global variables?

Node.js anticipated that new modules with new functionality, such as a MySQL access, would be developed by other people and need to be integrated into the `node` executable after Node.js was already installed on a user's computer. Since the names of data and functions in those modules would be unpredictable, a developer might accidentally choose the exact same name for a function in a module as a different developer might choose for another module. But since a module is contained in a namespace, the namespace would distinguish between the two functions. In fact, an important improvement over previous languages, such as C++ and Java, is that Node.js allows the user of the module to specify the name of the namespace because the user himself assigns the module to his variable, such as `http` or `xyzzybub`.

These new modules with new functionality are packages. A package is a module that can be added to the `node` executable later and is not built into the `node` executable by default. The difference between a module and a package is not very important; it is really just a change of terminology.

The `npm` (node package manager) executable adds new packages to the `node` executable.

To install a package, first use Google or another search engine to find the npm package that you want to install. Often, the package will be found on GitHub (*http:// github.com/*). An alternative to using a search engine is to use the npm executable itself to find the package using the search command.

Instead of the web server that always returns a "Hello world!" page, suppose we want to create a web server that actually serves up static web pages from files on the hard disk. To find a Node.js static file server module, a good search phrase to type into a search engine is "nodejs static file web server". Alternatively, "npm search static", "npm search file", or "npm search server" will list the npm packages that have the words "static", "file", or "server" in their names or descriptions. Using either of these two methods or both in combination (and with a little extra reading and browsing), you will find that Alexis Sellier, a.k.a. cloudhead, created a popular static file server module and hosted it here (*https://github.com/cloudhead/node-static*).

This package can be installed by running the following command line (additional options, such as the -g or --global command line switch, are available to configure the package installation):

```
npm install node-static
```

The npm executable will retrieve the package and, hopefully, install it successfully. Here's the output from a successful installation:

```
npm http GET https://registry.npmjs.org/node-static
npm http 200 https://registry.npmjs.org/node-static
npm http GET https://registry.npmjs.org/node-static/-/node-static-0.5.9.tgz
npm http 200 https://registry.npmjs.org/node-static/-/node-static-0.5.9.tgz
node-static@0.5.9 ./node_modules/node-static
```

The GET indicates that an HTTP GET was used to attempt to retrieve the package. The 200 indicates that the HTTP GET request returned "HTTP status 200 OK", meaning that the file was retrieved successfully.

There are hundreds of npm packages, but a few very popular ones are express, node-static, connect, sockets.io, underscore, async, and optimist.

To implement a web server that serves up static web pages, use the following *httpsvr.njs* source file:

```
var http = require('http');
var static = require('node-static');
var file = new static.Server();

http.createServer(function (req, res) {
  file.serve(req, res);
}).listen(1337, '127.0.0.1');
console.log('Server running at http://127.0.0.1:1337/');
```

At a basic level, this is how Node.js development happens. An editor is used to create and modify one or more *.njs* source files that contain Node.js code. When new functionality is needed that is not built into the node executable, the npm executable is used to download and install the needed functionality in the form of an npm package. The node executable is run on the *.njs* files to execute the Node.js code so the web application can be tested and used.

At this point, three Node.js servers have been presented: *hello.njs*, *hellosvr.njs*, and *httpsvr.njs*. These source files have been so simple that it did not matter how they were created. You could have used any text editor to create them and they would work fine. If you made a mistake, it was easily remedied by editing the source file.

It is safe to assume, though, that you already have a complicated PHP web application with dozens of files and tens of thousands of lines of PHP that you want to convert to Node.js. The conversion strategy will follow a straightforward but tedious step-by-step routine.

The first step will be to create a boilerplate Node.js source file, as described in detail in Chapter 2, that will support the new Node.js code. This boilerplate Node.js code will be enhanced to respond to the specific URLs that are available to be invoked by the client. A web application is, at its heart, a series of URL requests. The objective of conversion is to make a Node.js server that responds to the client in the exact same way as the PHP server. To make this happen, the boilerplate Node.js code is modified to handle each HTTP call and route it to specific Node.js code that will later implement the functionality of the specific PHP page in Node.js.

The second step will be to refactor the PHP code, as described in detail in Chapter 3 and Chapter 4, to make it easier to convert to Node.js code—that is, make the PHP code more Node.js friendly. It may come as a shock, but the conversion process is not just a matter of freezing the PHP code in whatever form it currently is, copying the PHP code into the Node.js source file, and then, line by line, converting the PHP code to Node.js code. Since both the PHP and Node.js code will be improved and have new features added going forward, it makes sense that both the PHP and Node.js code will need to "give" a little in their purity to smooth over the differences between how the two languages function. The PHP code will need to be refactored and make some sacrifices that will allow functional Node.js code to be created later on. At the end of the conversion process, both codebases will look very similar and will be written in a sort of hybrid metalanguage, a collection of idioms and algorithms that are easily ported from PHP to Node.js. The metalanguage will make both codebases look a little odd, but will be fully functional and, with time, will become very familiar and understandable to the developers who maintain and improve both codebases. Even if you plan to throw away the PHP code in the end and want to have pristine Node.js code, it is best to refactor the

PHP code anyway, convert both the PHP and Node.js code into the odd hybrid meta-language, throw away the PHP code, and then refactor the hybridized Node.js code into pure Node.js code. Refactoring PHP code is an essential step for any PHP to Node.js conversion, no matter what your eventual goal is.

The third step is to copy and paste one of the PHP pages from the PHP source file into the Node.js source file. Almost certainly, the Node.js server will then be broken; when the node executable is run on it, it will immediately exit with a stack trace.

The fourth step is to convert and fix the newly added code in the Node.js file, as described in detail in the remaining chapters, such that it becomes working Node.js code. Initially, the Node.js server will not run and will immediately exit with a stack trace. The stack trace will indicate the location of the error, which will be caused by some PHP code that was not completely converted or was not converted correctly to Node.js code. After the problem is analyzed, a conversion technique from one of the remaining chapters will be applied to the entire Node.js file; for example, Chapter 7 shows the technique to convert PHP array initialization using the array() function to Node.js object initialization using curly brackets ({ and }). When the Node.js server is run again, it will get a little further along, but will most likely continue to exit with a stack trace. Eventually, the Node.js code will be good enough such that it will not immediately exit with a stack trace.

It is surprising how much unconverted PHP code can exist in a Node.js source file and not cause the Node.js server to immediately exit with a stack trace. As you become familiar with the conversion process, you will learn just how similar PHP and Node.js are, even such that unconverted PHP code will be parseable by the node executable and will allow the node executable to run and accept HTTP requests and fail only when it needs to actually execute some unconverted PHP code.

Once the Node.js code is good enough that it does not immediately exit with a stack trace, you can begin to test the client against it. The client will usually be a browser, like Firefox or Google Chrome. Usually, when you start trying to use the client, the Node.js code will exit with a stack trace at some point, and then you will need to analyze the stack trace and apply a conversion technique to fix the problem. Over time, you will develop an ad hoc series of test cases that you can execute with the client to reveal unaddressed conversion issues or hopefully to confirm that the Node.js server is running correctly.

At times, it will also help to use a visual diff tool to compare the PHP code and Node.js code; by viewing it side by side with the original PHP code, you can more easily locate issues in the new Node.js code. This will help remind you of conversion techniques that you have not used yet but need to use. It will also help you keep the conversion process on track and under control.

The rest of the PHP to Node.js conversion process is simply a matter of applying a combination of previous steps many, many times until all the PHP code has been converted to Node.js code and the Node.js code works reliably and interchangeably with the PHP version. Depending on the size of the PHP codebase, the conversion process may take months, but—if you are determined—the conversion will be accomplished.

Stack Traces

During the conversion process, you will see a lot of stack traces. A lot. Here's an example stack trace that is generated because the `node-static` npm package was not installed using the npm executable before the *httpsvr.njs* was run:

```
module.js:337
    throw new Error("Cannot find module '" + request + "'");
                   ^
Error: Cannot find module 'node-static'
    at Function._resolveFilename (module.js:337:11)
    at Function._load (module.js:279:25)
    at Module.require (module.js:359:17)
    at require (module.js:375:17)
    at Object.<anonymous> (httpsvr.njs:2:14)
    at Module._compile (module.js:446:26)
    at Object..js (module.js:464:10)
    at Module.load (module.js:353:31)
    at Function._load (module.js:311:12)
    at Array.0 (module.js:484:10)
```

The top of the stack trace shows the code that threw the error. This is not the code that caused the error; this is the code that created and threw the error object.

Below that, the error message inside the `Error` object is shown. This error message indicates that the `node-static` module could not be found.

The remainder is the "call stack," a series of function calls indicated by the word "at" that show the chain of function calls that arrived at the code that threw the error. The call stack is listed from innermost call to outermost call. In this case, the `Function._resolveFilename()` function is the call at the top of the call stack, which indicates that it is the innermost call and thus the one that actually contains the code that threw the error. The `Function._resolveFilename()` function was called by the `Function._load()` function, which was called by the `Module.require()` function, which was called by the `require()` function, which was called by the `Object.<anonymous>()` function, and so on.

After each function call in the call stack, you will see the filename of the source file that contains that function, the last line that was executed (which is either the line that called the function above it or the line that actually threw the error object), and the position in the line that was last executed. In the example, you can see that two source files are involved: *module.js* and *httpsvr.njs*.

The *module.js* file resides inside the node executable; we can guess that because we do not recognize it as one of our files. The *httpsvr.njs* file is part of our own source code. Even though *httpsvr.njs* is referenced only once and is in the middle of the call stack, it is safe to assume that the error was caused by our source code. In general, we can assume that Node.js itself, its built-in modules, and even any installed npm modules are in perfect working order. Even if they are not, we must assume that they are working until we prove otherwise by eliminating all errors from our calling code. Even if we discover that the error originates elsewhere, we have control only over our own code, not over any other code. The solution would likely be to create a workaround in our own code rather than take on the long and slow process of lobbying other developers to fix their code. So, in the end, regardless of where the ultimate fault may be, the first place to focus our attention is on the *httpsvr.njs* file.

The part of the call stack to focus our attention on is:

```
Object.<anonymous> (httpsvr.njs:2:14)
```

This function call is on line 2 at position 14 in the *httpsvr.njs* file. Here's the *httpsvr.njs* file:

```
var http = require('http');
var static = require('node-static');
var file = new static.Server();

http.createServer(function (req, res) {
  file.serve(req, res);
}).listen(1337, '127.0.0.1');
console.log('Server running at http://127.0.0.1:1337/');
```

By cross-referencing the call stack with the source code, the require() function that attempts to load the node-static module is the function call in which the error occurred. This is consistent with the error message: "Cannot find module 'node-static'".

If we look up the call stack, we see the Function._load() function and the Function ._resolveFilename() function at the top. Looking at the name of these two functions, we guess that the Node.js environment is having difficulty loading the module because it cannot find the file that is associated with the module. We can guess that the module file (probably the npm package) is missing because it has not been installed yet. Again, this is consistent with the error message: "Cannot find module 'node-static'".

The Object.<anonymous> so-called function probably indicates that the require() function call was made in the global space, instead of within a user-defined function in *httpsvr.njs*. But that is not always the case. An anonymous object may be generated inside a user-defined function. But farther down the call stack, below the `Object.<anony mous>` function call, we see that the caller was the `Module._compile` function in the *module.js* file. The `require()` function call was made in the global space.

Using all this information, one solution is to try to install the `node-static` npm package:

```
npm install node-static
```

Admittedly, you won't need to do all this analysis every time you see a Node.js call stack. But since you will be seeing many, many call stacks, you should understand how to thoroughly analyze one—especially because catching and fixing errors is what takes 95% of the time in a PHP to Node.js conversion.

In summary, here's the process to analyze a call stack: read the error, look at the error message (if any), take a guess and focus on a particular function call in your own code, look at the code and find the line and perhaps even the position of the error, look up the stack to see if it indicates more detail about what the error might be, and look down the stack to see how the execution of the server got to that particular function call.

Eclipse PDT

Learning how to fully analyze a stack trace is one helpful skill for doing a successful PHP to Node.js conversion. A stack trace is a diagnostic tool for figuring out what is wrong with the code, like an x-ray is used by a doctor to figure out what is wrong with his patient. From a certain point of view, converting PHP to Node.js can be seen as similar to a complex surgery on a patient. You will be performing surgery on PHP and Node.js code. Like performing surgery, it takes a lot of skill and tenacity, but having a good environment can really help, too. Just like the x-ray is a tool used in the operating room, the stack trace will be a tool in the development environment for the conversion. Next, we will discuss integrated development environments, which will provide a sort of "operating room theater" for the conversion process.

Since you will probably be dealing with dozens of PHP files and tens of thousands of lines of PHP and, very soon, dozens of Node.js files and tens of thousands of lines of Node.js, a simple plain text editor will probably not be good enough to keep track of everything and keep the conversion process efficient. A plain text editor will be fine when you are typing in some simple examples to learn how to program using Node.js, but when you are dealing with a large amount of PHP and Node.js code, you will need something more effective.

If you were developing PHP or Node.js code by itself, you could choose a single language integrated development environment (IDE) and use it nearly straight out of the box. Eclipse PDT (PHP Development Tools) is a popular PHP IDE written in Java that is produced by the Eclipse Foundation. Some others are Zend Studio, PHPEdit, and Dreamweaver. On the Node.js side, there are fewer choices, and they are of more dubious popularity and effectiveness. At the time of this writing, I found Komodo Edit, nide, and Cloud9.

However, your objective is to convert PHP code to Node.js code while simultaneously improving and adding features to both codebases. To do this effectively, I recommend using the Eclipse PDT, but with some modifications to help it support Node.js code. Additional knowledge on how to easily compare PHP and Node.js code will be needed to support the conversion process.

Now, before I describe how to set up Eclipse PDT for PHP to Node.js conversion, I should briefly address developers who reject such tools and insist on using simple plain text editors. They say, "I only use vi!" If you are somebody who feels this way, you are free to skip the rest of this chapter and set up your conversion environment in any way that works for you. I am describing the installation and modification of Eclipse PDT here only because it was an essential tool for me to do my own PHP to Node.js conversion project and it will be an essential tool for a lot of other developers as well.

To install Elipse PDT, first download Java (*http://java.oracle.com/*). All the Eclipse IDEs are developed in Java and need Java to run, including the Eclipse PDT. I prefer to install the Java JDK instead of the JRE. At the time of this writing, I am using *jdk-6u29-windows-i586.exe*.

Next, browse to here (*http://eclipse.org/pdt/downloads*). Consider using the Zend Server Community Edition (CE) installation, which includes Eclipse PDT, the Zend Server HTTP server with built-in PHP debugging support, and even the MySQL database. I assume that your PHP web application uses the MySQL database or at least has the MySQL database as an option.

As of this writing, there is a PDT and Zend Server Community Edition link on the Eclipse PDT downloads page. If the link does not exist or you have a different web server already running, download the latest stable Eclipse PDT version that is appropriate for your operating system. Then, skip the next few paragraphs until the text describes installing and configuring the Eclipse PDT. Otherwise, follow the link and download the Eclipse PDT for Zend Server CE. For now, I am using *zend-eclipse-php-helios-win32-x86.zip*. Unzip but do not run the Eclipse PDT yet.

From the same web page, download Zend Server CE itself. At this time, I am using *ZendServer-CE-php-5.3.8-5.5.0-Windows_x86.exe*.

Install Zend Server CE. In brief, choose sensible, mostly default, selections until the Setup Type page. Select the Custom radio button on the Setup Type page, instead of the Typical radio button, and press the Next button. Check the "MySQL Server (separate download)" checkbox from the Custom Setup page. Then finish the installer.

Currently, Zend Server CE shows a browser to configure the way that it operates. In our case, no special configuration is needed for the server itself.

The MySQL database server is installed and configured as part of the Zend Server CE installer. By default, the root password for the MySQL database server is the empty string (a.k.a. "").

Run the Eclipse PDT. Zend Server CE is built on Apache 2 and has an *htdocs* folder. When the Eclipse PDT runs, find and select the *htdocs* folder as the Eclipse PDT Workspace folder. If you are using a different web server than Zend Server CE or Apache, select the document root as the Eclipse PDT Workspace folder so the PHP files that are deployed to the web server can be edited in place.

It is beyond the scope of this book, but if you wish, try to experiment with using the PHP debugger on your existing PHP codebase.

The Eclipse PDT and your web server will be the foundation of your "conversion development environment." Now, let's make some modifications and learn how to use the Eclipse PDT to effectively manage and implement the conversion process.

The Eclipse PDT, by itself, already supports JavaScript files, and since Node.js is JavaScript, it supports Node.js. But because the *.njs* file extension is nonstandard, Eclipse PDT does not recognize a *.njs* file as a Node.js file. So if a *.njs* file (e.g., *httpsvr.njs*) is opened in Eclipse PDT, it is shown as plain text with no syntax coloring or popup code completion like in a regular JavaScript (*.js*) file.

To modify Eclipse PDT to recognize *.njs* files as Node.js files, open the Window menu from the Eclipse PDT main menu and select the Preferences menu item. When you do this, you will see the Preferences dialog box with two inset panes (Figure 1-1). In the left pane, you will see a tree control with a hierarchically organized group of categories and subcategories of preferences. In the right pane, you will see a dialog that allows you to view and edit the preference items for the currently selected category in the left pane.

In the left pane, open the General tree folder item, then select the Content Types tree item. In the right pane, you will see a list of content types. Open the Text tree folder item in the "Content types" tree control in the right pane. Beneath the Text tree folder item, select the JavaScript Source File tree item. When you select the JavaScript Source File tree item, you should see a list box with a single item, "*.js (locked)", in the "File associations" list box along with an Add... button on the middle-right of the pane. Press the Add... button. Once the Add... button is pressed, the Add Content Type Association dialog box should pop up (Figure 1-2). You will type ***.njs** into the "Content type" edit box in that new dialog box.

Then, press the OK button on all the open dialog boxes to store the modifications.

When that modification is saved, JavaScript syntax coloring and code completion will work for Node.js source files that are stored as *.njs* files.

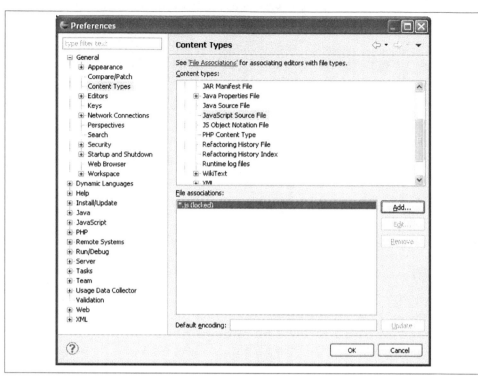

Figure 1-1. Eclipse PDT Preferences dialog box

With syntax coloring working for *.njs* files, you can spot simple Node.js syntax errors by noticing that some words have the wrong color. Visual inspection is an important part of any programming project, particularly in a PHP to Node.js conversion project. Another useful visual inspection technique is comparing the PHP and Node.js codebases using an advanced and very visual diff viewer to find out all kinds of things about the quality and progress of the conversion.

A diff program shows the difference between two files. Simple text-based diff programs usually print out the differences as monochrome lines of text, each line from a single file. That kind of diff program is useless for analyzing a PHP to Node.js conversion. A sophisticated visual diff program is needed. Instead of showing files as alternating lines of text, the files will be shown side by side. Instead of monochrome, color will be used. Instead of showing only which lines are different, the differences within the lines—down to the character level—will be reconciled and shown.

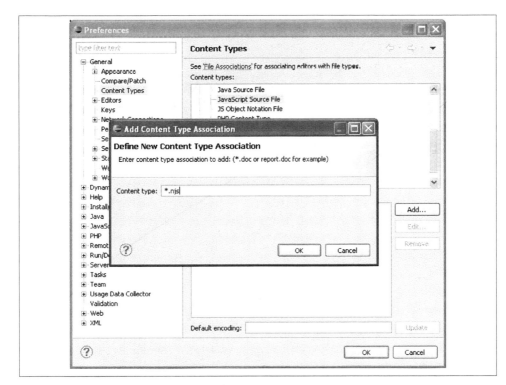

Figure 1-2. Eclipse PDT Add Content Type Association dialog box

Eclipse PDT has an advanced visual diff viewer built in. We can use this viewer to compare a *.php* file to its corresponding *.njs* file. To use the viewer of a *.php* file and a *.njs* file, select both files. Then, right-click one of them and select the Compare With submenu and then the Each Other menu item within that submenu. Figure 1-3 shows a screenshot of the Eclipse PDT viewer comparing a simple *.php* file with its corresponding *.njs* file.

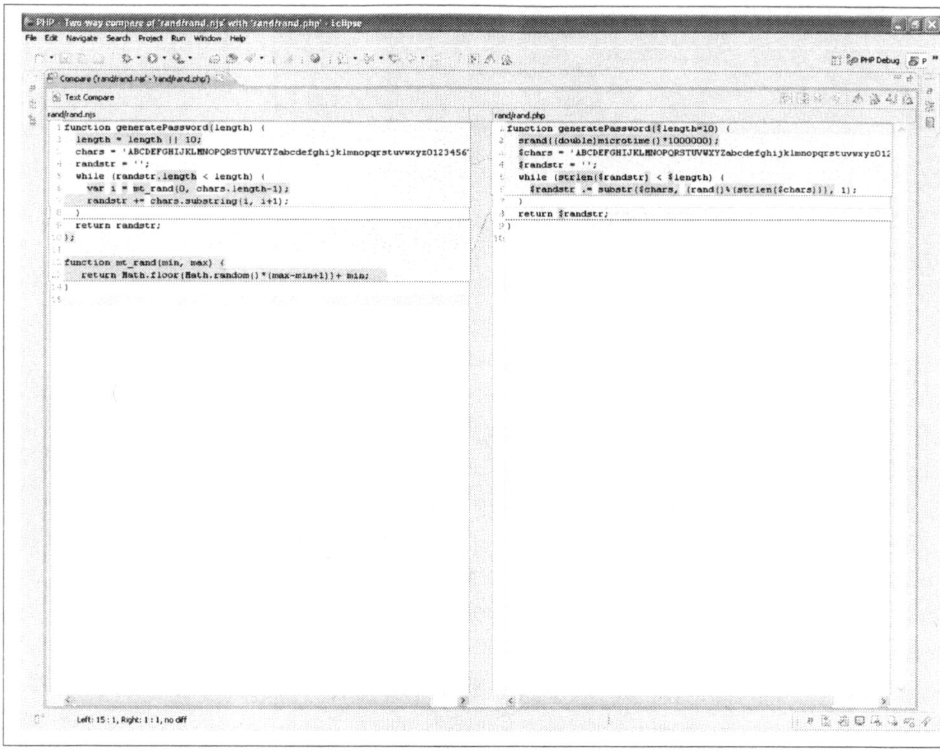

Figure 1-3. Eclipse PDT Compare view

You do not need to look at the figure in detail to either understand how it works or see just how similar PHP and Node.js are.

On the left is the *rand.njs* file. On the right is the *rand.php* file. The differences are in gray; the identical sequences of characters that have been matched are in white.

Notice how many of the lines are almost completely in white, except for a stray dollar sign ($) in gray. Both PHP and Node.js use the keyword `function` in the same place and put the name of the function in the same place. Over the years, it has become common for new languages to eschew variation in syntax structure and adopt a similar syntax for things like defining functions. Also, notice that the `while` statement is very similar.

It benefits the developer to make it easy for the visual diff to compare the *.php* file to its corresponding *.njs* file. The visual diff feature in Eclipse PDT is very good but it is not infallible. Sometimes, moving around code in either file may allow the comparison algorithm of the visual diff feature to find more matches; that is, the visual diff feature will show more white in both files. Copying a function so that it is earlier or later in a file might be irrelevant to the performance and functionality of the code, but might make the visual diff feature match up the code much more accurately. It is worth spending some time periodically throughout the conversion process to experiment with moving code around in each file and seeing the effect on the comparison.

In Eclipse PDT, the code can be edited in a separate window, in the comparison window itself, or in both. If it is edited in a separate window and saved, any comparison windows that show the same file will be reloaded and recompared. Making some tweaks in a separate window and saving the file so that the effect on the comparison can be determined is a common technique.

Naturally, it really helps to keep the code in the same format in both files to use the same names for everything (such as functions and variables), and even to refactor the code in one or both files such that the visual diff feature will find as many matches as possible.

To keep the PHP and Node.js code synchronized and simultaneously improve and add features to both codebases, you will often rely on the visual diff to make sure that the PHP and Node.js code are correct. In time, a developer will develop a finely tuned sense of what is not enough white and what is too much white.

When there isn't enough white, the visual diff feature usually is getting off track and trying to match PHP code in the *.php* file to Node.js code in the *.njs* file, which is not meant to be matched. There will be a lot of gray in the comparison, indicating differences, and not each matches. Experimentation will often correct this issue.

When there is too much white, it often means that there is some PHP code in the *.njs* file that has not been converted completely to Node.js code. Even though the *.njs* file can be parsed and run, too much white indicates that more conversion is needed. Often, eyeballing the Node.js code will indicate specific conversions that have not been done yet. One simple conversion that may be missed is that dollar signs ($) need to be added to PHP variables; dollar signs are not used on Node.js variables. Adding dollar signs to the PHP code will reduce the amount of white, bringing the comparison closer to having the right amount of white.

Visual inspection, especially using the visual diff feature, is much faster than interactively testing the PHP and the Node.js code. Visual inspection can act as a "smoke test" to determine if the conversion is approximately correct. Automated test cases, which are beyond the scope of this book, may also be used to quickly test the effectiveness of the conversion so far.

Throughout the book, there will be opportunities to convert a particular code element of a large amount of PHP code into the corresponding code element for Node.js code. For example, a PHP associative array is created by calling the PHP `array()` function, whereas in Node.js, it is often created by using the object literal notation, which uses curly brackets ({ and }). When the contents of an entire *.php* file are copied wholesale into a *.njs* file at the start of the conversion of the code, the *.njs* file will then obviously contain many PHP `array()` function calls that will need to be replaced by Node.js object literals. A simple way to address this particular conversion issue might be to simply use Eclipse PDT's Find/Replace feature to do a global search for `array(` and universally replace it with a left curly bracket ({); see Figure 1-4.

Figure 1-4. Eclipse PDT Find/Replace dialog box

The operation of this dialog box is straightforward.

Rather than including a screenshot of the Find/Replace dialog box every time that it is needed, this book uses a text shorthand. For the Find/Replace dialog box options in the figure, the text will have the following blurb inserted:

```
Operation: "Find/Replace" in Eclipse PDT
Find: array(
Replace: {
Options: Case sensitive
Action: Replace All
```

The Find/Replace dialog box can be used in two different ways.

One way is to do what I call a "blind" global find-and-replace action, like the example find-and-replace blurb in Figure 1-4. I call it "blind" because it finds and replaces every occurrence in the file all at once, with no warning and no manual inspection. If all the Find/Replace dialog box values are tested and determined to be foolproof, a "blind" global find-and-replace action is fast and accurate. Unfortunately, if the result causes an error, there are only two options: undo the action or perform a new action that corrects the previous action.

The second option for find-and-replace action repair work is worth pointing out. Some-times, it is better to do a simple-to-understand find-and-replace action that will correctly convert 298 code elements and incorrectly convert two code elements than it is to do a complicated find-and-replace action that correctly converts the same 300 code elements. Manually finding and fixing a few edge cases is a worthwhile technique; not everything needs to be fully automatic. Even though PHP to Node.js conversion is a lengthy task, it is not a task that you will be running over and over. This book is not describing "continuous conversion"; it is describing conversion as a one-time event. So manually finding and fixing a few edge cases is a perfectly acceptable technique to get the job done.

A second way to use the Find/Replace dialog box is to do a step-by-step global find-and-replace action. First, the Find/Replace dialog box is used to find the first instance. The developer then examines the instance and decides whether to modify the code manually (which he can do by clicking on the code and without dismissing the dialog box), or to execute the replace (by pressing the Replace/Find button), or to skip to the next instance without changing the current instance (by pressing the Find button again). Here's the blurb for a step-by-step global find-and-replace action:

```
Operation: "Find/Replace" in Eclipse PDT
Find: array(
Replace: {
Options: Case sensitive
Action: Find, then Replace/Find
```

The Find/Replace dialog box in the Eclipse PDT can also use regular expressions. Regular expressions are a pattern matching technique: instead of finding an exact phrase, a regular expression describes a pattern to search for. Each time that the pattern is found, the exact phrase that matches the pattern can be applied to the Replace field. For example, if the `array\((.*)\)` regular expression matches `array(id=>'name')`, the `(.*)` in the regular expression will save the `id=>'name'` text. This saved text is called a capture field, or less commonly, a capture group. In the Eclipse PDT Find/Replace dialog box, a capture field is captured by surrounding it with undelimited parentheses. To apply a capture field to the Replace field, the capture fields are enumerated according to the order that they were captured in the Find field. A dollar sign ($) indicates that a capture field is being specified, followed by the capture field number. For example, $1 in the Replace field indicates the first capture field, which, in the example earlier in this paragraph, would contain the `id=>'name'` text. Very often, there is only one capture field, so it is very common to only see $1 and rarely to see $2, $3, or beyond.

Here's a blurb for a blind global find-and-replace action using regular expressions:

```
Operation: "Find/Replace" in Eclipse PDT
Find: array\((.*)\)
Replace: {$1}
Options: Case sensitive, Regular expressions
Action: Replace All
```

In converting PHP to Node.js, regular expressions are only tangential to the process, so this book will not be giving a primer on how to understand and write your own regular expressions. The regular expressions will be provided as part of blurbs for find-and-replace actions that can be copied to the appropriate fields of the Find/Replace dialog box in the Eclipse PDT, usually verbatim, without requiring you to understand or modify them. If you need additional help with regular expressions or need to understand the rules and how they work, you are encouraged to consult the Eclipse PDT and to use Google or a similar search engine to find websites, blogs, and forums that will answer your questions.

Find-and-replace actions with regular expressions are often more comprehensive and effective than literal find-and-replace actions (i.e., actions where only one specific string is matched). A regular expression allows more variation in what it can match, and with capture fields, it can transport that variation to the Replace field. Often, a literal find-and-replace will be able to match only the beginning of a code element or the end of a code element at one time because the code element can vary in the middle. With a regular expression, the middle can be matched to a pattern that allows the entire code element to be matched in a single find-and-replace action. When the conversion of a code element can be done in a single find-and-replace action, instead of multiple ones, the chances for errors are reduced.

Until now, this chapter has described a range of activities and knowledge about how to set up a development environment for doing a PHP to Node.js conversion. The first thing to do was to download and install Node.js itself and become familiar with the two executables that it comes with. After that, we dug into Node.js stack traces to learn how to read them and how to use them to find what the real, underlying problem is such that the coding issue can be addressed and repaired. Then, we set up the Eclipse PDT as a foundation for a development environment, including a modification for it to understand *.njs* files, geared toward PHP to Node.js conversion. And finally, we learned how to use the visual diff feature and find-and-replace actions that will be very important when doing the conversion.

A capable development environment is essential to efficiency and is the way that big efforts get done. Too often, amateur developers will leap into coding with an inefficient or even an annoying development environment. At first, the development will go quickly in any environment because a small amount of code is simple to improve upon. But as the codebase grows larger, the complexity of the code will also grow and the pace of development will slow down. An inefficient or annoying development environment will do nothing to help the developer with the complexity, but a capable development environment will simplify the knowledge needed and help the developer such that the pace can be sustained and, ultimately, the project finished.

With a PHP to Node.js conversion, it is assumed that a large PHP codebase already exists. At the end of the conversion, it is expected that the codebase will more than double in size: the PHP code will be refactored for conversion, not brevity, so it will increase, and of course, an entire Node.js codebase will be added. The initial PHP codebase might have been created by many developers, but in conversions, there is often so much coupling between the activities that only a single developer will do the majority of the conversion. Even though a primitive development environment might have been acceptable for the creation of the original PHP codebase, a more sophisticated development environment will be needed to convert it to Node.js.

If a project already has an existing development environment, it may not be necessary to adopt the Eclipse PDT. The Eclipse PDT is presented as a workable, prototypical environment suitable only for conversion activities. Alternative development environments can work if they can support and be coupled with additional tools that support the features in this chapter. In summary, they need to be made to support the following syntax coloring for both *.php* and *.njs* files, visual side-by-side comparison between two files down to a word-by-word comparison and not just line-by-line comparison, and find-and-replace actions that support regular expressions.

Now that all the infrastructure for the conversion is ready, we can move on to creating the initial *.njs* file that will host the new Node.js code. In the next chapter, a template for an initial *.njs* file will be presented such that, in subsequent chapters, PHP code can be refactored for conversion and actual PHP code can be copied into Node.js files and transformed into working Node.js code.

CHAPTER 2

A Simple Node.js Framework

In the previous chapter, I presented a development environment along with a general education about how to use it to execute a conversion. In this chapter, we will start using that development environment and begin the actual conversion.

An HTTP Server

In PHP, a PHP file represents an HTML page. A web server, such as Apache, accepts requests and if a PHP page is requested, the web server runs the PHP. But in Node.js, the main Node.js file represents the entire web server. It does not run inside a web server like Apache; it replaces Apache. So, some bootstrap Node.js code is needed to make the web server work.

The *httpsvr.njs* file was presented as an example in the previous chapter. Here's the Node.js code for the *httpsvr.njs* file:

```
var http = require('http');
var static = require('node-static');
var file = new static.Server();

http.createServer(function (req, res) {
  file.serve(req, res);
}).listen(1337, '127.0.0.1');
console.log('Server running at http://127.0.0.1:1337/');
```

How does this work?

As described in the previous chapter, the Node.js `require()` API function makes a module available for use. The first two lines show a built-in module and an external module:

```
var http = require('http'); // built-in module
var static = require('node-static'); // external module
```

If you installed Node.js and followed the examples in the previous chapter, the node-static npm package, which contains the node-static external module, will already be installed. If not, install it now using the npm executable:

```
npm install node-static
```

The third line is a little tricky:

```
var file = new static.Server();
```

The node-static module wants to provide the Node.js server with as many file serving objects as needed rather than limit the client to a single file serving object. So, instead of using the module itself as the file serving object, the file serving object is created by calling a constructor function. A constructor function is a function that is designed to be used with the new keyword. Using the new keyword and invoking the constructor function creates a new object.

In this case, the module object is named static. Inside the module object, there is a key named Server, which has a value that is a constructor function. The dot (.) operator indicates this relationship such that the new operator is properly applied. A newly constructed file serving object is created and stored in the file variable.

The file serving object constructor can take zero or one arguments. If no arguments are provided, the file serving object uses the current directory (folder) as the HTTP server's top-level documents directory. For example, if the *httpsvr.njs* is run in the *ferris* directory and a web browser such as Google Chrome goes to *http://127.0.0.1:1337/hello.html*, the file serving object will look for the *hello.html* file in the *ferris* directory. However, if a web browser goes to *http://127.0.0.1:1337/exit/goodbye.html*, the file serving object will look for the *goodbye.html* file in the *exit* directory inside the *ferris* directory.

However, when one argument is passed to the file serving object constructor, the file serving object will look for files in the directory specified in the argument. For example, if the .. string is passed as the argument, the newly created file serving object will look for files in the parent directory of the current directory.

The require() function takes only one argument, the name of the module to load. There is no flexibility to pass additional arguments to the module while loading. Since it is desirable to specify a directory to load files from as an argument, it is best that loading the module be completely separate from specifying where to load files from.

After creating a file serving object, the HTTP server object is created to accept HTTP requests and return the file to the client, probably a web browser:

```
http.createServer(function (req, res) {
  file.serve(req, res);
}).listen(1337, '127.0.0.1');
```

This code can be rewritten as three statements to make it easier to understand:

```
var handleReq = function(req, res) {
  file.serve(req, res);
};
var svr = http.createServer(handleReq);
svr.listen(1337, '127.0.0.1');
```

The first statement takes up three lines. It defines a variable named handleReq that, instead of containing a "normal" value like a string or a number, contains a function. In Node.js, functions can be assigned to variables, just like strings and numbers. When a function is assigned to a variable, the function itself is called a *callback*, and for our convenience, the variable that it is assigned to is called a *callback variable*. A callback variable is defined nearly the same as a regular function is defined, except that a callback can be unnamed and is preceded by a variable assignment.

In this case, the callback expects two parameters. The first parameter, req, contains all the data related to the HTTP request. The second parameter, res, contains all the data related to the HTTP response. In this implementation, the file serving object, file, decodes the HTTP request, finds the appropriate file on the hard disk, and writes the appropriate data to the HTTP response such that the file will be returned to the browser. The node-static module was specifically written with this in mind, so that the file serving object could return hard disk files with only one line of code.

The fourth line creates an HTTP server and an HTTP request handling loop that will continuously wait for new HTTP requests and use the handleReq callback variable to fulfill them:

```
var svr = http.createServer(handleReq);
```

Inside the createServer() function, the handleReq callback variable will be invoked:

```
function createServer(handleReq) {
  while (true) {
    // wait for HTTP request
    var req = decodeHttpRequest(); // somehow decode the request
    var res = createHttpRequest(); // somehow create a response object
    handleReq(req, res); // invoke handleReq()
    // send HTTP response back to client based on "res" object
  }
}
```

Like functions (but unlike other types of variables), a callback variable can invoke the function that it contains. As you can see, invoking the handleReq callback argument is identical to calling a standard function; it just so happens that handleReq is not the name of a function but is the name of a callback variable or argument. Callback variables can be passed to functions as arguments just like other kinds of variables.

Why not just hardcode the file.serve() call into the createServer() function? Isn't serving files what a web server does?

```
function createServer(handleReq) {
  while (true) {
    // wait for HTTP request
    var req = decodeHttpRequest(); // somehow decode the request
    var res = createHttpRequest(); // somehow create a response object
    file.serve(req, res); // hardcode a reference to the "node static" module
    // send HTTP response back to the client based on "res" object
  }
}
```

Yes, but passing a callback to the createServer() function is more flexible. Remember: the http module is built into Node.js and the node static module is an npm package that was installed separately. If the file.serve() call was baked into the create Server() function, using a different module instead of the node static module or adding additional custom HTTP request handling code would require copying and pasting the entire createServer() function just so a line in the middle could be tweaked. Instead, a callback is used. So, if you think about it, a callback is a way for some calling code to insert some of its own code into a function that it is calling. It is a way to modify the function that it is calling without having to modify the code of the function itself. The function being called, createServer() in this case, has to expect and support the callback, but if it is written with the callback in mind, a caller can create a callback that matches what is expected and the called function can use it without knowing anything about the calling code. Callbacks enable two pieces of code to successfully work together, even though they are written by different people at different times.

In this case, a callback function is passed to allow the caller to handle an HTTP request in whatever way that it sees fit. But, in many other cases, a callback function is passed as an argument so that the callback function can be invoked when an asynchronous operation has been completed. In the next chapter, this use of callback functions will be covered in detail.

The fifth line uses the svr object to listen on port 1337 on the '127.0.0.1' computer, a.k.a. the "localhost" computer (meaning the computer that the Node.js server is running on):

```
svr.listen(1337, '127.0.0.1');
```

It should be pointed out that it is much more likely that the HTTP request handling loop is in the listen() function instead of the createServer() function. But for the purposes of explaining callbacks, it really does not matter.

Since the svr variable and the handleReq variable are used only once and can be replaced with more succinct code, the three statements are combined into one:

```
http.createServer(function(req, res) {
  file.serve(req, res);
}).listen(1337, '127.0.0.1');
```

The last statement of the *httpsvr.njs* file writes a message to the console so that the person who started the HTTP server will know how to access it:

```
console.log('Server running at http://127.0.0.1:1337/');
```

The *httpsvr.njs* file makes a basic Node.js HTTP server. Now we move all the files that constitute the web application from the current web server that supports PHP to the same directory that the *httpsvr.njs* file resides in. When the *httpsvr.njs* file is started, these files—which include all the HTML, CSS, client-side JavaScript, image files (e.g., PNG files), and other assorted files—will be delivered to the client, probably a web browser, and work just as they always have. The client needs to be directed only to the correct port (e.g., 1337) to load these files from Node.js instead of the original web server. The only reason that the web application will break is that it is still written in PHP, but since HTML, CSS, client-side JavaScript, and image files are all handled and executed exclusively on the client, they will work as much as they can until a PHP file is needed. The *.php* files can be moved to the Node.js server, too, but they will not work because Node.js cannot interpret *.php* files.

The key difference between the *.php* files and all the other files is that the *.php* files are interpreted and the result of the interpretation is passed back to the client as an HTTP response. For all other files, the contents of the file are read and then written directly into the HTTP response with no interpretation. If the *.php* file is not interpreted, the client receives the PHP source code, which it does not know how to use. The client needs the output of the source code, not the source code itself, in order to work. A PHP to Node.js conversion boils down to writing Node.js code that will produce the exact same HTTP response in all cases that the PHP source code would have produced. It seems simple, but it is still a ton of work.

To start with, a Node.js local module will be created for each *.php* file. For the purposes of this book, a local module is a local *.njs* file that can be loaded by the main *.njs* file (i.e., *httpsvr.njs*) using the Node.js require() API function. To create a Node.js local module for a *.php* file, we will create an empty *.njs* file in the same directory as the *.php* file using the same filename but a different extension. For example, for *admin/index.php*, create an empty *admin/index.njs* file.

For your own conversion effort, you will have to use your own judgment. In some cases, there may be so many *.php* files that creating the corresponding *.njs* files will be a lot of busywork, so it may be better just to do a few at first. In other cases, there may be only a few *.php* files, so it may make sense to create all the empty files at once.

Once there is a corresponding *.njs* file for some *.php* files, choose one of the *.php* files and edit its corresponding *.njs* file:

```
exports.serve = function(req, res) {
  res.writeHead(200, {'Content-Type': 'text/plain'});
  res.end('admin/index.njs');
};
```

Type this Node.js code into the *.njs* file and change the `res.end()` function call implementation to indicate the correct path (in this case, *admin/index.njs*) to the particular *.njs* file that is being edited.

With this simple code, the *.njs* file is now a Node.js module with an `exports.serve()` stub function implementation. A stub implementation is a placeholder with some very simple code that will be replaced with a serious implementation later. The `exports.serve()` stub function takes two parameters that correspond to the parameters to the callback function that is passed to the `http.createServer()` function in *httpsvr.njs*. The `req` parameter is the HTTP request object and the `res` parameter is the HTTP response object.

When the `exports.serve()` function is invoked, the stub implementation will return an HTTP response with a Content-Type HTTP header set to "text/plain" with the content containing the path name of the file that is being invoked. By customizing the stub implementation, it will be a little easier to debug later, in case a coding error leads to an HTTP request for one file accidentally ending up in another file.

Once you have a *.njs* file with a `exports.serve()` stub function, you should modify the *httpsvr.njs* file to invoke the `exports.serve()` function at the appropriate time. But first, the module with the `exports.serve()` function must be made accessible to the *httpsvr.njs* file. The Node.js `require()` API function can load local modules as well as built-in module and npm packages:

```
var admin_index = require('./admin/index.njs');
```

To load a local module, the argument must contain a path name with the `./` string at the beginning. The `./` indicates that this is a path name to a local module and not a name of a built-in module or npm package.

In this example, the local module is assigned to the `admin_index` variable. Depending on the number of *.php* files that are in a web application (and, thus, the number of corresponding *.njs* files), it may be convenient and less confusing to use a variation of the path name as the name of the variable that holds the module that contains the Node.js code that implements the functionality of a particular *.php* file.

To route an HTTP request for a particular PHP page to the correct Node.js local module, the callback passed to the `http.createServer()` function needs to be modified to identify and pass the HTTP request to the appropriate Node.js local module. Using a simple comparison in an `if` statement, the HTTP request is examined to see if it is requesting a particular *.php* file and if it is, it is routed to the appropriate Node.js local module instead of passing it to the `node static` npm package (i.e., the `file` variable):

```
http.createServer(function (req, res) {
  if (url.parse(req.url).pathname == '/admin/index.php') {
    admin_index.serve(req, res);
```

```
  } else {
    file.serve(req, res);
  }
}).listen(1337, '127.0.0.1');
```

This source code uses the `http` and `url` Node.js built-in modules to implement a simple but functional Node.js server. If desired, more sophisticated optional packages, such as the `express` Node.js npm package, could be installed and used instead.

For this implementation, the `url` built-in module is needed to parse the URL in the HTTP request. The following Node.js code uses the `require()` API function to access the `url` built-in module:

```
var url = require('url');
```

Here we continue with our previous example. If the HTTP request is requesting the */admin/index.php* URL resource, the `admin_index` local module interprets the request and provides the HTTP response instead of allowing the `file` variable to read the file and return it as a static page.

You may notice that the URL in the HTTP request is tested against */admin/index.php* instead of */admin/index.njs*. Since the browser handles requests for *.php* files with custom code, it can handle *.php* file requests in any way that it likes, including ignoring the *.php* file on the hard disk and running Node.js code instead. An HTTP request is a request, not a demand, and the Node.js server can force *.php* file requests to be handled without using PHP at all. In Node.js, the *.php* file reference becomes a unique identifier to perform a particular action; the *.php* extension no longer means PHP. The `if-else` statements in the callback now just match a unique path with a specific piece of Node.js code. The semantic meaning of the *.php* extension is ignored.

Most likely, the client is requesting *.php* files either because the user clicked on a link in an HTML page that had the *.php* file as a hyperlink reference or because it is part of a JavaScript AJAX call. To change this, the HTML and client-side JavaScript files would need to be modified to refer to *.njs* files instead of *.php* files. Whether or not you make these changes depends on your situation. On the plus side, removing the *.php* file references eliminates confusion by other developers accessing your code, who may wonder why there are PHP references in a Node.js codebase. On the minus side, removing the *.php* file references creates technically unnecessary differences between the PHP and Node.js codebases.

Having walked through a step-by-step explanation with a single *.php* file, let's put it all together and do the same thing with multiple *.php* files:

```
var http = require('http');
var static = require('node-static');
var file = new static.Server();
var url = require('url');
var index = require('./index.njs');
var login = require('./login.njs');
```

```
var admin_index = require('./admin/index.njs');
var admin_login = require('./admin/login.njs');

http.createServer(function (req, res) {
  if (url.parse(req.url).pathname == '/index.php') {
    index.serve(req, res);
  } else if (url.parse(req.url).pathname == '/login.php') {
    login.serve(req, res);
  } else if (url.parse(req.url).pathname == '/admin/index.php') {
    admin_index.serve(req, res);
  } else if (url.parse(req.url).pathname == '/admin/login.php') {
    admin_login.serve(req, res);
  } else {
    file.serve(req, res);
  }
}).listen(1337, '127.0.0.1');
console.log('Server running at http://127.0.0.1:1337/');
```

There are essentially two modifications: (1) a set of require() function calls have been added with one require() function call per *.php* file; and (2) a set of else-if statements have been added with one else-if statement per *.php* file. In this case, this modified version of *httpsvr.njs* is handling four *.php* files: */index.php*, */login.php*, */admin/index.php*, and */admin/login.php*. For any web application that is converted from PHP to Node.js, each *.php* file in the application will cause both a new require() function call and an else-if statement to be added so that the *httpsvr.njs* file can properly route an HTTP request for a *.php* file to a specific and separate *.njs* file that implements the PHP code in Node.js instead.

As described earlier, a corresponding *.njs* file will be created for each *.php* file. For the example with four *.php* files, there will be four *.njs* files: *index.njs, login.njs, admin/index.njs*, and *admin/login.njs*. The files will have the same code except for a slight modification to indicate the path name of the file:

```
exports.serve = function(req, res) {
  res.writeHead(200, {'Content-Type': 'text/plain'});
  res.end('admin/index.njs');
};
```

The exports.serve() function in each *.njs* file will ultimately contain the Node.js code that exactly and completely emulates the operation of its corresponding *.php* file. The stub implementation that just returns the name of the *.njs* file as an HTTP response will be erased. The PHP code from the corresponding *.php* file will be copied and pasted into the exports.serve() function, and through a series of transformations and conversion recipes, the PHP code will become Node.js code that does the exact same thing. But we are not quite ready to do that yet.

Predefined PHP Variables

When a web server that supports PHP executes a PHP page, it does not supply a raw HTTP request to the PHP page and then execute the page. If it did that, every PHP page would have to add a lot of code to decode the raw HTTP request and put the values in a more convenient format. Instead, the PHP engine decodes the raw HTTP request itself and populates a bunch of well-known PHP global variables with the equivalent data. PHP pages rely on these global variables to be correctly populated in order to work.

Since the basic approach is to copy the PHP page into the local module and transform it to Node.js code, we will need to implement these global variables in Node.js in order for the converted page to work. By analyzing the PHP page, we can determine which global variables it relies upon. It is not necessary to implement every single global variable that the PHP engine makes available. Instead, we can just implement the ones that are used.

Five PHP predefined global variables that are commonly used are $_GET, $_POST, $_COOKIE, $_REQUEST, and $_SESSION.

An HTTP request is sent with an HTTP action, also called a method or a verb. An HTTP GET action is very simple: the client is asking the server to retrieve a page. When a user types a URL into the address bar of a browser, he is typing in an HTTP GET request.

The HTTP GET request may have some arguments in the form of name/value pairs. These arguments are often called query arguments or the query string. A user can add these arguments manually to a browser's address bar by putting a question mark (?) at the end of the URL and typing name/value pairs separated by ampersands (&). The name/value pairs themselves separate the name from the value by using an equals sign (=). Here's an example:

```
http://localhost:1337/index.php?theme=green&tab=users&fastload=true
```

The name/value pairs in the example are: theme=green, tab=users, and fastload=true. When a PHP page gets an HTTP GET request like this one, the PHP engine extracts the name/value pairs from the raw HTTP GET request and puts them in the predefined PHP $_GET array. The name becomes the key or index into the $_GET array, and the value becomes, well, the value. For the previous example URL, the $_GET array looks like this:

```
$_GET['theme'] = 'green';
$_GET['tab'] = 'users';
$_GET['fastload'] = 'true';
```

When a PHP page is converted to Node.js code, the Node.js still expects these predefined arrays to exist and to be correctly populated. The following code shows a Node.js init GET() function, which can be used in any local module that contains a converted PHP page to create and populate a Node.js _GET variable that works very similarly to the PHP $_GET variable:

```
function initGET(req, pre, cb) {
  pre._GET = {};
  var urlparts = req.url.split('?');
  if (urlparts.length >= 2) {
    var query = urlparts[urlparts.length-1].split('&');
    for (var p=0; p < query.length; ++p) {
      var pair = query[p].split('=');
      pre._GET[pair[0]] = pair[1];
    }
  }
  cb();
}
```

The Node.js initGET() function takes three arguments: req, pre, and cb. The req argument contains the raw HTTP request. The pre argument is a Node.js object that contains all the predefined global variables, which are made available by the PHP engine to PHP pages. Instead of juggling a bunch of different variables, all predefined variables are stored in a pre variable that can be easily passed around. And finally, the cb contains a callback function to be invoked when the initGET() function is finished. Since the initGET() function does only simple memory manipulation and requires no operations that have callback functions, a callback function is not technically necessary. However, since the initPOST() function that will be implemented later will need a cb() callback function parameter, it is best that the initGET() and the initPOST() functions work as similarly as possible.

The first line of the Node.js initGET() function creates a _GET array in the pre argument. The pre._GET object will be the Node.js equivalent of the PHP $_GET array. Next, the query arguments will be separated from the main URL, which is found in the req.url property. Populating the Node.js pre._GET variable is as easy as using split() function calls to separate out the URL query arguments from each other to determine their name/value pairs. Finally, the cb argument is invoked to let the callback know that the pre._GET variable is ready for use.

To initialize the Node.js pre._GET variable, a modification will need to be made to the Node.js exports.serve() function. Here's the original exports.serve() function:

```
exports.serve = function(req, res) {
  res.writeHead(200, {'Content-Type': 'text/plain'});
  res.end('admin/index.njs');
};
```

Instead of implementing the actual page in the `exports.serve()` function, a new function called `page()` will actually implement the page and the `exports.serve()` function will be reserved for the initialization and other work that the PHP engine would provide to a PHP page:

```
function page(req, res, pre, cb) {
  res.writeHead(200, {'Content-Type': 'text/plain'});
  res.end('admin/index.njs');
  cb();
}
```

The `page()` function takes four arguments: `req`, `res`, `pre`, and `cb`. The `req` and `res` arguments are the HTTP request and the HTTP response, respectively. The `pre` argument is the predefined variables, including the _GET property that contains the query arguments. The `cb` argument is a callback function that will let the `exports.serve()` function know when the page has been completely handled.

For debugging purposes, it can be helpful to print out the `pre` object. By using the `require()` function to load the built-in module called `util` and then adding a `util`.`inspect()` function call to the `res`.`end()` function call, the contents of the `pre` variable, including the contents of its _GET property, will be shown in the HTTP response:

```
var util = require('util');

function page(req, res, pre, cb) {
  res.writeHead(200, {'Content-Type': 'text/plain'});
  res.end('admin/index.njs\n'+util.inspect(pre));
  cb();
}
```

Now that handling the page has moved to the `page()` function, the `exports.serve()` function will be changed to do an initialization, including calling the `initGET()` function:

```
exports.serve = function(req, res) {
  var pre = {};
  initGET(req, pre, function() {
    page(req, res, pre, function() {
    });
  });
};
```

The `pre` variable is created first. Then the `initGET()` function is called, and when it is finished, the `page()` function is called. There is no finalization or cleanup after the `page()` function, so its callback is empty.

Now that the _GET property is implemented, the `page()` function can be changed to use query arguments. The `page()` function can be modified to expect an x query argument and respond appropriately:

```
function page(req, res, pre, cb) {
  res.writeHead(200, {'Content-Type': 'text/plain'});
  if (pre._GET['x']) {
    res.end('The value of x is '+pre._GET['x']+'.');
  } else {
    res.end('There is no value for x.');
  }
  cb();
}
```

If the Node.js server is run and a browser is directed to *http://localhost:1337/index.php? x=4*, the browser page will show "The value of x is 4."

The HTTP POST request is similar to the HTTP GET request, except that the name/ value pairs are delivered in the body of the request instead of as a query string at the end of the URL. An HTTP request consists of HTTP headers and an HTTP body. The URL, which includes the query string, is specified as one of the HTTP headers. HTTP headers are meant to be short and limited in length. In particular, URLs, including the query string, are limited in length; extremely long URLs are not recommended. Instead, if a lot of data must be included in an HTTP request, it is recommended that the data be sent in the HTTP body as part of an HTTP POST. Unlike HTTP headers, which are limited in length, HTTP bodies can handle very large amounts of data. For an HTTP POST, the HTTP body is often referred to as the POST data.

Since the body of an HTTP POST can be very large, the POST data is not delivered all at once; it is delivered as it becomes available using events. Events are a way for Node.js to indicate that something happened. For example, a `data` event indicates that the next chunk of data has been read from the HTTP body. If there is a lot of data, Node.js may trigger several `data` events as each chunk of data is read.

An event can be associated with a callback function, also called an event handler. The event handler will execute some code each time that an event occurs.

The `on()` function associates an event with an event handler. The following example shows the on function being used to associate the `data` event with an event handler that writes the provided data to the console:

```
req.on('data', function(chunk) {
  console.log(chunk);
});
```

For the `initPOST()` function, the `_POST` property of the `pre` variable is initialized. As you will recall from the `initGET()` function, the `pre` argument is a Node.js object that contains all the predefined global variables, which are made available by the PHP engine to PHP pages. A `body` variable is created to hold the HTTP body as it is read. The `on()` function associates an event handler with the `data` event, which will add the data to the body variable as it becomes available:

```
pre._POST = {};
var body = '';
req.on('data', function(chunk) {
  body += chunk;
  if (body.length > 1e6) {
    req.connection.destroy();
  }
});
```

An `if` statement is added to the `data` event handler to detect if the HTTP body is too long, and will terminate the connection if so. Poorly written or malicious clients might send an endless amount of data, and this `if` statement protects the Node.js server by arbitrarily giving up on an HTTP request if it has already sent a very large amount of data.

Finally, the `on()` function associates an event handler with the end event, which occurs when the entire HTTP body has been read. Using simple `split()` function calls, the end event handler pulls apart the data and puts it into the `pre._POST` variable:

```
req.on('end', function() {
  var pairs = body.split('&');
  for (var p=0; p < pairs.length; ++p) {
    var pair = pairs[p].split('=');
    pre._POST[pair[0]] = pair[1];
  }
  cb();
});
```

The `cb()` callback is invoked at the very end to indicate that the `pre._POST` variable has been fully populated and is ready for use.

Putting the code all together, the `initPOST()` function is shown here in its entirety:

```
function initPOST(req, pre, cb) {
  pre._POST = {};
  var body = '';
  req.on('data', function(chunk) {
    body += chunk;
    if (body.length > 1e6) {
      req.connection.destroy();
    }
  });
  req.on('end', function() {
    var pairs = body.split('&');
    for (var p=0; p < pairs.length; ++p) {
      var pair = pairs[p].split('=');
      pre._POST[pair[0]] = pair[1];
    }
    cb();
  });
}
```

Just like pages that expect HTTP GET requests, the `exports.serve()` function must be updated. For pages that expect HTTP POST requests, the code in the `exports.serve()` function is almost identical, except that the `initGET()` function call is replaced with an `initPOST()` function call. This is by design. Even though the `initGET()` function does not need a callback, giving it a callback allows the `initGET()` function and the `initPOST()` function to take the same parameters and has almost the same code:

```
exports.serve = function(req, res) {
  var pre = {};
  initPOST(req, pre, function() {
    page(req, res, pre, function() {
    });
  });
};
```

By far, HTTP GET and HTTP POST are the most commonly used HTTP actions, and in most cases, will be the only HTTP actions that a web application needs. There are other HTTP actions, such as HTTP PUT, HTTP DELETE, and HTTP HEAD, but the PHP engine does not provide the same support for them, so a Node.js conversion usually does not need to provide support for them either.

A cookie is a name/value pair that is sent to a client (usually a browser) by the server; the client stores the cookie and adds it as an HTTP header to every subsequent HTTP request that the client sends to the server. The client usually stores cookies in a permanent place, such as a hard disk, so that future HTTP requests can include the cookie, even if the client is shutdown and restarted later. A cookie is a small piece of data that the server gives the client so that it can identify the client later, and automatically log the client into his account, for example.

An HTTP header for a cookie has the unsurprising name of "Cookie":

```
Cookie: user=admin;sessid=21EC33203BEA1169A2EA08332B313090
```

In a Node.js HTTP request, the cookies are stored in the `headers.cookie` property of the HTTP request, usually called `req` in the code examples in this book.

The `initCOOKIE()` function for extracting the cookies from the appropriate HTTP header and putting it into the `pre._COOKIE` variable is very similar to the `initGET()` function. Getting the cookies is even more convenient: the cookies are in their own property, not tacked on to the end of a URL as a query string. The `pre._COOKIE` variable will be a stand-in for the PHP `$_COOKIE` variable that is generated by the PHP engine for PHP pages:

```
function initCOOKIE(req, pre, cb) {
  pre._COOKIE = {};
  if (req.headers.cookie) {
    var cookies = req.headers.cookie.split(';');
    for (var c=0; c < cookies.length; ++c) {
      var pair = cookies[c].split('=');
```

```
      pre._COOKIE[pair[0]] = pair[1];
    }
  }
  cb();
}
```

Just like pages that expect HTTP GET and HTTP POST requests, pages that expect cookies will modify their exports.serve() function to call the initCOOKIE() function. The initCOOKIE() function has the same parameters as both the initGET() function and the initPOST() function so the same code can be used by calling the init COOKIE() function instead of those other functions:

```
exports.serve = function(req, res) {
  var pre = {};
  initCOOKIE(req, pre, function() {
    page(req, res, pre, function() {
    });
  });
};
```

A particular page handles both HTTP GET and HTTP POST requests as well as uses cookies. The exports.serve() function for that page can be enhanced to invoke the needed initialization functions by putting one function inside the callback of another function. This code will load the pre._GET, pre._POST, and pre._COOKIE properties, which will be substitutes for the PHP predefined variables, $_GET, $_POST, and $_COOKIE:

```
exports.serve = function(req, res) {
  var pre = {};
  initGET(req, pre, function() {
    initPOST(req, pre, function() {
      initCOOKIE(req, pre, function() {
        page(req, res, pre, function() {
        });
      });
    });
  });
};
```

In PHP, the $_REQUEST predefined variable contains all the name/value pairs that are in $_GET, $_POST, and $_COOKIE. To create a Node.js pre._REQUEST variable, the pre._GET, the pre._POST, and the pre._COOKIE variables are copied:

```
function initREQUEST(req, pre, cb) {
  pre._REQUEST = {};
  if (pre._GET) {
    for (var k in pre._GET) {
      pre._REQUEST[k] = pre._GET[k];
    }
  }
  if (pre._POST) {
    for (var k in pre._POST) {
      pre._REQUEST[k] = pre._POST[k];
```

```
    }
  }
  if (pre._COOKIE) {
    for (var k in pre._COOKIE) {
      pre._REQUEST[k] = pre._COOKIE[k];
    }
  }
  cb();
}
```

The Node.js for…in operator will find all the names of the properties (a.k.a. keys) in a Node.js object. The following code shows an `obj` object and prints out a list of all the property names:

```
var obj = { 'a': '1', 'b': '2', 'c': '3', 'd': '4', 'e': '5' };
for (var name in obj) {
  console.log('name:'+name);
}
```

Here's the output of the Node.js for…in loop:

```
name:a
name:b
name:c
name:d
name:e
```

In PHP, the foreach…as statement works similarly except that the foreach…as statement returns the property value in PHP, not the property name as the for…in statement does in Node.js.

As with the other Node.js predefined variable initialization functions, the init REQUEST() function must be called in the exports.serve() function. The init REQUEST() function is called after all the other initialization functions because it needs the pre variable to be populated with the _GET, _POST, and _COOKIE values in order to make the _REQUEST value, which is a composite of the first three:

```
exports.serve = function(req, res) {
  var pre = {};
  initGET(req, pre, function() {
    initPOST(req, pre, function() {
      initCOOKIE(req, pre, function() {
        initREQUEST(req, pre, function() {
          page(req, res, pre, function() {
          });
        });
      });
    });
  });
};
```

As expected, the initREQUEST() function takes the exact same parameters as the other initialization functions and performs in the exact same way.

There is one final commonly used PHP predefined variable: the $_SESSION variable. The $_SESSION variable is preserved for each user across calls to a PHP page.

The initSESSION() Node.js function uses the pre._COOKIE variable to maintain a reference to this user's session in the sessions variable. If a session does not exist, it is created; otherwise, it is retrieved from the sessions object:

```
/** All the sessions of all the users. */
var sessions = {};

function initSESSION(req, pre, cb) {
  if ((typeof pre._COOKIE['NODESESSID']) == 'undefined') {
    var pool = '0123456789ABCDEFGHIJKLMNOPQRSTUVWXYZabcdefghijklmnopqrstuvwxyz';
    var newid = '';
    for (var i = 0; i < 26; ++i) {
      var r = Math.floor(Math.random() * pool.length);
      newid += pool.charAt(r);
    }
    pre._COOKIE['NODESESSID'] = newid;
    sessions[pre._COOKIE['NODESESSID']] = {};
  }
  var id = pre._COOKIE['NODESESSID'];
  if ((typeof sessions[id]) == 'undefined') {
    sessions[id] = {};
  }
  pre._SESSION = sessions[id];
  cb();
}
```

A particular page must be made to handle sessions as well. The exports.serve() function for that page can be enhanced to invoke the needed initialization functions by putting one function inside the callback of another function. The following code will load the pre._GET, pre._POST, pre._COOKIE, and pre._REQUEST properties, which will be substitutes for the PHP predefined variables, $_GET, $_POST, $_COOKIE, and $_REQUEST.

The initSESSION() function is the final initialization function called in the exports .serve() function. It relies on the $_COOKIE PHP variable to maintain the session. To keep the cookie active, the callback function of the page() function is updated to return the cookie to the caller:

```
exports.serve = function(req, res) {
  var pre = {};
  initGET(req, pre, function() {
    initPOST(req, pre, function() {
      initCOOKIE(req, pre, function() {
        initREQUEST(req, pre, function() {
          initSESSION(req, pre, function() {
```

```
            page(req, res, pre, function() {
              var cookies = [];
              for ( var c in pre._COOKIE) {
                cookies.push(c + '=' + pre._COOKIE[c]);
              }
              res.setHeader('Set-Cookie', cookies);
              res.writeHead(200, {'Content-Type': 'text/plain'});
              res.end(res.content);
            });
          });
        });
      });
    });
  });
};
```

As expected, the initSESSION() function takes the exact same parameters as the other initialization functions and performs in the exact same way.

Instead of copying and pasting the initGET(), initPOST(), initCOOKIE(), init REQUEST(), and initSESSION functions into every local module, an *initreq.njs* local module can be created to share these functions with all the local modules. To make them available to callers that load the local module, they are assigned as properties to the exports variable:

```
exports.initGET = function(req, pre, cb) {
  pre._GET = {};
  var urlparts = req.url.split('?');
  if (urlparts.length >= 2) {
    var query = urlparts[urlparts.length-1].split('&');
    for (var p=0; p < query.length; ++p) {
      var pair = query[p].split('=');
      pre._GET[pair[0]] = pair[1];
    }
  }
  cb();
};

exports.initPOST = function(req, pre, cb) {
  pre._POST = {};
  var body = '';
  req.on('data', function(chunk) {
    body += chunk;
    if (body.length > 1e6) {
      req.connection.destroy();
    }
  });
  req.on('end', function() {
    var pairs = body.split('&');
    for (var p=0; p < pairs.length; ++p) {
      var pair = pairs[p].split('=');
      pre._POST[pair[0]] = pair[1];
```

```
      }
      cb();
    });
  };

exports.initCOOKIE = function(req, pre, cb) {
  pre._COOKIE = {};
  if (req.headers.cookie) {
    var cookies = req.headers.cookie.split(';');
    for (var c=0; c < cookies.length; ++c) {
      var pair = cookies[c].split('=');
      pre._COOKIE[pair[0]] = pair[1];
    }
  }
  cb();
};

exports.initREQUEST = function(req, pre, cb) {
  pre._REQUEST = {};
  if (pre._GET) {
    for (var k in pre._GET) {
      pre._REQUEST[k] = pre._GET[k];
    }
  }
  if (pre._POST) {
    for (var k in pre._POST) {
      pre._REQUEST[k] = pre._POST[k];
    }
  }
  if (pre._COOKIE) {
    for (var k in pre._COOKIE) {
      pre._REQUEST[k] = pre._COOKIE[k];
    }
  }
  cb();
};

/** All the sessions of all the users. */
var sessions = {};

exports.initSESSION = function(req, pre, cb) {
  if ((typeof pre._COOKIE['NODESESSID']) == 'undefined') {
    var pool = '0123456789ABCDEFGHIJKLMNOPQRSTUVWXYZabcdefghijklmnopqrstuvwxyz';
    var newid = '';
    for (var i = 0; i < 26; ++i) {
      var r = Math.floor(Math.random() * pool.length);
      newid += pool.charAt(r);
    }
    pre._COOKIE['NODESESSID'] = newid;
    sessions[pre._COOKIE['NODESESSID']] = {};
  }
  var id = pre._COOKIE['NODESESSID'];
```

```
    if ((typeof sessions[id]) == 'undefined') {
      sessions[id] = {};
    }
    pre._SESSION = sessions[id];
    cb();
}
```

To use the *initreq.njs* local module, a call to the `require()` function loads it. Then, the references to the initialization functions exported by the *initreq.njs* file need to have the module name `initreq` prepended to each call. This code shows these changes:

```
var initreq = require('./initreq.njs');

exports.serve = function(req, res) {
  var pre = {};
  initreq.initGET(req, pre, function() {
    initreq.initPOST(req, pre, function() {
      initreq.initCOOKIE(req, pre, function() {
        initreq.initREQUEST(req, pre, function() {
          initreq.initSESSION(req, pre, function() {
            page(req, res, pre, function() {
              var cookies = [];
              for ( var c in pre._COOKIE) {
                cookies.push(c + '=' + pre._COOKIE[c]);
              }
              res.setHeader('Set-Cookie', cookies);
              res.writeHead(200, {'Content-Type': 'text/plain'});
              res.end(res.content);
            });
          });
        });
      });
    });
  });
};
```

Now you should have an even better idea about the parts of the PHP to Node.js conversion and how the process is going to work.

The *httpsvr.njs* file is the Node.js HTTP server. In a common PHP setup, the *httpsvr.njs* file would be analogous to the Apache web server with the PHP module installed. If you need to tweak the Node.js web server to add pages, route URLs to specific pages, or perform other general-purpose web server configuration, the *httpsvr.njs* file will be modified. The previous *httpsvr.njs* example file is repeated here for reference:

```
var http = require('http');
var static = require('node-static');
var file = new static.Server();
var url = require('url');
var index = require('./index.njs');
var login = require('./login.njs');
var admin_index = require('./admin/index.njs');
```

```
var admin_login = require('./admin/login.njs');

http.createServer(function (req, res) {
  if (url.parse(req.url).pathname == '/index.php') {
    index.serve(req, res);
  } else if (url.parse(req.url).pathname == '/login.php') {
    login.serve(req, res);
  } else if (url.parse(req.url).pathname == '/admin/index.php') {
    admin_index.serve(req, res);
  } else if (url.parse(req.url).pathname == '/admin/login.php') {
    admin_login.serve(req, res);
  } else {
    file.serve(req, res);
  }
}).listen(1337, '127.0.0.1');
console.log('Server running at http://127.0.0.1:1337/');
```

For each PHP page, an *index.njs* file or other local module file will be created. The exports.serve() function will be the Node.js stand-in for the page handling code in the PHP engine for this specific page. If additional predefined variables, initialization code, or finalization code (i.e., code that needs to be run after the page completes) is needed, the exports.serve() function can be modified. The exports.serve() function is not the page itself; it is the code that "wraps" around the page:

```
var initreq = require('./initreq.njs');

exports.serve = function(req, res) {
  var pre = {};
  initGET(req, pre, function() {
    initPOST(req, pre, function() {
      initCOOKIE(req, pre, function() {
        initREQUEST(req, pre, function() {
          initSESSION(req, pre, function() {
            page(req, res, pre, function() {
              var cookies = [];
              for ( var c in pre._COOKIE) {
                cookies.push(c + '=' + pre._COOKIE[c]);
              }
              res.setHeader('Set-Cookie', cookies);
              res.writeHead(200, {'Content-Type': 'text/plain'});
              res.end(res.content);
            });
          });
        });
      });
    });
  });
};

function page(req, res, pre, cb) {
```

```
    res.writeHead(200, {'Content-Type': 'text/plain'});
    res.end('admin/index.njs\n'+util.inspect(pre));
    cb();
}
```

A PHP Example Page

The page() function is the page itself. In broad terms, the process will be to copy the
PHP code from the *.php* file into the page() function. Then transformations will be
applied to the PHP code in the page() function to make it into Node.js code. When the
page() function contains only Node.js code and no remnants of the copied-in PHP code
remain, the page() function will perform in exactly the same way that the PHP
code does, except that it will be in Node.js instead of PHP.

A simple example of the transformation will be illustrative.

Suppose that you have this simple *showx5.php* page, which contains both some PHP
code mixed with some HTML:

```
<?php
  $x = $_REQUEST['x'];
  $x += 5;
?>
<html><head></head><body>
The value of x plus 5 is <?php echo $x; ?>.
</body></html>
```

The PHP code will first be copied and pasted into the page() function, yielding weird
looking, nonfunctional PHP/Node.js hybrid code:

```
function page(req, res, pre, cb) {
  var content = '';
  <?php
    $x = $_REQUEST['x'];
    $x += 5;
  ?>
  <html><head></head><body>
  The value of x plus 5 is <?php echo $x; ?>.
  </body></html>
  res.writeHead(200, {'Content-Type': 'text/html'})
  res.end(content);
  cb();
}
```

Next, the first block of PHP code will be converted. Here's the snippet before conversion:

```
<?php
  $x = $_REQUEST['x'];
  $x += 5;
?>
```

After conversion, it still looks very similar, except now it is Node.js code:

```
var x = parseInt(pre._REQUEST['x']);
x += 5;
```

Then, the remaining HTML code is converted:

```
<html><head></head><body>
The value of x plus 5 is <?php echo $x; ?>.
</body></html>
```

Its Node.js equivalent is very similar to its PHP counterpart, too:

```
content += '<html><head></head><body>';
content += 'The value of x plus 5 is '+x+'.';
content += '</body></html>';
```

And here's the fully converted page() function in the *showx5.njs* file that implements the Node.js equivalent of *showx5.php*:

```
function page(req, res, pre, cb) {
  var content = '';
  var x = parseInt(pre._REQUEST['x']);
  x += 5;
  content += '<html><head></head><body>';
  content += 'The value of x plus 5 is '+x+'.';
  content += '</body></html>';
  res.writeHead(200, {'Content-Type': 'text/html'})
  res.end(content);
  cb();
}
```

And the complete *showx5.njs* file:

```
var initreq = require('./initreq.njs');

exports.serve = function(req, res) {
  var pre = {};
  initreq.initGET(req, pre, function() {
    initreq.initPOST(req, pre, function() {
      initreq.initCOOKIE(req, pre, function() {
        initreq.initREQUEST(req, pre, function() {
          initreq.initSESSION(req, pre, function() {
            page(req, res, pre, function() {
              var cookies = [];
              for ( var c in pre._COOKIE) {
                cookies.push(c + '=' + pre._COOKIE[c]);
              }
              res.setHeader('Set-Cookie', cookies);
              res.writeHead(200, {'Content-Type': 'text/plain'});
              res.end(res.content);
            });
          });
        });
      });
    });
```

```
      });
    });
  };

  function page(req, res, pre, cb) {
    var content = '';
    var x = parseInt(pre._REQUEST['x']);
    x += 5;
    content += '<html><head></head><body>';
    content += 'The value of x plus 5 is '+x+'.';
    content += '</body></html>';
    res.writeHead(200, {'Content-Type': 'text/html'})
    res.end(content);
    cb();
  }
```

The *httpsvr.njs* file is modified to route the *showx5.php* URL to the showx5.njs local module:

```
var http = require('http');
var static = require('node-static');
var file = new static.Server();
var url = require('url');
var showx5 = require('./showx5.njs');

http.createServer(function (req, res) {
  if (url.parse(req.url).pathname == '/showx5.php') {
    showx5.serve(req, res);
  } else {
    file.serve(req, res);
  }
}).listen(1337, '127.0.0.1');
console.log('Server running at http://127.0.0.1:1337/');
```

If you put the *httpsvr.njs*, *initreq.njs*, and *showx5.njs* files in the same directory and run the Node.js server, both the PHP and Node.js code will perform the same. Using a client such as a web browser to visit the following URLs will show the same result:

```
http://localhost/showx5.php?x=22
http://localhost:1337/showx5.php?x=22
```

The first URL will go to the PHP web server. The second URL will go to its equivalent Node.js web server.

The showx5 example is trivial, but it does demonstrate three things:

- You have a development environment setup to do PHP to Node.js conversion.
- You have a Node.js framework setup to support the conversion of individual PHP pages to Node.js.
- You can convert trivial PHP pages to Node.js easily.

With trivial PHP pages able to be converted to Node.js, the remaining chapters in this book focus on converting sophisticated, real-world PHP pages into Node.js. In the next chapter, a discussion of callbacks and the concept of code linearity will be presented to show how PHP code can be refactored to ease its conversion to Node.js before it is copied and pasted into the `page()` function.

CHAPTER 3

Simple Callbacks

Of all the differences between PHP and JavaScript, here's the most difficult: PHP is, at its heart, a sequential language, whereas JavaScript is an event-driven one.

Being sequential or event-driven is essentially an assumption that is built into a language. Languages do not develop in a vacuum. With both PHP and JavaScript, each language was developed in a hurry, with a particular purpose in mind, and deployed to users within months of its creation.

Rasmus Lerdorf invented PHP in 1994 as a replacement for CGI scripts. CGI scripts were usually C (or C++) programs that executed when a browser requested a specific URL and the output from the program was sent back as a web page. These C programs were single threaded and ran from beginning to end in a step-by-step fashion. Lerdorf developed PHP as a substitute. When a browser requested a specific URL, instead of running a C program, the PHP script (page) would be quickly compiled and run, and the output from the script would be sent back as a web page. Since PHP was a drop-in substitute for single-threaded C programs, PHP naturally adopted the single-threaded approach.

Those CGI scripts and early PHP pages really did not have any concept of or need for events. The only two events that might make sense and have any kind of use would be: (1) a URL-invoked event, or (2) a URL invocation completed event. The URL-invoked event was handled by running the PHP script; essentially, the entire PHP script itself was the URL-invoked handler. When the PHP script completed running and all its output was generated, that could be considered the URL invocation completed event. To handle this event, additional code would be added to the end of the PHP page. So, a PHP page can be looked at as a single monolith of eventless code sandwiched between two events.

This whole discussion of events is only to explain that there is one way into a PHP page and one way out. There is no concept or purpose for multithreading: basically, doing something while waiting for something else to be done is useless. In PHP, if you have a task that takes a long time, you might as well just wait until it is done because you cannot get to the end of the page any faster.

CGI scripts and early PHP pages were single threaded because it was assumed that the web server would multithread them. Individual PHP pages would not benefit from threads, but if a web server was simultaneously serving multiple PHP pages, it could multithread its operations with them. PHP pages are the individual operations inside a web server that make a web application work, but they are not the web server itself.

Brendan Eich developed JavaScript in 1995 for a completely different purpose—and with a completely different mindset—than PHP was developed the previous year. Java-Script was designed to run within the Netscape Navigator browser and was primarily designed to handle events. In an Internet browser, users are expected to click buttons and links, type into forms, select items in select boxes, and do all kinds of other inter-active operations. Whereas PHP was essentially eventless, JavaScript was eventful. Early website developers desired to catch all the different kinds of events that might occur when a user interacts with a web page and associate a handler to run specific code with each event.

While waiting for the user to click a certain button, an Internet browser cannot just hang and wait. In fact, when there are multiple controls on a web page (and there almost always are), the order in which the controls might be manipulated and how they might be manipulated is totally unpredictable. This is completely different from PHP, where the number and order of events is completely predictable.

Since it was designed for event handling, JavaScript had the concept of switching be-tween tasks baked into its design from the very start: basically, doing something while waiting for something else to be done was the whole point. In JavaScript, event handlers could be set up for handling user interaction events or to handle completion events from long running operations. Many operations could be provided an event handler, be kicked off, and more code could be run. When the operation completed, the event handler would be invoked, even if other JavaScript code farther along was still being run.

When Ryan Dahl developed Node.js in 2009, he saw no reason to change JavaScript's heritage. Rather than modeling Node.js on single-threaded, single-page PHP scripts, he modeled it on the multiple-task, multiple page–handling web server itself. Each PHP page represents a single unit of work, but each Node.js script represents an entire web server. In fact, it is possible to create a single Node.js script that serves up any number of PHP pages!

But our objective here is to convert PHP functionality to Node.js functionality, not merely to code up a web server in Node.js, instead of C, to serve up PHP web pages.

Instead of creating a PHP handler in Node.js, the PHP functionality will be converted to Node.js and run inline, entirely in JavaScript, without switching back and forth between two languages. Everything that is implemented in PHP will be reimplemented in Node.js.

Both PHP and Node.js have very similar functions for many operations, including relatively complex operations, such as file and database access. Even better, both PHP and JavaScript were originally implemented in C and the developers of both adopted much of the style and many of the conventions of the C language. And, even better than that, by the time Ryan Dahl took JavaScript and developed Node.js roughly 15 years after PHP and JavaScript were developed, the industry had already formed a strong consensus about a very, very large number of standard operations, from simple to complex, not only about how the APIs should look and operate but even about what the specific APIs should be named. To his credit and the credit of the many contributors to Node.js who helped, Node.js adopted the consensus rather than ignoring it.

Linearity

Let us use file handling as a concrete example of how similar C, PHP, and Node.js can be. In C, here is a simple example to write "Hello world!" to a file named *fp.txt*:

```
#include <stdio.h>

FILE * fp = fopen("fp.txt", "w");
fwrite("Hello world!", 12, 1, fp);
fclose(fp);
```

It's simple. The C fopen() API function creates the file, the C fwrite() API function writes content to the file, and the C fclose() API function tells the library that we are done with the file. The fp variable is the file pointer so the C API functions can keep track of which file you are dealing with. The *stdio.h* file is included so the program can access the C filesystem APIs.

The following PHP code shows the corresponding code in that language:

```
<?php
$fp = fopen('fp.txt', 'w');
fwrite($fp, 'Hello world!');
fclose($fp);
?>
```

As you can see, it is very, very similar. The PHP API functions use the exact same names: fopen(), fwrite(), and fclose().

Now, let's look at the Node.js version of this example:

```
var fs = require('fs');

fs.open('fp.txt', 'w', 0666, function(error, fp) {
  fs.write(fp, 'Hello world!', null, 'utf-8', function() {
    fs.close(fp, function(error) {
    });
  });
});
```

The Node.js version has some things that are similar and some things that are different.

To use the filesystem library, Node.js requires the functions from the Node.js fs module. Similar to C but unlike PHP, a special Node.js declaration is needed to access the file handling functions.

The Node.js API functions themselves are similarly named but not the same. In C and PHP, to open a file, the fopen() API function is used, but in Node.js, the API function is called fs.open(). Similarly, the fwrite() and fclose() API functions are used in C and PHP, but the fs.write() and fs.close() API functions are used in Node.js.

If you take the PHP example code and substitute the Node.js API names for the PHP API names, it creates the following PHP/Node.js hybrid code:

```
$fp = fs.open('fp.txt', 'w');
fs.write($fp, 'Hello world!');
fs.close($fp);
```

A few other minor differences are easily corrected, such as removing dollar signs and adding extra arguments that are required by Node.js but not by PHP. With these corrections, the PHP/Node.js hybrid code becomes a little more like Node.js and less like PHP:

```
fp = fs.open('fp.txt', 'w', 0666);
fs.write(fp, 'Hello world!', null, 'utf-8');
fs.close(fp);
```

One step remains. In Node.js, the fp variable is not the return value from the Node.js fs.open() API function; it is passed as an argument to the callback function, which is the last argument in the Node.js fs.open() API function call. Let us change just that one call and move the fp variable to the right place:

```
fs.open('fp.txt', 'w', 0666, function(error, fp) {
});
fs.write(fp, 'Hello world!', null, 'utf-8');
fs.close(fp);
```

The fp variable is no longer accessible to the Node.js fs.write() API function because it is outside the scope of the callback function. Even if we could somehow provide access, the Node.js fs.write() API function might be called too early, possibly before the Node.js fs.open() API function call is finished and before the fp variable is given the correct value from the Node.js fs.open() API function.

This simple example highlights the biggest challenge to converting between PHP and Node.js. The challenge is to somehow bring together the different origins of PHP and Node.js. The single-threaded, sequential mentality of PHP needs to be reconciled with the multiple task handling, nonsequential nature of JavaScript. The eventless nature of PHP needs to be made eventful, like Node.js, so that the JavaScript code has a possibility of working.

PHP is composed of sequential, also known as blocking, APIs. Each statement is executed in order and the next statement does not start to execute until the statement before it is completely done. When the PHP `fopen()` API function is called, its return value contains the file pointer because the PHP `fopen()` API function call does not return until the file is actually open. If the disk is slow and takes a long time to open a file, then the API blocks and waits for the disk.

Node.js is composed mostly of nonblocking APIs. Each statement is still executed in order, but a function passed as an argument to the call is invoked when the statement is completely done. The next statement in order might execute before or after that happens.

In terms of conversion, at least for converting blocking PHP APIs to nonblocking Node.js APIs, the next statement is not really the statement after the Node.js `fs.open()` API function call, it is the first statement in the callback function that is passed as the last argument. When we convert, we need to take the PHP code and move the next statement into the callback function.

Let's make that modification and examine the resulting code:

```
fs.open('fp.txt', 'w', 0666, function(error, fp) {
  fs.write(fp, 'Hello world!', null, 'utf-8');
});
fs.close(fp);
```

Now, the Node.js `fs.write()` API function call is inside the callback function. The Node.js `fs.write()` API function call will not be made until the Node.js `fs.open()` API function call completely finishes. The Node.js `fs.write()` API function call is in the correct scope, so it has access to the `fp` variable, and since we are using the Node.js API function as it was intended, the `fp` variable will always have the correct value when the Node.js `fs.write()` API function is invoked.

It is obvious that that is not enough, though. The Node.js `fs.write()` API function has its own callback function and the Node.js `fs.close()` API function call does not have access to the `fp` variable in the same way that the Node.js `fs.write()` API function call did not have access before it was moved into the callback function. The solution is obvious: add a callback function to the Node.js `fs.write()` API function call and move the Node.js `fs.close()` API function call into it:

```
fs.open('fp.txt', 'w', 0666, function(error, fp) {
  fs.write(fp, 'Hello world!', null, 'utf-8', function() {
    fs.close(fp);
  });
});
```

Finally, a callback function is added to the Node.js `fs.close()` API function call itself to finish the conversion:

```
fs.open('fp.txt', 'w', 0666, function(error, fp) {
  fs.write(fp, 'Hello world!', null, 'utf-8', function() {
    fs.close(fp, function(error) {
    });
  });
});
```

The original PHP sample code was three blocking PHP API calls. The conversion to Node.js rewrites those three blocking calls into three nonblocking Node.js calls.

It always reminds me of an accordion: the Node.js `fs.open()` API function call is expanded to contain the Node.js `fs.write()` API function call, which is expanded to contain the Node.js `fs.close()` API function call, which could be expanded to contain more code.

In the simplest cases, a sequence of PHP statements can be converted to Node.js by adding callback statements to the corresponding Node.js API function calls and copying and pasting the rest of the code into the callback statement.

From this observation, we can make what I call a conversion recipe. A conversion recipe is a semi-mechanical series of steps that can be applied to a line of PHP code to convert it into code that is more compatible with Node.js code.

Notice that I wrote "more compatible." A conversion recipe does not necessarily convert a line of running PHP code into running Node.js code. A conversion recipe may only address one issue in a line of code, leaving the semi-converted code as a PHP/Node.js hybrid that runs in neither language.

Conversion recipes have other important features.

A conversion recipe should be able to be applied mechanically or semi-mechanically so that PHP code can be converted quickly and without a deep understanding of the surrounding code. A conversion recipe should not lose any information or code; it should never require that code be recreated later. A conversion recipe keeps the code readable and with the correct flow (even though it is probably nonfunctional); it should never leave the code with a broken syntax, like unbalanced curly brackets or parentheses, nor should it move code to a place that it does not make sense.

The file-handling API explanation is not really a conversion recipe; it is meant to illustrate the conversion issues. If used, it could leave the code with the wrong flow. The following is a conversion recipe based on what we have learned.

Given the original PHP code:

```php
$fp = fopen('fp.txt', 'w');
fwrite($fp, 'Hello world!');
fclose($fp);
```

convert the PHP `fopen()` API function call to a Node.js `fs.open()` API function call, fix up the call's arguments, and cut and paste the remaining statements into the callback function of the Node.js `fs.open()` API function call, like this:

```js
fs.open('fp.txt', 'w', 0666, function(error, fp) {
  fwrite(fp, 'Hello world!');
  fclose(fp);
});
```

Notice how the `fs.open()` API function call is now converted to Node.js but its callback contains PHP code. Putting all the PHP code in the callback keeps the order of execution of the statements clear.

To convert the PHP `fwrite()` API function call, we apply the same conversion operations. That is, convert the PHP `fwrite()` API function call to a Node.js `fs.write()` API function call, fix up the call's arguments, and cut and paste the remaining statements into the callback function of the call:

```js
fs.open('fp.txt', 'w', 0666, function(error, fp) {
  fs.write(fp, 'Hello world!', null, 'utf-8', function() {
    fclose(fp);
  });
});
```

To convert the `fclose()` call, it is the same, except that since there are no operations after the `fclose()` call, an empty callback function is created:

```js
fs.open('fp.txt', 'w', 0666, function(error, fp) {
  fs.write(fp, 'Hello world!', null, 'utf-8', function() {
    fs.close(fp, function(error) {
    });
  });
});
```

This is a very simple and effective conversion recipe. This might have been the end of this chapter except for one thing: this conversion recipe breaks down fairly quickly for code that is even slightly more complex.

The conversion recipe works because the PHP code is linear. Statements are executed one after another with no significant conditional statements, such as `if` branches or `for` or `while` loops. I use the word "linear" because I visualize it as all the significant code paths going off in straight lines away from each other and not trying to cross or recombine with each other again.

If there are no conditional statements at all, let us call the PHP code fully linear. Here is some fully linear PHP code:

```php
$msg = 'start';
$fp = fopen('fp.txt', 'w');
$msg = 'opened';
fwrite($fp, 'Hello world!');
$msg = 'written';
fclose($fp);
$msg = 'closed';
```

Since the conversion recipe works on all fully linear PHP code, it easily converts the PHP code into the following Node.js code:

```javascript
var msg = 'start';
fs.open('fp.txt', 'w', 0666, function(error, fp) {
  msg = 'opened';
  fs.write(fp, 'Hello world!', null, 'utf-8', function() {
    msg = 'written';
    fs.close(fp, function(error) {
      msg = 'closed';
    });
  });
});
```

However, if the PHP code contains conditional statements, the PHP code might be effectively linear, meaning that the conditional statements do not affect the conversion recipe. To be effectively linear, any blocking PHP calls that will be converted to non-blocking Node.js calls are linear from that call until the end of the code.

PHP code is effectively linear if every conditional is self-contained and separated from all the blocking PHP calls. For example:

```php
$msg = 'start';
$fp = fopen('fp.txt', 'w');
if ($fp !== null) {
  $msg = 'opened';
}
fwrite($fp, 'Hello world!');
fclose($fp);
```

The if statement is self-contained and the code keeps its linear quality before, during, and after the branch. The conversion recipe will yield the following Node.js code:

```javascript
var msg = 'start';
fs.open('fp.txt', 'w', 0666, function(error, fp) {
  if (fp !== null) {
    msg = 'opened';
  }
  fs.write(fp, 'Hello world!', null, 'utf-8', function() {
```

```
      fs.close(fp, function(error) {
      });
    });
  });
```

PHP code is also effectively linear if all conditionals, even if they contain blocking PHP calls that will be converted to nonblocking Node.js calls, maintain linearness to the end of the code. For example:

```
$fp = fopen('fp.txt', 'w');
if ($fp !== null) {
  fwrite($fp, 'Hello world!');
  fclose($fp);
}
```

This PHP code will easily become the following Node.js code:

```
fs.open('fp.txt', 'w', 0666, function(error, fp) {
  if (fp !== null) {
    fs.write(fp, 'Hello world!', null, 'utf-8', function() {
      fs.close(fp, function(error) {
      });
    });
  }
});
```

Not all code is linear or effectively linear; some PHP code is nonlinear. Nonlinear code happens when the code "comes back together" and tries to recombine in a way that breaks the previous conversion recipe. When the conversion recipe is applied, all the remaining code is moved into the callback of the Node.js API call. But with nonlinear PHP code, the new Node.js code will also require the exact same code to remain outside of the callback as well so that it can service the code paths that do not use the non-blocking Node.js API. This will be clearer in subsequent examples.

Nonlinear PHP code can occur when a blocking PHP API call is in an `if` statement block that has more statements after the `if` statement block ends. The PHP `fwrite()` call makes this code nonlinear:

```
$fp = fopen('fp.txt', 'w');
if ($msg == 'say') {
  fwrite($fp, 'Hello world!');
}
$msg = 'done';
```

If the conversion recipe is applied to the PHP code, the Node.js code would not compile or even be syntactically valid! The following code is broken because the conversion recipe was applied to nonlinear PHP code when it only works for linear PHP code:

```
fs.open('fp.txt', 'w', 0666, function(error, fp) {
  if (msg == 'say') {
    fs.write(fp, 'Hello world!', null, 'utf-8', function() {
    } // oops!
```

```
      msg = 'done'; // oops!
    });
  }
});
```

The key difficulty is the final statement where the msg variable is set to 'done'. It is not the if statement itself nor is it the fs.write() call that turns the PHP code from effectively linear to nonlinear; it is the seemingly simple and seemingly irrelevant statement at the very end. That final statement pulls the "lines" back together. It requires that the code path (i.e., line) that enters the if statement and the code path that skips the if statement to both execute the same code and the blocking PHP API that is in one path but not in the other path will result in a callback in one place and not in the other. If the final statement was removed, the PHP code would be linear instead of nonlinear. Also, if the blocking PHP API was removed or replaced with other code that would not result in a callback, the PHP code would be linear instead of nonlinear.

Until now, "the end of the code" has been rather vague.

The end of the code is where the PHP code stops running, the PHP page is finished, and the web server retakes control. Each PHP page has a limited lifetime when it is running; it runs from the URL-invoked pseudo-event to the URL invocation completed pseudo-event. The end of the code is when the URL invocation completed pseudo-event occurs.

As you can see, the conversion recipe is most effective when you work your way backward. If you start at where the PHP page exits, you can trace your way backward, identifying exit points and applying the conversion recipe to PHP code that is linear until each exit point. The entry point into the page and its linearness is irrelevant to the conversion recipe.

Like if statements, for statements and while statements can be effectively linear or nonlinear. An effectively linear for statement would be:

```
$total = 0;
$fp = fopen('fp.txt', 'w');
for ($i=0; $i < 10; ++$i) {
  $total += $i;
}
fwrite($fp, 'Total = '.$total);
```

The for statement is irrelevant and does not interfere with the conversion recipe. The Node.js code will work fine:

```
var total = 0;
fs.open('fp.txt', 'w', 0666, function(error, fp) {
  for (var i=0; i < 10; ++i) {
    total += i;
```

```
      }
      fs.write(fp, 'Total = '+total, null, 'utf-8', function() {
      });
   });
```

`for` statements can also be nonlinear. The conversion recipe will not work on this PHP code:

```
$fp = fopen('fp.txt', 'w');
for ($i=0; $i < 3; ++$i) {
   fwrite($fp, 'Hello world!');
}
```

If you try to apply the conversion recipe, the Node.js code will be syntactically invalid and unfixable:

```
fs.open('fp.txt', 'w', 0666, function(error, fp) {
   for (var i=0; i < 3; ++i) {
      fs.write(fp, 'Hello world!', null, 'utf-8', function() {
      } // oops!
      });
   });
```

With some practice, you can train your eye to easily identify the linearness of code, and thus know whether or not the conversion recipe will work and what the converted Node.js code will look like.

With any PHP page that you want to convert, you will want to identify any linear code before exit points in the page and trace the code paths backward until you find nonlinear code.

Making Code Linear

Sometimes, nonlinear code can be refactored to be linear. It is worthwhile to refactor the PHP page such that it contains minimal nonlinear code, regardless of whether you intend to keep the PHP code in sync with the Node.js code or dispose of the PHP code and move forward with the converted Node.js code only.

Consider this previous example of nonlinear code:

```
$fp = fopen('fp.txt', 'w');
if ($msg == 'say') {
   fwrite($fp, 'Hello world!');
}
$msg = 'done';
```

This code is nonlinear because the `fwrite()` PHP API call is in an `if` statement block and the code paths recombine after the `if` statement ends. If either one of these two conditions of nonlinearity can be removed, the statement will become effectively linear. When removing nonlinearity, each condition should be examined for ways that it can be removed.

An `if` statement only has two code paths: `true` or `false`. Since there are only two paths, it is often sensible to simply duplicate the remaining code. If it is possible and not too long, the duplicated code will separate the code paths and make the code linear. The previous nonlinear PHP code will become the following linear PHP code:

```php
$fp = fopen('fp.txt', 'w');
if ($msg == 'say') {
  fwrite($fp, 'Hello world!');
  $msg = 'done';
} else {
  $msg = 'done';
}
```

The `else` clause is added and the `msg` variable manipulation is duplicated. This code is now linear. By applying the conversion recipe, it becomes:

```js
fs.open('fp.txt', 'w', 0666, function(error, fp) {
  if (msg == 'say') {
    fs.write(fp, 'Hello world!', null, 'utf-8', function() {
      msg = 'done';
    });
  } else {
    msg = 'done';
  }
});
```

Refactoring `if` statements using duplication is often a good way to create linearity. Adding the `else` clause (if it is not already there) and then copying and pasting the remaining statements into both the `if` clause and the `else` clause works.

In other cases, nonlinearity can be removed by a good understanding of the operation of the APIs themselves and refactoring to reduce multiple PHP API calls to a single PHP API call. Consider the previous example of a nonlinear `for` statement:

```php
$fp = fopen('fp.txt', 'w');
for ($i=0; $i < 3; ++$i) {
  fwrite($fp, 'Hello world!');
}
```

In this case, it is worth pointing out that the issue and any possible solution is quite thorny. When the loop is unrolled, it is clear that the `fs.write()` calls cannot be in a loop anymore; they need to be chained together in nested callbacks:

```js
fs.open('fp.txt', 'w', 0666, function(error, fp) {
  fs.write(fp, 'Hello world!', null, 'utf-8', function() {
    fs.write(fp, 'Hello world!', null, 'utf-8', function() {
      fs.write(fp, 'Hello world!', null, 'utf-8', function() {
      });
    });
  });
});
```

If the number of times is a discrete number, the loop can be unrolled, but if the number of times is a variable, unrolling the loop will be impossible.

Fortunately, insight into what the `fwrite()` PHP API does tells us that multiple `fwrite()` PHP API calls can often be replaced with a single `fwrite()` PHP API call that writes all the data at once. So the PHP code is factored to the following:

```
$fp = fopen('fp.txt', 'w');
$data = '';
for ($i=0; $i < 3; ++$i) {
  $data .= 'Hello world!';
}
fwrite($fp, $data);
```

The data for the file is first collected into the data variable and then written with a single `fwrite()` PHP API call. This refactored code is effectively linear. This linear PHP code can be converted using the conversion recipe to yield:

```
fs.open('fp.txt', 'w', 0666, function(error, fp) {
  var data = '';
  for (var i=0; i < 3; ++i) {
   data += 'Hello world!';
  }
  fs.write(fp, data, null, 'utf-8', function() {
  });
});
```

Analyzing PHP code, line by line, to identify nonlinearity and refactor the nonlinear PHP code into linear PHP code is a necessary and worthwhile first step to preparing PHP code to be converted to Node.js code. Until now, you have seen how to take PHP code with simple statements, conditional statements, and blocking PHP calls and convert them to more easily converted PHP code, which will ultimately lead to functional nonblocking Node.js code. But PHP code contains more than statements and PHP API calls: it also contains functions and function calls.

If you recall, earlier in this chapter we covered how Node.js models its built-in library APIs on an industry-wide consensus formed over many years, often tracing its heritage back to the naming, functionality, and operation of the original C APIs. When the conversion recipe seeks to convert a blocking PHP API call into a nonblocking Node.js API call, it relies heavily on finding a very similar Node.js API for each PHP API. This almost always works, and even when it does not work, the required Node.js API can almost always be manufactured easily from existing Node.js APIs and be just as good.

However, PHP functions in the existing code, as opposed to built-in blocking PHP functions, are more difficult to handle. It is hard to predict whether or not they use blocking PHP APIs, so it is hard to predict whether they will require a callback or not.

Consider a PHP user-defined function, `prefixAndConcat()`. This function takes two parameters: a string and an array. It also returns a string value. The return value is a long string that has the string argument prepended to each element in the array and then concatenates all the prepended strings together. For example, given a string argument of `prefix_` and an array argument of `['a','b','c']`, it will return a string like `prefix_aprefix_bprefix_c`:

```php
function prefixAndConcat($str, $a) {
  // unknown code that may or may not call blocking PHP APIs
}

$n = prefixAndConcat('prefix_', array('a', 'b', 'c'));
$msg = 'prefixed string: '.$n; // last statement before PHP exit point
```

Compare the `prefixAndConcat()` function to a PHP user-defined function and its calling code that writes "Hello world!" multiple times to a file and stores the return value in the `msg` variable:

```php
function writeMultipleStrings($str, $a) {
  // unknown code that may or may not call blocking PHP APIs
}

$n = writeMultipleStrings('fp.txt', array('a', 'b', 'c'));
$msg = 'wrote '.$n.' times'; // last statement before PHP exit point
```

They are essentially the same. However, the `prefixAndConcat()` function only does string manipulation, which never requires a nonblocking API call, even in Node.js. But, the `writeMultipleStrings()` function will ultimately use the nonblocking Node.js file-handling APIs.

When converted to Node.js, the calling code for `prefixAndConcat()` will be:

```javascript
var n = prefixAndConcat('prefix_', ['a', 'b', 'c']);
var msg = 'prefixed string: '+n; // last statement before PHP exit point
```

By contrast, the calling code for `writeMultipleStrings()` will be:

```javascript
writeMultipleStrings('fp.txt', array('a', 'b', 'c'), function(n) {
  var msg = 'wrote '+n+' times'; // last statement before PHP exit point
});
```

Moving the return value from the front of the PHP expression to be a parameter to the Node.js callback function is quite a challenge to keep track of when the PHP and Node.js code are both maintained and kept synchronized. It is yet another nonblocking Node.js function to track and to understand how it affects linearity.

One way to cope is to provide a naming convention that would indicate whether a user-defined function is blocking or nonblocking in Node.js (it is always blocking in PHP). By adding an indicator to the function name, it would be easier to visualize what the converted Node.js code would look like even when looking at the pre-converted PHP calling code. A conversion recipe is to add _cb (for "callback") to the end of each PHP user-defined function name that uses a nonblocking Node.js API call.

So, the `writeMultipleStrings()` is renamed to `writeMultipleStrings_cb()`:

```
function writeMultipleStrings_cb($str, $a) {
  // unknown code that may or may not call blocking PHP APIs
}
```

If this conversion recipe is applied, it will be clearer that the Node.js calling code for `writeMultipleStrings_cb()` will be:

```
writeMultipleStrings_cb('fp.txt', array('a', 'b', 'c'), function(n) {
  var msg = 'wrote '+n+' times'; // last statement before PHP exit point
});
```

The `prefixAndConcat()` function would remain the same and not have _cb in its name:

```
var n = prefixAndConcat('prefix_', ['a', 'b', 'c']);
var msg = 'prefixed string: '+n; // last statement before PHP exit point
```

This conversion recipe will be effective for relatively simple PHP code, but in more complex PHP code, nearly every user-defined function will touch a blocking PHP API. Adding _cb to the end of every PHP user-defined function will not be much help. To be useful, some of the PHP functions need to have _cb and some do not in order to make that indicator useful.

A more effective conversion strategy is to limit nesting of functions that contain blocking PHP API calls. If a PHP user-defined function calls a function that calls another function that calls another function, and so on, the code is considered to have deep nesting. If the calls only go one or two calls deep, the code is considered to have shallow nesting. In regular PHP code that is not destined to be converted to Node.js, deep nesting is desirable because the lower functions abstract away details from the higher functions. However, to analyze and remove nonlinear situations from PHP code that is maintained and synchronized with a Node.js version, shallow nesting is desirable. It is desirable because an understanding of the code at all levels is necessary when dealing with non-linearity issues. Abstraction is an obstacle, not a help.

One way to remove abstraction and make PHP code more easily analyzed and refactored for linearity is to unroll nested PHP user-defined functions. This conversion recipe removes a level of nesting that makes PHP code easier to analyze and refactor for linearity. Consider an implementation of the `writeMultipleStrings()` user-defined function. The use of this function was described earlier in this chapter but the following provides an actual implementation:

```
function writeMultipleStrings($str, $a) {
  $fp = fopen($str, 'w');
  $data = '';
  for ($i=0; $i < count($a); ++$i) {
    $data .= $a[$i];
  }
  fwrite($fp, $data);
  fclose($fp);
```

```
    return $data;
}

$n = writeMultipleStrings('fp.txt', array('a', 'b', 'c'));
$msg = 'wrote '.$n.' data'; // last statement before PHP exit point
```

To unroll the function, the writeMultipleStrings() implementation is copied and pasted to the calling code. If the parameter names can be kept the same, the parameters can be declared and assigned at the beginning of the implementation. The return value can be assigned to the variable at the end of the implementation:

```
$str = 'fp.txt'; // argument #1
$a = array('a', 'b', 'c'); // argument #2
$fp = fopen($str, 'w');
$data = '';
for ($i=0; $i < count($a); ++$i) {
  $data .= $a[$i];
}
fwrite($fp, $data);
fclose($fp);
$n = $data; // return value
$msg = 'wrote '.$n.' data'; // last statement before PHP exit point
```

By unrolling the PHP writeMultipleStrings() call, this code can be more easily made linear. Here is the corresponding Node.js code:

```
var str = 'fp.txt'; // argument #1
var a = ['a', 'b', 'c'];  // argument #2
fs.open(str, 'w', 0666, function(error, fp) {
  var data = '';
  for (var i=0; i < a.length; ++i) {
    data += a[i];
  }
  fs.write(fp, data, null, 'utf-8', function() {
    fs.close(fp, function(error) {
      var n = data; // return value
      var msg = 'wrote '.$n.' data'; // last statement before PHP exit point
    });
  });
});
```

As you can see, unrolling a PHP function call will eliminate a level of nesting, which makes the code easier to convert.

A second but rather vague conversion recipe for removing nesting is to inspect the PHP code for opportunities to eliminate it, concentrating on PHP user-defined functions that may involve blocking PHP APIs. PHP user-defined functions that do not involve blocking PHP APIs are harmless and irrelevant. By identifying and carefully refactoring to avoid unnecessary PHP user-defined functions, the PHP code will be converted to Node.js more easily.

As this chapter has demonstrated, an important part of converting PHP code to Node.js code is refactoring the original PHP code so it is more easily converted to Node.js. Linearity is best handled in the PHP code so the Node.js and PHP code will parallel each other closely. Since it is anticipated that both the PHP and Node.js code will be kept synchronized and will improve in parallel, the developer can use his understanding of linearity and other Node.js conversion issues to write the new features with an eye toward making them conversion-friendly.

Linearity is a goal, but it is not always possible. Several basic conversion recipes have been presented in this chapter to convert nonlinear PHP code into linear PHP code. But there is certain nonlinear code that needs a more complex strategy to cope with it.

Certain for statements are particularly challenging. A linearity concern occurs when a for statement contains a blocking PHP API call that, when converted to Node.js, will turn into a nonblocking Node.js API call:

```php
$fp = fopen('fp.txt', 'w');
for ($i=0; $i < $n; ++$i) {
  fwrite($fp, 'Hello world!');
}
```

When this PHP code is converted to Node.js code, the for statement completely disappears and is replaced with a "callback chain" structure:

```js
fs.open('fp.txt', 'w', 0666, function(error, fp) {
  fs.write(fp, 'Hello world!', null, 'utf-8', function() {
    fs.write(fp, 'Hello world!', null, 'utf-8', function() {
      fs.write(fp, 'Hello world!', null, 'utf-8', function() {
        // and on and on for a total of "n" times
      });
    });
  });
});
```

Earlier in this chapter, a conversion recipe was presented to remove the blocking PHP API call from the loop. Using insight into the way that the Node.js fs.write() API works, the blocking PHP API call could be moved outside the for statement. Instead of converting the for statement into a callback chain, the for statement was preserved but iterated over code that only had a single path and, after the for statement completed, a single Node.js fs.write() API call was made. Refactoring the code from multiple Node.js fs.write() API calls to a single call was the key. Instead of the Node.js callback chain, the code had the same effect and looked more like the original PHP code:

```js
fs.open('fp.txt', 'w', 0666, function(error, fp) {
  var data = '';
  for (var i=0; i < n; ++i) {
    data += 'Hello world!';
```

```
    }
    fs.write(fp, data, null, 'utf-8', function() {
    });
  });
```

What if insight fails us? Maybe there is no way to remove the blocking PHP API call from the for statement. Instead of writing a piece of data an arbitrary number of times to the same file, consider a for statement that writes a piece of data to an arbitrary number of different files (e.g., a set of log files):

```
for ($i=0; $i < $n; ++$i) {
    $fp = fopen($str+$i, 'w');
    fwrite($fp, $data);
    fclose($fp);
}
```

When translated to Node.js without refactoring, the for statement is replaced with a callback chain:

```
fs.open('fp.txt', 'w', 0666, function(error, fp) {
  fs.write(fp, data, null, 'utf-8', function() {
    fs.close(fp, function(error) {
      fs.open('fp.txt', 'w', 0666, function(error, fp) {
        fs.write(fp, data, null, 'utf-8', function() {
          fs.close(fp, function(error) {
            // and on and on for a total of "n" times
          });
        });
      });
    });
  });
});
```

How can the callback chain be avoided? Each file has to be written individually; there is no special nonblocking Node.js API that can write multiple files with a single callback. If each file is written individually, then multiple Node.js API calls must be made, each with its own callback and each nested in the callback of the previous API call.

In the next chapter, a more sophisticated conversion recipe will be presented to address this problem. That conversion recipe involves PHP continuations, a way to simulate callbacks in PHP code and even older PHP 4 code, which does not support new language features introduced in PHP 5 (e.g., lambdas and anonymous functions) that would be helpful in making Node.js-style callbacks work.

CHAPTER 4

Advanced Callbacks

In the previous chapter, the concept and use of linearity was explained. Making PHP code linear makes it easier to convert to Node.js code. But what if PHP code cannot be made linear?

A good example of PHP code that cannot simply be made linear is a for statement that writes to multiple files. The PHP code remains stubbornly linear because the for statement cannot be eliminated and the blocking PHP API calls cannot be moved outside of it:

```
for ($i=0; $i < $n; ++$i) {
  $fp = fopen('fp.txt'+$i, 'w');
  fwrite($fp, $data);
  fclose($fp);
}
```

The Node.js "callback chain" illustrates how the Node.js code will work. A callback chain is formed where each subsequent nonblocking Node.js API call is nested inside the callback of the previous nonblocking Node.js API call, forming an arbitrarily long chain:

```
fs.open('fp.txt0', 'w', 0666, function(error, fp) {
  fs.write(fp, data, null, 'utf-8', function() {
    fs.close(fp, function(error) {
      fs.open('fp.txt1', 'w', 0666, function(error, fp) {
        fs.write(fp, data, null, 'utf-8', function() {
          fs.close(fp, function(error) {
            // and on and on for a total of "n" times
          });
        });
      });
    });
  });
});
```

Although this example illustrates how the Node.js code needs to function, it is not practical because the value of the n variable might only be known at runtime. To actually implement the callback chain in Node.js, the code must use three relatively sophisticated JavaScript features: anonymous functions, lambdas, and closures.

Anonymous Functions, Lambdas, and Closures

An anonymous function is a function without a name. Named functions are general-purpose tools, ready and available for other JavaScript code to invoke at any time. In contrast, anonymous functions are usually special purpose and specific to the code that they are declared in.

How can you call a function without a name? An anonymous function is often also a lambda function. A lambda function is a function that can be assigned to a variable and that variable functions very much like any other variable. A lambda function can also be invoked using the usual function call syntax with the variable that the lambda function is assigned to. An anonymous function is assigned to a variable (or passed to a function where it is assigned to one of the function arguments) and can be invoked using the variable and the function call syntax. For example:

```
var f = function(a) {
  // lambda function
  return a + 1;
};

var b = f(4); // b takes the value of 5
```

The word "lambda" may sound highfalutin and complicated but it hides the simple concept that functions are first-class values, like numbers and strings, and can mostly be treated and manipulated in the same ways that numbers and strings can.

To make anonymous functions easier and more capable, JavaScript supports closure. Closure is a language feature where, when the function is defined, the outer context of a function is preserved and is made available to the function when it is invoked. The value of any variables in the saved context is persistent over time and there is only one value at any given time; all invocations of the function share the same context and refer to the same variables. An example of closure is:

```
function f() {
  var b = 6;
  function g() {
    // b is closed over by this function
    ++b;
    return b;
  }
  return g;
}
```

```
var h = f();
var c = h(); // c is 7
var d = h(); // d is 8
```

In this example, the b variable, even though it is not a local variable of the g() function, is still available to the g() function even after the f() function has exited. The b variable (also called an "upvalue" in closure terminology) behaves sort of like a private global variable. It behaves like a global variable to the g() function but is hidden from all other code that is outside of the f() function.

Anonymous functions, lambdas, and closures are needed to implement a callback chain that can be arbitrarily long:

```
var f = function() {
};
for (var i=n-1; i >= 0; --i) {
  f = function(g, j) {
    return function() {
      fs.open('fp.txt'+j, 'w', 0666, function(error, fp) {
        fs.write(fp, data, null, 'utf-8', function() {
          fs.close(fp, function(error) {
            g();
          }
        });
      });
    };
  } (f, i);
}
f();
```

The Node.js code is quite complicated. The overall algorithm is to build the callback chain in reverse order, from the most deeply nested call to the outermost call, and then to kick off the callback chain by calling the first one. Let us go through it, step by step.

A do-nothing, default lambda function is created that will be the "no-op" (empty) callback for the innermost fs.close() call:

```
var f = function() {
};
```

In the PHP code, the for statement goes from 0 to n-1 but, since callbacks need to be built from the inside out, Node.js requires the for statement to go from n-1 to 0:

```
for (var i=n-1; i >= 0; --i) {
  // create the callback
}
```

The current callback is held in the f variable to capture the value during this specific iteration of the for loop. The callback just outside the current callback will be created by using a new lambda function that does the work for the outer callback and then calls the current (inner) callback. The new lambda function is a return value for syntax reasons that will be explained next:

```
return function() {
  fs.open('fp.txt'+j, 'w', 0666, function(error, fp) {
    fs.write(fp, data, null, 'utf-8', function() {
      fs.close(fp, function(error) {
        g(); // current callback
      }
    });
  });
}
```

The newly created callback function is returned as an anonymous function. An anonymous function is an unnamed function that can be used as a value. The inner anonymous function takes zero arguments and is used as the return value for an outer function that takes two arguments. The outer function is needed to defeat closure.

In this case, closure must be defeated so that the values of the f and i variables during this iteration of the loop are preserved, instead of their values at some later time, such as when the f function is invoked. Closure is defeated by making new variables, actually, arguments, that will always have the same values. The g variable holds the value of the f variable during this iteration of the for loop; likewise, the j variable holds the value of the i variable during this iteration of the for loop. The outer anonymous function (which takes two arguments) is invoked immediately, as indicated by the (f, i) string at the end of the function definition. When invoked, it captures the f and i values and returns the inner anonymous function. The inner anonymous function actually contains the callback code:

```
f = function(g, j) {
  return function() {
    // implement outer callback
    // call g() to invoke inner callback
  };
} (f, i);
```

The for statement loops from n-1 to 0, creating inner callbacks and nesting them into outer callbacks. When the for statement exits, the f variable contains the outermost callback, which will properly invoke its subsequent callback, which will invoke its subsequent callback, and so on, all in the correct order. All that is left is to invoke the outermost callback:

```
f();
```

This Node.js code works but it has two drawbacks. First, the PHP code looks nothing like the Node.js code. If callback chains occur often (which is common), maintaining and improving the PHP version and the Node.js version simultaneously is going to be very difficult if they are very different. Second, the Node.js code by itself is pretty complicated and requires three advanced JavaScript concepts: lambdas, anonymous functions, and closure.

PHP 5.3

PHP 5.3 introduced anonymous functions, lambdas, and closure to the PHP language. To make the PHP similar to the Node.js code, the PHP code could be refactored from its step-by-step algorithm to the complicated algorithm used by the Node.js function.

Lambdas and anonymous functions in PHP 5.3 are very similar to lambdas in Node.js. The only difference is syntactic. PHP variables use the dollar sign ($) while Node.js variables do not; Node.js variables are required to be declared using the var keyword:

```
$f = function($a) {
  // lambda function
  return $a + 1;
};

$b = $f(4); // $b takes the value of 5
```

PHP 5.3 also supports closure. Unlike Node.js, the entire outer context is not automatically preserved in PHP 5.3 like it is in Node.js. In PHP 5.3, the use keyword must be used to indicate the specific variables (upvalues) that will be captured (closed over) by the function. Variables can be captured in two ways: they can be captured by value or by reference.

If a PHP variable is captured by value, each invocation of the lambda function will reset the variable to its value when the lambda function was created. A variable captured by value freezes its value in time.

If a PHP variable is captured by reference, each invocation of the lambda function shares the same variable. If one invocation modifies the variable, future invocations will see the modification. Capturing by reference might be considered real or true closure and is equivalent to how closure works in Node.js:

```
function f() {
  $b = 6;
  $g = function() use (&$b) {
    // b is closed over by this function
    ++$b;
    return $b;
  }
  return $g;
}
```

```
$h = f();
$c = $h(); // c is 7
$d = $h(); // d is 8
```

This example captures the $b variable by reference. Since the $b variable will be preserved across invocations, the $d variable is assigned the value of 8. Initially, the $b variable is set to 6. Then, when the $c variable is assigned, the $b variable is incremented to 7. Finally, when the $d variable is assigned, the $b variable is incremented to 8.

If the $b variable was captured by value instead of by reference, any call to the $g function would always return 7. In that case, when the $c variable is assigned, the $b variable is incremented to 7. But when the $d variable is assigned, the $b variable is reset to 6 and then incremented to 7. The $d variable would receive a value of 7 instead of a value of 8.

What is the purpose of capturing by value if it is not really closure? Capturing by value is how PHP 5.3 defeats closure.

Earlier, it was shown that Node.js needs to defeat closure in order to take the current value of a variable when a function is defined, instead of its current value at the time of invocation. Here's a simple example of defeating closure in Node.js:

```
for (var i=0; i < n; ++i) {
  f[i] = function(j) {
    return function() {
      return j;
    };
  } (i);
}
```

In Node.js, an outer function and an inner function are used to defeat closure. The outer function, which takes a single argument, is declared and then immediately invoked as indicated by the (i) string at the end of the function definition. When it is invoked, the value of the i variable is "frozen" in the j argument. The inner function captures the j variable instead of the i variable. Even though the j variable is captured (essentially by reference), a new j variable is declared each time through the loop. The j variable is many variables that take the value of the i variable when the function is defined; the i variable itself is a single variable with a single value that is shared across all invocations.

Consider alternative Node.js code where closure is not defeated:

```
for (var i=0; i < n; ++i) {
  f[i] = function() {
    return i;
  };
}
```

In this Node.js example, a single i variable is shared across all the functions. The i variable breaks out of the loop when the i variable reaches the value of n. Since the i variable now has the value of n, all the functions that were generated will return the current value of i, which is n.

PHP 5.3 is much simpler. Instead of declaring two functions where an outer function is required to defeat closure in the inner function, PHP 5.3 allows closure values to be captured by value, instead of reference. Defeating closure is a language feature that results in simpler code:

```php
for ($i=0; $i < $n; ++$i) {
    $f[$i] = function() use ($i) {
        return $i;
    };
}
```

Closure (i.e., true closure) is enabled by using the ampersand (&) in the use clause of the code; removing the ampersand (&) defeats closure. The extra complication of outer and inner functions and immediate invocation in Node.js is not needed in PHP 5.3.

Using anonymous functions, lambdas, and closure by value (i.e., defeating closure), the Node.js callback chain algorithm can be implemented in PHP 5.3. The new PHP 5.3 code is more complex than the original code, but by design, it is very similar to the Node.js code:

```php
$f = function() {
};
for ($i=$n-1; $i >= 0; --$n) {
    $f = function() use ($f, $i) {
        $fp = fopen('fp.txt'+$i, 'w');
        fwrite($fp, $data);
        fclose($fp);
        $f();
    }
}
$f();
```

The corresponding Node.js code is:

```javascript
var f = function() {
};
for (var i=n-1; i >= 0; --i) {
    f = function(g, j) {
        return function() {
            fs.open('fp.txt'+j, 'w', 0666, function(error, fp) {
                fs.write(fp, data, null, 'utf-8', function() {
                    fs.close(fp, function(error) {
                        g();
                    }
                });
            });
        });
}
```

```
    };
  } (f, i);
  }
  f();
```

Since the PHP 5.3 code now looks so similar to the Node.js code, it is much easier to improve the code and add features while maintaining both the PHP and Node.js versions simultaneously.

The PHP 5.3 code can be improved to parallel the Node.js code more closely. The definition of the f function inside the for statement looks like this:

```
$fp = fopen('fp.txt'+$i, 'w');
fwrite($fp, $data);
fclose($fp);
$f();
```

The corresponding Node.js code looks like this:

```
fs.open('fp.txt'+j, 'w', 0666, function(error, fp) {
  fs.write(fp, data, null, 'utf-8', function() {
    fs.close(fp, function(error) {
      g();
    }
  });
});
```

Notice anything familiar? The linearity-based conversion recipes from Chapter 3 can be applied here! The PHP 5.3 implementation of the f function can be made linear and converted to Node.js code easily and independently. The outer context of the function is irrelevant and is totally orthogonal to converting the implementation of function f.

One annoyance is that the PHP 5.3 code uses $i and $f, the original names of the variables captured using closure by value, whereas the Node.js renames these variables to j and g. This annoyance is easily remedied by creating temporary variables, $j and $g, in the PHP 5.3 code:

```
$g = $f;
$j = $i;
$fp = fopen('fp.txt'+$j, 'w');
fwrite($fp, $data);
fclose($fp);
$g();
```

The final PHP 5.3 implementation of the callback chain algorithm is:

```
$f = function() {
};
for ($i=$n-1; $i >= 0; --$n) {
  $f = function() use ($f, $i) {
    $g = $f;
    $j = $i;
    $fp = fopen('fp.txt'+$j, 'w');
```

```
        fwrite($fp, $data);
        fclose($fp);
        $g();
    }
  }
}
$f();
```

So, a useful conversion recipe is to rewrite PHP 5.3 code from a step-by-step algorithm to a callback chain algorithm.

A pattern is developing. Converting PHP code to Node.js code often involves refactoring the PHP code so it is more like Node.js, not simply taking the PHP code as is and grinding through a bunch of conversion steps to output Node.js code at the other end. Refactoring the PHP code can even be seen as converting Node.js features and algorithms to PHP such that when the "official" conversion process begins, the PHP code is already primed for easy conversion to Node.js code. The conversion process is two-way: the PHP code is converted to Node.js, but in some sense, the Node.js code is converted to PHP code. An acceptable medium is developed between the two languages and the two codebases. Most likely, the developer will decide to compromise the PHP code the most but there will be some cases where the Node.js code makes some minor compromises to keep the PHP code from being too difficult.

PHP 4

PHP 5.3 introduced anonymous functions, lambdas, and closure, which are all needed to easily create Node.js-style callback chain algorithms. What about PHP 4 and other PHP versions below PHP 5.3? Does PHP code that is converted to Node.js have to drop support for PHP versions below 5.3?

Many web hosting companies no longer support or provide PHP 4 or PHP versions below 5.3. Similarly, as cloud computing increases in popularity and virtual machines become the de facto standard for delivering cloud computing, the user can choose any version of PHP that he wants to run and there really is not any reason to choose a PHP version less than 5.3. If your PHP code is targeted for specific users, perhaps you can require those users to install PHP 5.3 and above. If your PHP code is targeted at the general public, perhaps it is not a serious burden or inconvenience to require them to install PHP 5.3 or above or to insist that your users select only services that support PHP 5.3 and above.

Still, there are some good reasons to support PHP 4 and PHP versions below 5.3. One reason is to remove the PHP version as a requirement. Why have a requirement when you do not have to? If your PHP code supports PHP versions below 5.3, you can loosen the requirement from "PHP 5.3 and above" to just "PHP." The user no longer needs to figure out the PHP version; he only needs to know that he can serve PHP code. Another reason is that the codebase will rely on fewer language features. If you decide to convert your PHP code to even more languages, do you really want to require those languages to support advanced language features like anonymous functions, lambdas, and closure and assume that they are supported in a similar way? In the past, software was written and functioned in languages without these advanced features, so it is probably doable. It may even be easier for novice developers to follow and understand your code. A final reason is that there may be some legacy or custom requirement that forces your users to use a PHP version below 5.3.

For the rest of this chapter, I will present a way to support PHP 4 and PHP versions below 5.3 that will still allow conversion to Node.js code. With this method, the code can still be improved and features can be added while maintaining both the PHP and Node.js versions simultaneously. For simplicity, I will use the phrase "PHP 4" to loosely refer to "PHP 4 and PHP versions below 5.3."

Anonymous functions, lambdas, and closure are not supported in PHP 4. However, these language features can be simulated in PHP 4 and even the simulations of these features can be converted to Node.js code. Instead of using its built-in versions of anonymous functions, lambdas, and closure, the Node.js code can convert the algorithms that implements the simulations from PHP and run them. Both the PHP and Node.js code will eschew language support for anonymous functions, lambdas, and closure so their code can closely parallel each other.

A simulation of a language feature always uses a subset of the language. Basic features of the language are built upon to accomplish what the more advanced feature could accomplish simply and directly. The Node.js code will always be able to use its basic features to simulate its more advanced features. With trivial differences, it will always be possible for the PHP code that simulates an anonymous function, a lambda, or closure to be directly converted to Node.js code that supports it in the same way. The basic features of PHP and Node.js are nearly identical in functionality, though not in syntax, such that it can confidently be said that "whatever can be built with PHP's basic features can be built with Node.js' basic features." As a result, the PHP code that simulates anonymous functions, lambdas, and closures can be converted and will work the same way in Node.js.

In Node.js, this anonymous function increments its argument and returns the incremented value as its return value:

```
function(a) {
  return a + 1;
};
```

In PHP 4, this anonymous function can be simulated by giving it a name. It is now a "simulated anonymous PHP function":

```
function anon_increment($a) {
  return $a + 1;
}
```

This simulated anonymous PHP function can be converted back to Node.js:

```
function anon_increment(a) {
    return a + 1;
}
```

If the Node.js code has 20 anonymous functions, they can be simulated by making 20 named functions in PHP and those 20 named PHP functions can be converted back to Node.js as 20 named Node.js functions. For now, it may seem pointless but it can be done.

A lambda function, which is generally an anonymous function, is stored in a lambda variable. The f variable stores a lambda function in the following Node.js code:

```
var f = function(a) {
    return a + 1;
};
```

In PHP 4, a lambda variable can be simulated using a PHP array. A PHP array can store all the information to "freeze" a function call. Instead of passing around a lambda variable, a PHP array variable can be passed around. If supported properly, the PHP array can do everything that a lambda variable can do:

```
function anon_increment($a) {
    return $a + 1;
}

$f = array('func'=>'anon_increment');
```

The $f variable above encapsulates a lambda variable by storing the name of the function that it represents. The func key indicates which lambda function it is pointing to.

This simulated lambda PHP variable and function can be converted back to Node.js:

```
function anon_increment(a) {
    return a + 1;
}

var f = {'func':'anon_increment'};
```

In Node.js, the PHP array becomes a Node.js object. Node.js objects work similarly to PHP arrays and have a similar syntax.

In Node.js, a lambda function can be invoked:

```
var f = function(a) {
    return a + 1;
};

var b = f(4); // b takes the value of 5
```

To simulate the invocation of a lambda function in PHP 4, the target function must accept a call object, a PHP array that represents the lambda function call. The invoking code will create this call object before it invokes the simulated lambda function. The call object combines both the lambda variable and the details of the call, such as the argument values.

The call object will contain several properties. These properties are:

func
:   A string with the name of the function to invoke

args
:   An array of objects that are the arguments to the call

ret
:   An object that is the return value of the call

Each function that will be a target of a simulated lambda function call will need to have a version of itself that accepts a call object instead of ordinary arguments and return values. Accepting a call object will give the utmost flexibility to the target function in terms of handling the call. By convention, the lf_ prefix is added to the function name to indicate that it is a "lambda function" handler. The lambda function handler will unpack the call arguments and repack the return value into the call object.

A side-by-side comparison of the PHP anon_increment() function and the PHP lf_anon_increment() lambda function will demonstrate how the $a argument is unpacked from the lambda call object, the $lc argument, and how the return value is repacked into the same:

```php
function anon_increment($a) {
  return $a + 1;
}

function lf_anon_increment($lc) {
  $a = $lc['args']['a']; // unpack the arguments
  $ret = $a + 1;
  $lc['ret'] = $ret; // pack the return value
};
```

At the start of the function, the argument array is unpacked into individual variables that have the same name. When the function exits, the return value is packed into the call object.

Of course, the simulated lambda function can be converted to Node.js:

```js
function anon_increment(a) {
  return a + 1;
}

function lf_anon_increment(lc) {
```

```
      var a = lc['args']['a']; // unpack the arguments
      var ret = a + 1;
      lc['ret'] = ret; // pack the return value
};
```

A helper function is needed to translate the simulated lambda call object into an actual function call. This PHP function works like a very poor man's JavaScript eval() function call. It takes a string and turns it into running code. In our case, it takes a string and turns it into a single function call:

```
function lc_call($lc) {
    if ($lc['func'] == 'anon_increment') {
      lf_anon_increment($lc);
    }
    return $lc;
}
```

For convenience of the callers, the lc_call() function returns the same call object, which is passed as an argument. The calling code can sometimes have more compact code by taking advantage of the returned call object.

The lc_call() function will grow as you add new lambda functions. You simply add more if…else clauses. If you have many lambda functions, the lc_call() function will become very long.

The lc_call() function can be converted to Node.js:

```
function lc_call(lc) {
    if (lc['func'] == 'anon_increment') {
      lf_anon_increment(lc);
    }
    return lc;
}
```

To simulate a lambda function call, the call object is created by merging the function object with the arguments. The PHP array_merge() function takes the $f array variable, which simulates the lambda variable and merges or adds an array that represents the function arguments to be applied. Then, the lc_call() function is called on the call object to execute the call. The lc_call() function finds the function to call and calls it. The target function, the lf_anon_increment() function in our previous example, un-packs the arguments, increments the argument, and then packs the return value in the ret key. The lf_anon_increment() function returns to lc_call(), which returns the call object to the caller. Since the call object is returned from the lc_call() function, the ret key can be accessed inline to get the return value. Here's the "long" form of the code to invoke the simulated lambda function:

```
$b = lc_call(array_merge($f, array('args'=>array('a'=>4))))['ret'];
```

Although this PHP code makes it as straightforward as possible to trace the code through the `lc_call()` function call then through the `lf_anon_increment()` function call and back again, it is unnecessarily verbose in practice. A helper function, the `lf_call()` function, can shorten the code for lambda functions to be turned into calls:

```
function lf_call($lf, $a) {
  $lf['args'] = $a;
  return lc_call($lf);
}

$b = lf_call($f, array('a'=>4))['ret'];
```

Instead of calling the `array_merge()` PHP API, assigning the arguments array to the `args` key of the lambda variable works just as well. In practice, it is harmless to reuse a lambda function as a call object. `lf_call()` is much simpler than `lc_call()`.

Of course, this PHP code can be converted to Node.js code easily:

```
function lf_call(lf, a) {
  lf['args'] = a;
  return lc_call(lf);
}

var b = lf_call(f, array('a'=>4))['ret'];
```

We now have everything needed to simulate the Node.js example code. If you will recall, the Node.js code created an anonymous function, assigned it to the f lambda variable, invoked the f lambda function, and assigned the return value to the b variable:

```
var f = function(a) {
  // anonymous function
  return a + 1;
};

var b = f(4); // b takes the value of 5
```

The four pieces of the simulated lambda call are: the `lf_anon_increment()` function, the `lc_call()` helper function, the `lf_call()` convenience function, and the calling code where the $f lambda variable is invoked. The following code puts all four pieces together for a complete demonstration of how PHP 4 can support lambda (callback) functions:

```
function lf_anon_increment($lc) {
  // anonymous function
  $a = $lc['args']['a'];
  $ret = $a + 1;
  $lc['ret'] = $ret;
};

function lc_call($lc) {
  if ($lc['func'] == 'anon_increment') {
    lf_anon_increment($lc);
```

```
  }
  return $lc;
}

function lf_call($lf, $a) {
  $lf['args'] = $a;
  return lc_call($lf);
}

$f = array('func'=>'anon_increment');
$b = lf_call($f, array('a'=>4))['ret'];
```

This PHP 4 code can be converted to Node.js in a straightforward way:

```
function lf_anon_increment(lc) {
  // anonymous function
  var a = lc['args']['a'];
  var ret = a + 1;
  lc['ret'] = ret;
};

function lc_call(lc) {
  if (lc['func'] == 'anon_increment') {
    lf_anon_increment(lc);
  }
  return lc;
}

function lf_call(lf, a) {
  lf['args'] = a;
  return lc_call(lf);
}

var f = {'func':'anon_increment'};
var b = lf_call(f, {'a':4})['ret'];
```

This example shows definitively that Node.js anonymous functions and lambda variables can work in PHP 4 code and be converted to Node.js code. Now, let us turn our attention to the real world example presented at the start of this chapter. In PHP, writing multiple files was straightforward:

```
for ($i=0; $i < $n; ++$i) {
  $fp = fopen('fp.txt'+$i, 'w');
  fwrite($fp, $data);
  fclose($fp);
}
```

Converting this PHP code to Node.js was problematic. The code was nonlinear and could not be made linear. As a result, the Node.js code had to be completely rewritten with a callback chain algorithm:

```
var f = function() {
};
```

```
for (var i=n-1; i >= 0; --i) {
  f = function(g, j) {
    return function() {
      fs.open('fp.txt'+j, 'w', 0666, function(error, fp) {
        fs.write(fp, data, null, 'utf-8', function() {
          fs.close(fp, function(error) {
            g();
          }
        });
      });
    };
  } (f, i);
}
f();
```

To effectively maintain and improve the PHP and Node.js code simultaneously, it was
unacceptable that the two codebases be so dramatically different. Since the PHP algorithm, a simple for statement, could not be converted into Node.js code, the Node.js
callback chain algorithm was converted to PHP 5.3 code:

```
$f = function() {
};
for ($i=$n-1; $i >= 0; --$n) {
  $f = function() use ($f, $i) {
    $g = $f;
    $j = $i;
    $fp = fopen('fp.txt'+$j, 'w');
    fwrite($fp, $data);
    fclose($fp);
    $g();
  }
}
$f();
```

To convert this PHP 5.3 code to PHP 4, the first step is to identify and implement the
anonymous functions. At the top of the code, there is a "do nothing" anonymous function; a good name for this function is lf_anon_noop() because it is a "no operation"
function or "noop" for short. Inside the for statement, there is a "write file" anonymous
function; a good name for this function is lf_anon_writefile(). Here's the code for
these functions:

```
function lf_anon_noop($lc) {
}

function lf_anon_writefile($lc) {
  $j = $lc['args']['j'];
  $g = $lc['args']['g'];
  $fp = fopen('fp.txt'+$j, 'w');
  fwrite($fp, $data);
  fclose($fp);
  lc_call($g);
}
```

In the PHP 4 `if_anon_writefile()` function, the arguments are unpacked from the lambda call object. After that, the file is written; the PHP 4 code for that is unsurprising. Finally, the `$g` lambda variable is invoked to execute the next step in the callback chain.

These PHP 4 anonymous functions can be converted to Node.js:

```
function lf_anon_noop(lc) {
}

function lf_anon_writefile(lc) {
  var j = lc['args']['j'];
  var g = lc['args']['g'];
  fs.open('fp.txt'+j, 'w', 0666, function(error, fp) {
    fs.write(fp, data, null, 'utf-8', function() {
      fs.close(fp, function(error) {
        lc_call(g);
      }
    });
  });
}
```

Notice how the implementation of the `lf_anon_writefile()` function in Node.js can have the linearity-based conversion rules from Chapter 3 applied independently of the outer context of the function. A callback chain algorithm works because it forces the nonblocking Node.js API calls into an anonymous function that prevents those APIs from affecting the surrounding code. The anonymous function serves as a "prison" for the nonlinear code, breaking it apart from the `for` statement that causes it to be non-linear. Since it is effectively no longer in a `for` statement, the `for` statement becomes linear.

The second step to make the PHP 4 code work is to implement the `lc_call()` and `lf_call()` functions. The `lc_call()` function is unsurprising; it is modified from the example to execute the `lf_anon_noop()` and `lf_anon_writefile()` functions instead of the `lf_anon_increment()` function from the previous example. The `lf_call()` function is unchanged. It is completely independent of the specifics of the rest of the PHP 4 code:

```
function lc_call($lc) {
  if ($lc['func'] == 'anon_noop') {
    lf_anon_noop($lc);
  } else if ($lc['func'] == 'anon_writefile') {
    lf_anon_writefile($lc);
  }
  return $lc;
}

function lf_call($lf, $a) {
  $lf['args'] = $a;
  return lc_call($lf);
}
```

The PHP 4 `lf_anon_noop()` and `lf_anon_writefile()` functions are converted to Node.js with very few changes:

```
function lc_call(lc) {
  if (lc['func'] == 'anon_noop') {
    lf_anon_noop(lc);
  } else if (lc['func'] == 'anon_writefile') {
    lf_anon_writefile(lc);
  }
  return lc;
}

function lf_call(lf, a) {
  lf['args'] = a;
  return lc_call(lf);
}
```

The third and final step is to convert the PHP 5.3 calling code into PHP 4. To more clearly see the PHP 5.3 calling code, the implementations of the anonymous functions have been removed and replaced with comments here:

```
$f = function() {
  // the lf_anon_noop() anonymous function
};
for ($i=$n-1; $i >= 0; --$n) {
  $f = function() use ($f, $i) {
    // the lf_anon_writefile() anonymous function
  }
}
$f();
```

This PHP 5.3 calling code will be translated line by line to PHP 4 and Node.js.

The following PHP 5.3 code assigns a "noop" (no operation) lambda function to the `$f` lambda variable:

```
$f = function() {
  // the lf_anon_noop() anonymous function
};
```

In PHP 4, the `$f` lambda variable becomes an array variable that points to the `lf_anon_noop()` simulated anonymous function:

```
$f = array('func'=>'anon_noop');
```

Next, in PHP 5.3, the `for` statement builds the callback chain by repeatedly redefining the `$f` lambda variable in terms of its initial value or its value from the last time through the loop. The `use` keyword is used in such a way to defeat closure for the `$f` and `$i` variables. The `$f` lambda variable is used inside the anonymous function (i.e., `lf_anon_writefile()`) as the next link in the chain:

```
for ($i=$n-1; $i >= 0; --$n) {
  $f = function() use ($f, $i) {
    // the lf_anon_writefile() anonymous function
  }
}
```

In PHP 4, the for statement remains the same. The inside of the for statement is very interesting, though:

```
for ($i=$n-1; $i >= 0; --$n) {
  $f = array('func'=>'anon_writefile', 'args'=>array('j'=>$i, 'g'=>$f));
}
```

The $f lambda variable is redefined as a call object that passes the current value of the $i index variable and the value of the $f lambda variable from the previous time through the loop as arguments. But in the PHP 5.3 code, these variables are not passed as arguments; they are passed to the use keyword in such as a manner as to defeat closure. Closure and arguments are two different things. What happened to closure?

With Node.js and PHP 5.3 lambda variables, only a function can be stored in a variable, not any predefined arguments. Arguments can only be applied when the lambda variable is invoked, not at the time of definition. In PHP 4, though, lambda variables are simulated using an array. Since lambda variables are just arrays, arguments can be added at the time of definition or at the time of invocation or any other time. In some sense, simulated lambda variables are more powerful than real lambda variables because they can add their arguments at any time, not just at the time of invocation.

In light of this idea, closure can be seen as a way to add arguments at the time of definition. When using closure, arguments are added to the lambda function by reference. When defeating closure, arguments are added by value. Simulating a lambda variable using an array and manipulating the arguments at definition time is a drop-in replacement for defeating closure.

To simulate the PHP 5.3 use clause in PHP 4, a call object is assigned to the $f lambda variable with the use variables passed as arguments. It is that simple:

```
$f = array('func'=>'anon_writefile', 'args'=>array('j'=>$i, 'g'=>$f));
```

Once the callback chain has been created, it needs to be triggered. A PHP 4 lc_call() call starts the callback chain:

```
lc_call($f);
```

Put together, here's the PHP 4 calling code:

```
$f = array('func'=>'anon_noop');
for ($i=$n-1; $i >= 0; --$n) {
  $f = array('func'=>'anon_writefile', 'args'=>array('j'=>$i, 'g'=>$f));
}
lc_call($f);
```

The Node.js version is similar:

```
f = {'func':'anon_noop'};
for (var i=n-1; i >= 0; --n) {
  f = {'func':'anon_writefile', 'args':{'j':i, 'g':f}};
}
lc_call(f);
```

Although using arrays directly will work, some convenience functions would be nice for PHP 4 production code.

A PHP 4 lf_create() convenience function is useful for creating lambda functions instead of direct array definition:

```
function lf_create($name) {
  return array('func'=>$name);
}
```

Here's the Node.js version of the lf_create() function:

```
function lf_create(name) {
  return {'func':name};
}
```

A PHP 4 lc_create() convenience function is useful for creating call objects:

```
function lc_create($name, $args) {
  return array('func'=>$name, 'args'=>$args)
}
```

The lc_create() function is easily converted to Node.js:

```
function lc_create(name, args) {
  return {'func':name, 'args':args};
}
```

With the three PHP 5.3 steps converted to PHP 4, plus the two convenience functions, the PHP 4 code can be put together.

Here's the PHP 5.3 version:

```
$f = function() {
};
for ($i=$n-1; $i >= 0; --$n) {
  $f = function() use ($f, $i) {
    $g = $f;
    $j = $i;
    $fp = fopen('fp.txt'+$j, 'w');
    fwrite($fp, $data);
    fclose($fp);
    $g();
  }
}
$f();
```

Here's the PHP 4 version, which also works on PHP 5.3:

```php
function lf_anon_noop($lc) {
}

function lf_anon_writefile($lc) {
  $j = $lc['args']['j'];
  $g = $lc['args']['g'];
  $fp = fopen('fp.txt'+$j, 'w');
  fwrite($fp, $data);
  fclose($fp);
  lc_call($g);
}

function lf_create($name) {
  return array('func'=>$name);
}

function lf_call($lf, $a) {
  $lf['args'] = $a;
  return lc_call($lf);
}

function lc_create($name, $args) {
  return array('func'=>$name, 'args'=>$args)
}

function lc_call($lc) {
  if ($lc['func'] == 'anon_noop') {
    lf_anon_noop($lc);
  } else if ($lc['func'] == 'anon_writefile') {
    lf_anon_writefile($lc);
  }
  return $lc;
}

$f = lf_create('anon_noop');
for ($i=$n-1; $i >= 0; --$n) {
  $f = lc_create('anon_writefile', array('j'=>$i, 'g'=>$f));
}
lc_call($f);
```

Here's the PHP 4 version converted to Node.js:

```javascript
function lf_anon_noop(lc) {
}

function lf_anon_writefile(lc) {
  var j = lc['args']['j'];
  var g = lc['args']['g'];
  fs.open('fp.txt'+j, 'w', 0666, function(error, fp) {
    fs.write(fp, data, null, 'utf-8', function() {
      fs.close(fp, function(error) {
```

```
        lc_call(g);
      }
    });
  });
}

function lf_create(name) {
  return {'func':name};
}

function lf_call(lf, a) {
  lf['args'] = a;
  return lc_call(lf);
}

function lc_create(name, args) {
  return {'func':name, 'args':args};
}

function lc_call(lc) {
  if (lc['func'] == 'anon_noop') {
    lf_anon_noop(lc);
  } else if (lc['func'] == 'anon_writefile') {
    lf_anon_writefile(lc);
  }
  return lc;
}

var f = lf_create('anon_noop');
for (var i=n-1; i >= 0; --n) {
  f = lc_create('anon_writefile', {'j':i, 'g':f});
}
lc_call(f);
```

The simulated anonymous functions and lambda variables are compatible with every-thing: PHP 4, PHP 5.3, and Node.js. These simulation techniques allow arbitrary PHP 4 code to be refactored such that it can be converted to Node.js and both the PHP and Node.js codebases kept closely synchronized while both are improved and new features added.

Some optional improvements are worth mentioning.

Although implementing simulated anonymous functions as standalone functions works fine, there may be cases when anonymous functions either need to be attached to existing classes or a class full of anonymous functions is useful for organizational reasons.

Adding an `obj` key to the lambda variable allows simulated anonymous functions to be added to classes. The `lfo_create()` and `lco_create()` convenience functions, where the "o" stands for "object," are object-based versions of the `lf_create()` and `lc_create()` convenience functions. When these alternative functions are used, the `lc_call()` function can invoke simulated anonymous functions that are attached to objects. Here's the PHP 4 code:

```php
function lfo_create($obj, $name) {
  return array('obj'=>$obj, 'func'=>$name);
}

function lco_create($obj, $name, $args) {
  return array('obj'=>$obj, 'func'=>$name, 'args'=>$args);
}

function lc_call($lc) {
  if ($lc['func'] == 'anon_noop') {
    $lc['obj']->lf_anon_noop($lc);
  } else if ($lc['func'] == 'anon_writefile') {
    $lc['obj']->lf_anon_writefile($lc);
  }
  return $lc;
}
```

These PHP 4 functions can be converted to Node.js:

```javascript
function lfo_create(obj, name) {
  return {'obj':obj, 'func':name};
}

function lco_create(obj, name, args) {
  return {'obj':obj, 'func':name, 'args':args};
}

function lc_call(lc) {
  if (lc['func'] == 'anon_noop') {
    lc['obj'].lf_anon_noop($lc);
  } else if (lc['func'] == 'anon_writefile') {
    lc['obj'].lf_anon_writefile(lc);
  }
  return lc;
}
```

Chapter 8 shows how to convert PHP classes to Node.js classes. The implementation and usefulness of adding simulated anonymous functions to classes will become more apparent in that chapter.

In the next chapter, the differences between sending an HTTP response in PHP and in Node.js will be addressed. As might be expected, HTTP responses in PHP are sent using a blocking technique whereas HTTP responses in Node.js are sent using a nonblocking technique. The linearity-based conversion recipes from Chapter 3 and the simulation-based conversion recipes from this chapter will be the foundation for refactoring PHP HTTP response code to be easily converted to Node.js.

CHAPTER 5

HTTP Responses

In previous chapters, a development environment suitable for PHP to Node.js conversion was set up, a Node.js framework for hosting Node.js code converted from PHP pages was written, and the original PHP code was refactored to make it friendlier to PHP to Node.js conversion (in particular, in terms of handling callbacks). With that done, we are ready to copy and paste the PHP code from the *.php* file into the corresponding *.njs* file.

At this point, some or all of your *.php* files will have a corresponding *.njs* file in the same directory. All the *.njs* files in your project will have a stub implementation of the page similar to the following Node.js code:

```
var initreq = require('./initreq.njs');

exports.serve = function(req, res) {
  var pre = {};
  initGET(req, pre, function() {
    initPOST(req, pre, function() {
      initCOOKIE(req, pre, function() {
        initREQUEST(req, pre, function() {
          page(req, res, pre, function() {
          });
        });
      });
    });
  });
};

function page(req, res, pre, cb) {
  res.writeHead(200, {'Content-Type': 'text/plain'});
  res.end('index.njs');
  cb();
}
```

The page() function has a stub implementation. We will copy and paste the PHP code from the *.php* file into the implementation of the page() function soon. But first, let's examine how HTTP responses are returned in both PHP and Node.js.

An HTTP response is similar to an HTTP request: it can contain multiple HTTP response headers and a single HTTP response body. In actual implementation, the HTTP response headers are separated from the HTTP response body by a single blank line. The stub implementation of the page() function will produce an HTTP response similar to this:

```
HTTP/1.1 200 OK
Content-Type: text/plain

index.njs
```

In the first header, the one containing HTTP/1.0 200 OK, the 200 is the important part. 200 is an HTTP status code that means that the HTTP request succeeded completely normally. The OK after 200 is just a short description of the status code.

In the second header, Content-Type says that this is a plain text web page, instead of an HTML web page. If it was an HTML web page, the second header would set text/html as the content type instead of text/plain.

The blank line between Content-Type: text/plain and index.njs separates the HTTP response header for the HTTP response body.

Finally, the index.njs line is the HTTP response body. If the user goes to a particular PHP page or clicks a hyperlink, the HTTP response body would contain a full page of HTML. If a browser is running JavaScript and that JavaScript makes an AJAX call, the HTTP response body might contain plain text or data in the JSON format.

Headers

In Node.js, sending an HTTP response is straightforward and transparent. The raw HTTP response object is passed to the page() function as the res parameter. The writeHead() function writes the HTTP response headers. The HTTP status code, 200 in this case, is the first argument and any additional HTTP response headers, such as the Content-Type header, can be passed as the second argument:

```
res.writeHead(200, {'Content-Type': 'text/plain'});
```

Technically, a reason phrase, such as OK, is passed as the second argument and the additional HTTP response headers are passed as a third argument. However, the write Head() function is flexible enough to detect the difference between a reason phrase and HTTP response headers, and can handle HTTP response headers passed as the second argument.

The HTTP response body is just as obvious as the HTTP response headers in Node.js. The HTTP response body can be sent using the end() function of the HTTP response object. The end() function indicates that this is the end of the HTTP response. Any data passed to the end() function will be sent to the client and the HTTP response will be considered complete. The end() function must be called at some point; if it is not, the HTTP response hangs and stays open, which is considered a bug:

```
res.end('index.njs');
```

There is also another Node.js function for writing the HTTP response. The write() function writes some data to the HTTP response body, but instead of considering the HTTP response complete, allows for additional write() function calls and eventually an end() function call:

```
res.write('Some data');
res.write('Some more data');
res.end();
```

By having the raw HTTP response object, res, and using the writeHead(), write(), and end() functions, it is easy to understand how an HTTP response is sent in Node.js.

In contrast, the PHP engine makes certain assumptions about every PHP page that, unless they are changed, are secretly and opaquely applied. By default, a PHP page returns 200 as the HTTP status code. Also by default, a PHP page sets its content type to text/html.

By default, the PHP engine assigns the following HTTP response headers (and a few more of no particular consequence) to the HTTP response object:

```
HTTP/1.1 200 OK
Content-Type: text/html
```

Unlike Node.js, the PHP page does not take the raw HTTP response object and manipulate it directly. There is no corresponding PHP object for the res variable that exists in Node.js. Instead, the PHP engine creates a default HTTP response before it executes the PHP page. Later, when the PHP page is being processed, the PHP page can make PHP API calls to replace any default setting with a new setting. If no changes are made, that is, if the PHP page ignores the HTTP response object, the default HTTP response object is returned.

The PHP header() API changes an HTTP response header. To change the HTTP status code from 200 to 404, the following code would be used. The HTTP status code 404 means that the requested web page was not found:

```
header('HTTP/1.1 404 Not Found');
```

To change the Content-Type header for an HTTP response from the default text/html to text/plain, the same PHP header() API would be used, as follows:

```
header('Content-Type: text/plain');
```

In PHP, existing HTTP response headers are modified and new HTTP response headers are added using the same PHP header() API.

Body

To set the HTTP response body, PHP has the print and echo keywords. In PHP, the print and echo keywords work similarly to the way that the Node.js write() function works in Node.js. The print and echo keywords write some data to the HTTP response body, but instead of considering the HTTP response complete, they allow additional calls to print and echo. Here's a trivial example using print:

```
print 'Some data';
print 'Some more data';
```

The difference between print and echo is minor and not worth discussing here. For all practical purposes, they work the same.

A PHP page has another way that it can write to the HTTP response body. All content that is outside a PHP tag, that is, all content that is not between <?php and its corresponding ?> is considered to be part of the HTTP response body. In the following example, The value of x plus 5 is and the final . are part of the HTTP response body:

```
The value of x plus 5 is <?php echo $x; ?>.
```

PHP does not have an equivalent to the end() function in the Node.js HTTP response object. When the PHP engine finishes processing a PHP page, it assumes that the HTTP response is complete. As you will recall from the previous chapter, the PHP engine has fine control and understanding over the lifetime of a PHP page; the PHP engine controls before, during, and after PHP page processing. Using this control, the PHP engine knows when the PHP page is done and does not need an API call to indicate it. But because Node.js operates at the server level and not the page level, it does not have any built-in control or understanding about the concept of a web page. The only way that it can know that an HTTP response is complete is by telling it to use the end() function.

There is one other minor difference in terms of HTTP responses: PHP has a flush() API and Node.js does not. The flush() API tells the PHP engine to do its best to send all HTTP response headers and the HTTP response body that have been created so far in case they are being buffered in a cache. Here's an example PHP flush() API call:

```
print 'Some data';
print 'Some more data';
flush();
```

The PHP engine supports HTTP response caching, so when a PHP print or echo is executed, it may write to a cache instead of being sent out immediately. The PHP flush()

API sends the contents of this cache to the client and empties the cache. In contrast, Node.js has no built-in buffering or caching. If buffering or caching is desired, it must be written manually or imported as a Node.js module. Since the HTTP response is never buffered, the Node.js `write()` function always sends its content immediately.

In both PHP and Node.js, the PHP response headers always have to come before the HTTP response body. Recall the raw HTTP response presented at the beginning of this chapter:

```
HTTP/1.1 200 OK
Content-Type: text/plain

index.njs
```

The HTTP response headers are separated from the HTTP response body by a blank line. Since the HTTP response headers are always before the blank line and the HTTP response body is always after the blank line, all HTTP headers have to be sent before any part of the HTTP body can be sent. If no HTTP response headers have been explicitly specified, both Node.js and PHP send the default HTTP response headers when a call is first made to write to the HTTP response body. If an attempt is made to write the HTTP response headers after the HTTP response body has already been written, the attempt is ignored because the default HTTP response headers have already been sent. The HTTP response always follows a strict order: HTTP response headers, then HTTP response body.

Now that we have a detailed understanding of how HTTP responses work in both PHP and Node.js, we can turn our attention to one big challenge of converting HTTP responses from PHP to Node.js: ensuring that the `end()` function is called on the HTTP response in Node.js.

Recall the stub implementation of the Node.js `page()` function:

```
function page(req, res, pre, cb) {
  res.writeHead(200, {'Content-Type': 'text/plain'});
  res.end('index.njs');
  cb();
}
```

Notice that any `write()` function calls will be inserted between the `writeHead()` function call and the `end()` function call. The `end()` function call is always right before the page is finished; it signals that the HTTP response is complete. The `cb()` function call is always right after that to call back to the `exports.serve()` function to do any post processing after a page is completed. If new HTML or new PHP is inserted into the page and converted to Node.js, the new Node.js code will always go somewhere before the `end()` and `cb()` function calls because both those functions essentially indicate the ends of different things. A call to the end() function indicates that the HTTP response is complete and nothing more can be added to the HTTP response body. The cb() function call indicates that the page is complete and control should be returned to the Node.js server.

If the PHP page is mostly HTML with a few sections of PHP that use PHP functions, which, when converted to Node.js, will not use callbacks, it is easy. In that case, the end() and cb() function calls go at the end of the page() function.

However, if the PHP page is complicated with classes and with many PHP API calls that will be converted to Node.js APIs with callbacks, the "end of the function" is not so clear and could be in many places.

Consider this simple PHP page, which reads the *message.html* file and shows it:

```php
<?php
$contents = file_get_contents('message.html');
print $contents;
?>
```

When converted to Node.js, the call to the PHP file_get_contents() API function will be replaced with a call to the Node.js readFile() API function in the fs module. Here's the page() function that implements this example PHP page in Node.js:

```
var fs = require('fs');

function page(req, res, pre, cb) {
  res.writeHead(200, {'Content-Type': 'text/html'});
  fs.readFile('message.html', 'ascii', function(err, contents) {
    res.end(contents);
    cb();
  }
  // do nothing here!
}
```

Notice how the end() and cb() function calls have shifted from the end of the page() function to the end of the callback used by the readFile() function. The end() function must be called when the HTTP response is complete, and in this case, the HTTP response requires the contents of the *message.html* file, which is only available when the callback passed to the readFile() function is invoked. When callbacks are involved, the end of the page() function does not necessarily indicate that the HTTP response is complete or that the page is done processing. Callbacks allow a function to continue even after the function itself has returned.

The comment that reads "do nothing here!" is important, too. The end() and cb() function calls must be removed from here. Otherwise, the end() and cb() functions would be called twice: once when the readFile() function returned, and a second time when the callback to the readFile() function was invoked. The HTTP response can be completed once and only once because the end() function declares the HTTP response complete and closes the connection. When an HTTP response is considered complete, it is complete and fully sent. Adding additional content would mean that it was not complete the first time. Calling it complete again, by calling the end() function a second time without an argument, is invalid too, because the HTTP response has already been sent. Similarly, when the cb() function is invoked, it means that the page is done processing and ready for post processing and, if this is called more than once, it means that one of the calls was an error.

In Chapter 3, the concept of linearity was described. It was largely about keeping a single code path through the PHP page, but when a code path needed to be split, keeping both subsequent code paths independent and not allowing them to recombine. The end() and cb() function calls will be at the end of some of these code paths, although they will not be at the end of some others. However, they will not ever need to be put in the middle of a code path or somewhere else in the code. Logically, making the HTTP response complete by calling the end() function and doing post-processing on the page by calling the cb() function can only happen at the end of a code path. By knowing and understanding the code paths generated by the linearity concept in Chapter 3, you have a finite set of locations to consider putting the end() and cb() function calls.

A helpful technique can be to add a "do nothing" function call to the PHP codebase to remind yourself where the end() and cb() function calls will need to be added when the code is converted to Node.js. The following PHP code shows an eocp() function, which stands for "end of code path"; it will only print out the data argument when invoked on the PHP side, but can serve as a marker to indicate that the Node.js code will need to make its end() and cb() function calls at this location:

```php
$res = '';
$cb = '';
function eocp($res, $cb, $data) {
  print $data;
}
...
eocp($res, $cb, '');
```

In fact, the eocp() function can be converted and implemented in Node.js as a quick-and-dirty way to call the end() and cb() functions in the correct places:

```javascript
function eocp(res, cb, data) {
  res.end(data);
  cb();
}
...
eocp(res, cb, '');
```

When the PHP and Node.js codebases are compared using a visual diff feature or program as described in Chapter 1, the eocp() function calls in both codebases should be matched and able to be visually verified to be in all the correct places.

The eocp() function can work and is a good approach but there is an alternative.

An alternative approach is to remove all the end() function calls from the page() function and put them into the callback function, the cb callback variable, that is passed from the exports.serve() function. The following code shows the exports.serve() function with the end() function call:

```
exports.serve = function(req, res) {
  var pre = {};
  initGET(req, pre, function() {
    initPOST(req, pre, function() {
      initCOOKIE(req, pre, function() {
        initREQUEST(req, pre, function() {
          page(req, res, pre, function() {
            res.end();
          });
        });
      });
    });
  });
};
```

With this approach, the eocp() function and the end() function call isn't needed in the page() function implementation. Instead, an empty cb() function can be used in PHP to serve as a marker:

```
function cb() {
}
...
cb();
```

In Node.js, the cb() function is already defined, so a new function is not needed. The cb() function is called in the same place that it would normally be called. The end() function call is removed since it is now done inside the exports.serve() function:

```
function page(req, res, pre, cb) {
  ...
  cb();
}
```

The only caveat of this alternative approach is that no data can be passed to the end() function call. All PHP print and echo statements must be converted to the Node.js res.write() function and even the last one must use the res.write() function instead of the res.end() function.

A PHP Example Page

Now, let's take some PHP example code and see how we would convert it to Node.js using these ideas and this information. The following is a piece of PHP code that prints an error page. The cb() marker function and a call to it has already been added, and we will use the approach where we add the end() function call to the exports.serve() function:

```php
<?php
  function cb() {
  }
?>
<?php
  $site = $_REQUEST['site'];
  header('HTTP/1.1 404 Not Found');
?>
<html><head></head><body>
<?php
  $header = file_get_contents('header.html');
  print $header;
?>
The page could not be found on <?php echo $site; ?>.
<?php
  $footer = file_get_contents('footer.html');
  print $footer;
?>
</body></html>
<? cb(); ?>
```

Now let's do the conversion step by step for this particular PHP page. The conversion consists of nine steps:

1. Copy and paste the PHP code into the Node.js page() function.

2. Remove the unneeded cb() function definition manually.

3. For all text outside the PHP tags, put the text in a res.write() function call, possibly putting a newline escape sequence (\n) at the end.

4. Remove the <?php text using the Find/Replace feature in Eclipse PDT.

5. Remove the ?> text.

6. Replace $_REQUEST with pre._REQUEST.

7. Replace print with res.write(, and at each occurrence, add); to the end of the line.

8. Replace echo with res.write(, and at each occurrence, add); to the end of the line.

9. Remove $, and at each occurrence, determine whether or not the Node.js `var` keyword should be added to the beginning of the line to declare the variable.

Now let's look at each step in more detail. The first step is to copy and paste the PHP code into the Node.js `page()` function of the appropriate *.njs* file. Here is the Node.js `page()` function with the PHP code pasted in the middle:

```
function page(req, res, pre, cb) {
  res.writeHead(200, {'Content-Type': 'text/plain'});
  <?php
    function cb() {
    }
  ?>
  <?php
    $site = $_REQUEST['site'];
    header('HTTP/1.1 404 Not Found');
  ?>
  <html><head></head><body>
  <?php
    $header = file_get_contents('header.html');
    print $header;
  ?>
  The page could not be found on <?php echo $site; ?>.
  <?php
    $footer = file_get_contents('footer.html');
    print $footer;
  ?>
  </body></html>
  <?php cb(); ?>
}
```

The second step is to remove the unneeded `cb()` function definition manually.

Next, we move onto step 3: for all text outside the PHP tags, put the text in a `res.write()` function call, possibly putting a newline escape sequence (\n) at the end.

If you are clever, perhaps you can figure out a way to use regular expressions using the Find/Replace in Eclipse PDT to avoid doing this manually.

After step 3, the state of the Node.js `page()` function will look like this:

```
function page(req, res, pre, cb) {
  res.writeHead(200, {'Content-Type': 'text/plain'});
  <?php
    $site = $_REQUEST['site'];
    header('HTTP/1.1 404 Not Found');
  ?>
  res.write('<html><head></head><body>\n');
  <?php
    $header = file_get_contents('header.html');
    print $header;
  ?>
```

```
    res.write('The page could not be found on ');<?php echo $site; ?>
    res.write('.\n');
    <?php
      $footer = file_get_contents('footer.html');
      print $footer;
    ?>
    res.write('</body></html>\n');
    <?php cb(); ?>
}
```

Step 4 is to remove the <?php text using the Find/Replace in Eclipse PDT.

In Chapter 1, a book convention for specifying a find-and-replace operation was defined. Perform the following find-and-replace operation:

```
Operation: "Find/Replace" in Eclipse PDT
Find: <?php
Replace:
Options: Wrap search
Action: Replace All
```

Step 5 is to remove the ?> text:

```
Operation: "Find/Replace" in Eclipse PDT
Find: ?>
Replace:
Options: Wrap search
Action: Replace All
```

After step 5, the code should resemble this Node.js page() function:

```
function page(req, res, pre, cb) {
  res.writeHead(200, {'Content-Type': 'text/plain'});
  $site = $_REQUEST['site'];
  header('HTTP/1.1 404 Not Found');
  res.write('<html><head></head><body>\n');
  $header = file_get_contents('header.html');
  print $header;
  res.write('The page could not be found on '); echo $site; res.write('.\n');
  $footer = file_get_contents('footer.html');
  print $footer;
  res.write('</body></html>\n');
  cb();
}
```

Step 6 is to replace $_REQUEST with pre._REQUEST:

```
Operation: "Find/Replace" in Eclipse PDT
Find: $_REQUEST
Replace: pre._REQUEST
Options: Wrap search
Action: Replace All
```

Step 7 is to replace `print` with `res.write(`, and at each occurrence, add `)`; to the end of the line:

```
Operation: "Find/Replace" in Eclipse PDT
Find: print
Replace: res.write(
Options: None
Action: Find, then Replace/Find
```

Step 8 is to replace `echo` with `res.write(` and at each occurrence add `)`; to the end of the line.

```
Operation: "Find/Replace" in Eclipse PDT
Find: echo
Replace: res.write(
Options: None
Action: Find, then Replace/Find
```

After step 8, the code should resemble this Node.js `page()` function:

```
function page(req, res, pre, cb) {
  res.writeHead(200, {'Content-Type': 'text/plain'});
  $site = pre._REQUEST['site'];
  header('HTTP/1.1 404 Not Found');
  res.write('<html><head></head><body>\n');
  $header = file_get_contents('header.html');
  res.write($header);
  res.write('The page could not be found on '); res.write($site);
  res.write('.\n');
  $footer = file_get_contents('footer.html');
  res.write($footer);
  res.write('</body></html>\n');
  cb();
}
```

Step 9 is to remove $, and at each occurrence, determine whether or not the Node.js `var` keyword should be added to the beginning of the line to declare the variable:

```
Operation: "Find/Replace" in Eclipse PDT
Find: $
Replace:
Options: None
Action: Find, then Replace/Find
```

After these nine steps, the `page()` function looks like it might almost work:

```
function page(req, res, pre, cb) {
  res.writeHead(200, {'Content-Type': 'text/plain'});
  var site = pre._REQUEST['site'];
  header('HTTP/1.1 404 Not Found');
  res.write('<html><head></head><body>\n');
  var header = file_get_contents('header.html');
  res.write(header);
  res.write('The page could not be found on '); res.write(site);
```

```
  res.write('.\n');
  var footer = file_get_contents('footer.html');
  res.write(footer);
  res.write('</body></html>\n');
  cb();
}
```

At this point, it might be worth trying to run the code and see if it breaks. The Node.js server will come up, but when a client tries to access this page, the Node.js server will exit with a stack trace that indicates that Node.js does not have a header() function.

With a little investigation, it can be determined that the following section of code can be rewritten:

```
res.writeHead(200, {'Content-Type': 'text/plain'});
var site = pre._REQUEST['site'];
header('HTTP/1.1 404 Not Found');
```

The following is a working Node.js version. The header() function call is removed and the writeHead() function call is modified to produce the desired effect:

```
res.writeHead(400, '404 Not Found', {'Content-Type': 'text/html'});
var site = pre._REQUEST['site'];
```

Seeing this improvement, we might return to the original PHP code and refactor it in the same way so a visual diff feature or program will match more directly the PHP code with its corresponding Node.js code. Here's the original PHP code:

```
$site = $_REQUEST['site'];
header('HTTP/1.1 404 Not Found');
```

Logically, we can determine that the order of these PHP statements makes no difference. But by switching the order of the statements, the visual diff feature or program will find a closer match:

```
header('HTTP/1.1 404 Not Found');
$site = $_REQUEST['site'];
```

After making this change, the Node.js server will now break with a stack trace because Node.js does not have a file_get_contents() function. Using the linearity concepts from Chapter 3 and knowing from earlier in this chapter that the Node.js fs.read File() function is a substitute for the PHP file_get_contents() function, the page() function is changed:

```
var fs = require('fs');

function page(req, res, pre, cb) {
  res.writeHead(400, '404 Not Found', {'Content-Type': 'text/html'});
  var site = pre._REQUEST['site'];
  res.write('<html><head></head><body>\n');
  fs.readFile('header.html', 'ascii', function(err, header) {
    res.write(header);
    res.write('The page could not be found on '); res.write(site);
```

```
      res.write('.\n');
      fs.readFile('footer.html', 'ascii', function(err, footer) {
        res.write(footer);
        res.write('</body></html>\n');
        cb();
      });
    });
  }
```

This code will work if the end() function call is added to the exports.serve() function.

Inspection of this working code in the page() function will show an odd line of three write() function calls:

```
res.write('The page could not be found on '); res.write(site); res.write('.\n');
```

These three write() function calls can be rewritten as a single write() function call:

```
res.write('The page could not be found on '+site+'.\n');
```

Here's the original PHP code that caused these three write() function calls.

```
The page could not be found on <?php echo $site; ?>.
```

The interaction of steps 3 and 8 caused these three write() function calls. The PHP code could be refactored to have the echo statement print the entire line, rather than just a part of it:

```
<?php echo 'The page could not be found on '+$site+'.'; ?>
```

If that had been the case, step 8 would convert the PHP code into almost working Node.js code and the PHP code would be very, very similar to the Node.js code. This is another case where refactoring the PHP code, even if there are plans to throw it away at the end of the conversion, is worthwhile. Comparing the PHP code and the Node.js code is a powerful tool in ensuring that the conversion from PHP to Node.js is successful.

The last two statements in the innermost callback are worth studying. They can be rewritten in several different ways, depending on what is most convenient for you. These statements rely on the end() function call being in the exports.serve() function:

```
res.write('</body></html>\n');
cb();
```

Alternatively, they can be rewritten using an eocp() function call. The end() function call will be in the eocp() function and not in the exports.serve() function:

```
eocp(res, cb, '</body></html>\n');
```

They can also be rewritten so it is explicit. Although there are more statements here, the following code will be the most straightforward, and anticipates Node.js developers who do not refer to the corresponding PHP code:

```
res.end('</body></html>\n');
cb();
```

How you address these last two statements is an important part of your conversion strategy. In this page and in some of your pages, it will not matter because there are only a few code paths that need an end() function call. But in really complicated PHP pages, there may be dozens of code paths that require an end() function call, and having a strategy in place can keep things organized and keep the conversion on track.

In the page() function, a single writeHead() function call is the first statement and a single end() function call is as close to being the last statement as possible. This is an intentional strategy. By calling the writeHead() function as early as possible, there is less chance that a write() function call will slip in ahead of it under some circumstance. And similarly, by calling the end() function as late as possible, possibly moving it to the export.serve() function, there is less chance that a write() function call will accidentally be made after it. The writeHead() and end() function calls "bookend" the page() function. After all, the most important job of the page() function is to produce an HTTP response. If the PHP page does not set HTTP response headers as early as possible, it is worth looking and seeing if it can be refactored to move its calls to the PHP header() API further toward the top of the PHP page.

One important challenge that has not been mentioned yet is keeping the res and cb variables in scope, meaning that arguments or variables containing the values are within the same block or a block that contains their block, for the code that needs access to them. The following simple PHP page outputs the *error.html* file instead of the current PHP file that will demonstrate the issue when converted to Node.js:

```php
<?php
  function forward($filename) {
    $contents = file_get_contents($filename);
    print $contents;
  }
  forward('error.html');
?>
```

When converted from PHP to Node.js, a desirable conversion looks as follows:

```
function forward(filename) {
  fs.readFile(filename, 'ascii', function(err, contents) {
    res.end(contents);  // res variable not in scope
    cb();  // cb variable not in scope
  });
}

function page(req, res, pre, cb) {
  res.writeHead(200, {'Content-Type': 'text/html'});
  forward('error.html');
}
```

As is noted in the comments, the res and cb variables are not in scope in the for ward() function. Both functions and classes provide a challenge of keeping these variables available so that the HTTP response can be completed and post-processing can be run on the page.

One obvious way to keep the res and cb variables in scope is to pass them as arguments to any function or class that might need them or call a function or class that might need them, and so on and so forth. Here's a modified version of the forward() function example:

```
function forward(filename, res, cb) {
  fs.readFile(filename, 'ascii', function(err, contents) {
    res.end(contents);  // res variable in scope
    cb();  // cb variable in scope
  });
}

function page(req, res, pre, cb) {
  res.writeHead(200, {'Content-Type': 'text/html'});
  forward('error.html', res, cb); // pass res and cb
}
```

The weakness of this way is obvious: the res and cb arguments are passed everywhere.

Another way is to move the forward() function inside the page() function. The benefit of this way is that the Node.js forward() function remains more like the original PHP forward() function, in that both functions take only one argument and no arguments need to be passed:

```
function page(req, res, pre, cb) {
  function forward(filename) {
    fs.readFile(filename, 'ascii', function(err, contents) {
      res.end(contents);  // res variable in scope
      cb();  // cb variable in scope
    });
  }
  res.writeHead(200, {'Content-Type': 'text/html'});
  forward('error.html');
}
```

The weakness of putting everything in the page() function is that the page() function can become very, very long and difficult to understand, but generally, I have found this way to work the best for many situations.

Classes can be handled similarly to functions, and will be more fully addressed in Chapter 8.

This chapter has given you a full explanation of the similarities and differences between the way that PHP and Node.js handle HTTP responses. It has provided practical examples and effective techniques to get the converted Node.js code to put the same data in the HTTP response that the original PHP code does. It has also shown how to organize the code paths and address scoping issues such that the HTTP response can be properly sent by the end( ) function and control can be returned to the Node.js server.

But that's not enough. Both PHP and Node.js are programming languages. Although the PHP syntax has some similarities to the Node.js syntax, any PHP to Node.js conversion will need to convert from one syntax to the other.

In the next chapter, the differences between the PHP syntax and the Node.js syntax will be explained and conversion recipes will be provided to convert between them.

CHAPTER 6

Syntax

By now, the Node.js server is running and routing HTTP requests to the correct handler function, the `page()` function, in the correct Node.js local module for that page request. The local modules contain a simple framework based on the `exports.serve()` function that is correct Node.js code but the `page()` function itself mostly contains PHP code with a few Node.js modifications mixed in. When a client requests a page, the Node.js server probably stops with a stack trace.

The good news is that the Node.js server infrastructure is done. From here on out, all our conversion efforts are focused on making transformations to the hybrid PHP/Node.js code that constitutes the page itself.

Initially, the hybrid code will be mostly PHP with a little bit of Node.js, but as the conversion techniques from this chapter and the remaining chapters are applied, the balance in hybrid code will shift from being mostly PHP to being a balance of PHP and Node.js, then being mostly Node.js with a little bit of PHP, and finally, being fully working pure Node.js code.

In this chapter, we will deal with syntax, the "standard parts" of a language. The syntax of a language consists of the keywords and symbols used to create different statements. For example, in Node.js and every other computer language ever invented, the plus (+) operator is the syntax used to add two numbers together; in the code fragment 4+5, the plus (+) operator is a piece of syntax. In contrast, the semantics of a language is the knowledge that the plus (+) operator means "add these two numbers together"; in the 4+5 example, the semantics indicate that the answer is 9. For our purposes, we will not quibble over syntax versus semantics. This chapter will show how to convert some of the PHP syntax to Node.js syntax while keeping an eye on semantic differences so that the converted code will function the same way as the original code did.

Fortunately, PHP and Node.js have a lot of syntax and semantics in common. We already know from Chapter 3 that both PHP and Node.js have common roots in the C language, and even where they depart from the C language, they have often departed in the same way.

Both PHP and Node.js use the `if` and `else` keywords. In both languages, `if` and `else` statements have the same syntax and the same semantics. Both PHP and Node.js have the `switch`, `case`, and `break` keywords, and they have the same punctuation and function in the same way in each language. They both have `for` statements, and in both languages, the `for` statements have an initialization clause, a conditional clause, and an increment clause, separated by semicolons (;). They both have `while` and `do…while` statements that operate the same. These control statements are the same for many other languages, including the C language.

Statements in both languages end in semicolons (;). Statement blocks in both languages use curly brackets ({ and }). It is the same in the C language. Here is a PHP example of an `if` statement with a statement block (which, of course, uses curly brackets):

```
if ($var1 == 1) {
    $var1 += 10;
    $var1 += 12;
}
```

The Node.js example is almost the same, except that variables in PHP are required to start with a dollar sign ($), whereas in Node.js, they do not:

```
if (var1 == 1) {
    var1 += 10;
    var1 += 12;
}
```

PHP and Node.js use the same set operators. To access a value at a particular index (also known as a "key"), the square brackets notation ([and]) can be applied to PHP arrays, Node.js arrays, and Node.js objects. Parentheses ((and)) are used to define precedence. Plus (+) for addition, minus (-) for subtraction, asterisk (*) for multiplication, slash (/) for division, and percent sign (%) for remainder work the same way in both languages. The double plus (++) increment and double minus (--) decrement operators work the same in both languages.

Both languages use the same conditional operators: greater than (>), less than (<), greater than or equal (>=), and less than or equal (<=) are the same. The equals (==) and the does not equal (!=) operators work the same. Even the triple equals (===) and triple does not equal (!==) work the same. In both languages, the triple versions compare both the type and the value, while the regular equals (==) and does not equal (!=) compare the values, possibly coercing the values to be the same type in order to do the comparison.

Both PHP and Node.js support the inline conditional, using the question mark (?) and colon (:), in the same way.

Functions in both languages use the `function` keyword. However, the C language does not have the `function` keyword. Fortunately, despite the fact that they do not share the same syntax as the C language, both PHP uses the same syntax and the same semantics for functions as Node.js does. All three languages use the `return` statement in the same way for the same purpose. Here's a simple PHP function with a `return` statement:

```
function add($a, $b) {
   return $a + $b;
}
```

The corresponding Node.js function is the same, except for the dollar sign ($) discrepancy mentioned earlier:

```
function add(a, b) {
   return a + b;
}
```

Function calling is as similar as function definition. In both languages, functions are called by name, arguments are enclosed in parentheses ((and)) and separated from each other by commas (,). The following example function call works in both PHP and Node.js:

```
add(4, 5);
```

All these similarities between PHP and Node.js are shown to demonstrate just how similar the two languages are in terms of syntax and semantics. Converting from PHP to Node.js is not as enormous a job as might be initially imagined. Now, let us turn to the relatively few syntactic or semantic differences between the two languages.

String Literals

For string literals, which are not to be confused with string variables, both a single quote (') and a double quote (") can be used in both PHP and Node.js. In Node.js, both kinds of quotes are interchangeable with each other and perform in exactly the same way. But, in PHP, the single quote (') means a literal string with no substitutions while a double quote (") will substitute variables and delimited special characters. Here's a PHP example using both kinds of quotes:

```
$name = "Bill";
print 'My name is $name.\n';
print "\n"; // so the next line will display on a new line
print "My name is $name.\n";
```

The output of the preceding PHP code shows the same string for single quotes ('), and for the double quotes ("), substitutes the string `Bill` for the `$name` variable and converts the `\n` text into an new line rather than printing a literal backslash-n:

```
My name is $name.\n
My name is Bill.
```

By comparison, in Node.js, both single quotes (') and double quotes (") will never substitute variables and will always substitute delimited special characters. The following Node.js example corresponds to the preceding PHP example. For the time being, simply accept and ignore the var keyword (it will be covered in the next chapter, which explains variables and scoping):

```
var name = "Bill";
console.log('My name is name.\n');
console.log("My name is name.\n");
```

The output of the Node.js code shows two strings, both without variable substitution and both with the special newline character \n, removed and replaced by an actual new line:

```
My name is name.
My name is name.
```

Lots of existing PHP code has single quotes (') and double quotes (") arbitrarily used for string literals with little rhyme or reason, only dependent on the whim of the developer at the time. A more rigorous approach for both PHP and Node.js is to always use single quotes (') unless either a literal double quote (") is needed or the substitution semantics of a double quote (") is needed. The following example, applicable to both PHP and Node.js, shows why preferring single quotes (') by default is a good approach:

```
'The man said, "Throw the ball to me."'
```

The string literal above produces what is expected in both PHP and Node.js.

To fix up PHP or Node.js code, the following find-and-replace action can be taken. In PHP and Node.js, it can be performed on the entire file:

```
Operation: "Find/Replace" in Eclipse PDT
Find: "
Replace: '
Options: None
Action: Find, then Replace/Find
```

Each occurrence should be manually examined to see if any single quotes (') are used inside the string literal, needing to be converted to double quotes (") or needing to be delimited by becoming a backslash-single quote (\'). Each occurrence will also need to be examined to ensure that it is not inside a comment and that the code will perform as expected.

With some tweaking of both the PHP code and the Node.js code, the visual diff feature or program should be able to match all the string literals in both codebases fairly closely.

With string literals reconciled between PHP and Node.js, we can turn to the matter of the plus (+) operator and string concatenation in both languages. In Node.js, the plus

(+) operator is used both to add two numbers together and to concatenate strings. In PHP, the plus (+) operator is only used to add two numbers, and in a rather obscure and unwise case, to add two PHP arrays in a special way. Instead, in PHP, the dot (.) operator is used to concatenate strings.

For example, the following PHP code adds two numbers and concatenates two strings:

```
$total = $trees + $plants;
$html = 'The total number of trees and plants is '.$total.'.'
```

The dot (.) operator is used in the second statement while the plus (+) operator is used in the first statement.

However, in Node.js, the plus (+) operator is used for both statements:

```
total = trees + plants;
html = 'The total number of trees and plants is '+total+'.'
```

To make string concatenation work in Node.js, the PHP dot (.) operator must be converted to a plus (+) operator. An incremental find-and-replace action can be executed to make this happen:

```
Operation: "Find/Replace" in Eclipse PDT
Find: .
Replace: +
Options: Selected lines
Action: Find, then Replace/Find
```

For each occurrence, it must be verified that the dot (.) is being used to do a string concatenation and is not being used in one of the following other ways:

- In a comment for any purpose, including to end a sentence
- In a string literal
- As part of a floating-point number

While the dot (.) operator is used in PHP to do string concatenation, the dot (.) operator is used in Node.js to access a property of a Node.js object. In the following Node.js example, the number "14" will be printed to the console because the dot (.) operator accesses the length property of the s object. The length property of a string object contains its length in characters:

```
var s = 'Copyright 2013';
console.log(s.length);
```

Since both the dot (.) operator and the plus (+) operator are used in both PHP and Node.js but serve different important purposes in some instances, careful track must be kept of whether or not the hybrid PHP/Node.js code in the page() function is using the dot (.) operator in the PHP way or the Node.js way. When the dot (.) operator is converted from PHP to a Node.js plus (+) operator, it must be fully converted and any attempt to convert an already converted operator will introduce errors and confusion. It is recommended that a comment be placed in the Node.js code of each *.njs* file to indicate the status. Here's an example Node.js comment:

```
// dot concatenation converted: yes
```

Earlier, it was mentioned briefly that the plus (+) operator can be used in PHP to add two PHP arrays together in a special way. The plus (+) operator in PHP can be used to create an array that is the union of two PHP arrays. In Node.js, there is no corresponding operator. Rather than attempting to convert a plus (+) operator used in this way, it is recommended that the PHP code be refactored to remove the plus (+) operator for this case and replace it with a call to a PHP function, perhaps an `array_union()` function, that does the same operation. Then, the `array_union()` function can be converted from PHP to Node.js just one time rather than each and every time that the PHP code uses the plus (+) operators with arrays directly.

Syntax Differences

A minor difference between PHP and Node.js is one facet of how it handles `if...else` statements.

In both PHP and Node.js, the standalone `if` and `else` statements are used in exactly the same way and work the same way. The difference is the `else if` statement, an optional statement that occurs after the beginning `if` statement but before the `else` statement, if an `else` statement actually exists.

In PHP, the `else if` statement uses the `elseif` keyword. Here's a PHP example using the `elseif` keyword:

```
if ($a == $b) {
  print 'a is equal to b';
} elseif ($a > $b) { // elseif, not else if
  print 'a is greater than b';
} else {
  print 'a is less than b';
}
```

In Node.js, there is not a special keyword for the `else if` statement. The `else` and `if` keywords are separated by whitespace, and when they are arranged in this way, they perform the same function as the `elseif` keyword does in PHP. Here's an example using the Node.js `else if` keywords:

```
if (a == b) {
  console.log('a is equal to b');
} else if (a > b) { // else if, not elseif
```

```
    console.log('a is greater than b');
  } else {
    console.log('a is less than b');
  }
```

Since the elseif keyword is a PHP keyword and has no other use, it is safe to do a blind, global find-and-replace action to replace all elseif text with else if text in any *.njs* file that contains a page() function. The find-and-replace action can even be repeated with no ill effects:

```
Operation: "Find/Replace" in Eclipse PDT
Find: elseif
Replace: else if
Options: Case sensitive
Action: Replace All
```

Both string concatenation and the else if statement can be handled mechanically but the PHP foreach statement requires more insight when each occurrence is examined. The PHP foreach statement has a rough equivalent in the Node.js for...in statement.

In PHP, the values in an array can be any kind of object. However, keys can only be an integer or a string. In PHP terminology, a PHP array with integer keys is called an "indexed array." A PHP array with string keys is called an "associative array." Beyond terminology, PHP does not differentiate much between an indexed array and an associative array.

In Node.js, a PHP-style indexed array is just called an array. A PHP-style associative array is called an "object" in Node.js terminology.

The PHP foreach statement can take two forms.

The first form returns only the values of the array. Here's a PHP example showing a foreach statement, which shows the values of the $a array:

```
foreach ($a as $value) {
  print $value;
}
```

The second form returns both the keys and the values of the array. The following PHP example shows a foreach statement using the second form:

```
foreach ($a as $key => $value) {
  print $key.' contains '.$value;
  print $key.' contains '.$a[$key];  // $a[$key] is the same as $value
}
```

In this Node.js code, you should note that even though the value is returned in its own variable, the value is also obtained from the array itself by using the square brackets ([and]) operator on the array.

In Node.js, the `for...in` statement (which roughly corresponds to the PHP `foreach` statement) only has one form. It looks similar to the PHP `foreach` statement, except that instead of returning values, it returns keys. In Node.js, it is more common to use the terminology "properties" or "property names" instead of "keys." Here's a Node.js `for...in` statement:

```
for (var key in a) {
    console.log(key+' contains '+a[key]);
}
```

To convert PHP `foreach` statements to Node.js `for...in` statements, it is best to address PHP indexed arrays separately from PHP associative arrays.

For indexed arrays, it is recommended that PHP `foreach` statements be refactored as regular `for` statements so, when they are converted to Node.js, they are converted into regular `for` statements and not into `for...in` statements. For the following PHP example, assume that the `$colors` array is an indexed array that contains three values: `red`, `blue`, and `green`:

```
foreach ($colors as $value) {
    print $value."\n";
}
```

Here's output of this code:

```
red
blue
green
```

To refactor the preceding `foreach` statement, the PHP `count()` API function is used to determine the number of indexes in the `$colors` array variable. The `$key` variable iterates over the keys, not the values, so the value needs to be extracted from the `$colors` array variable each time through the loop:

```
for ($key=0; $key < count($colors); ++$key) {
    print $colors[$key]."\n";
}
```

This refactoring is wordy and probably executes a little slower than the `foreach` version. However, it can be converted from PHP to Node.js in a straightforward way:

```
for (var key=0; key < colors.length; ++key) {
    console.log(colors[key]+"\n");
}
```

By refactoring these `foreach` statements into regular `for` statements, no find-and-replace action is needed to convert from PHP to Node.js. In both PHP and Node.js, the keywords and punctuation for `for` statements are identical to the C language and to each other. Only the variables and the way to find the number of elements in an array must be converted. Chapter 7 covers converting all kinds of variables, including variables in `for` statements, and their associated functions, including how to get the number of elements in an array. The `for` statement does not need any special conversion.

If the PHP `foreach` version was converted to Node.js to use a `for…in` statement, it would look like this code:

```
for (var key in colors) {
    console.log(colors[key]+"\n");
}
```

In many cases, this `for…in` statement would work. But in Node.js, properties can be arbitrarily added to any object, including arrays. The regular `for` statement is explicit about looping through the numbered indexes but the `for…in` statement only assumes that there are no other properties except the indexes. It is safer to be explicit; that is, it is better to be safe than sorry.

For associative arrays in PHP, it is recommended that PHP `foreach` statements be refactored to always use the form where both a key and value are provided. Let us assume that the following PHP code has an associative `colors` array variable where 0 is the value associated with the red key, 128 is the value associated with the blue key, and 255 is the value associated with the green key:

```
foreach ($colors as $value) {
    print $value."\n";
}
```

The preceding PHP code may rely on the keys being inserted in a certain order: red, then blue, and, finally, green. Here's output of the PHP `foreach` statement:

```
0
128
255
```

The PHP code above should be refactored to add the $key variable to the `foreach` statement:

```
foreach ($colors as $key => $value) {
    print $value."\n";
}
```

The find-and-replace action will be run on the *.php* file, not the *.njs* file. This action refactors PHP and is not a conversion from PHP to Node.js:

```
Operation: "Find/Replace" in Eclipse PDT
Find:  as
Replace: as $key =>
Options: None
Action: Find, then Replace/Find
```

At each occurrence, the foreach statement will be examined to see if it already uses the => syntax or not. If it already uses it, it will be skipped. If it does not use it, it will be added, possibly replacing the $key variable with a more appropriately named variable.

Refactoring the PHP code to add a $key variable does nothing for the PHP, but when converted to Node.js, the Node.js code can create the value variable from the array variable and the current key, as shown here:

```
for (var key in colors) {
    var value = colors[key];
    console.log(value+"\n");
}
```

To convert a PHP foreach statement into a Node.js for...in statement, the following find-and-replace action will be used with two manual steps executed at each occurrence:

```
Operation: "Find/Replace" in Eclipse PDT
Find: foreach (
Replace: for (
Options: None
Action: Find, then Replace/Find
```

At each occurrence, the PHP $colors as $key => $value will need to be manually converted to the Node.js var key in colors. It is up to the developer doing the conversion to execute this first step, although a clever developer might come up with a regular expression that would accomplish the same thing.

The second manual step needed at each occurrence will be to add an extra statement at the beginning of the Node.js for...in statement similar to var value = colors[key];. The name of the newly defined variable and the name of the array are dictated by the names given in the original PHP foreach statement.

With the $key variable added to the PHP code, the visual diff feature or program will more easily match the $key variable when comparing the PHP and Node.js codebases, and by doing so, it is easier to visually confirm that both codebases are correct. If you really want to make the visual diff feature or program match up nicely, the Node.js statement that assigns the value variable can be converted back to the corresponding PHP foreach statement:

```
foreach ($colors as $key => $value) {
    $value = $colors[$key]; // redundant but makes "visual diff" very happy
    print $value."\n";
}
```

The preceding PHP improvement is not optional, but will make the PHP and Node.js codebases more similar and easier to compare. The improvement can be made by executing the following find-and-replace action:

```
Operation: "Find/Replace" in Eclipse PDT
Find: foreach
Replace:
Options: None
Action: Find, then Replace/Find
```

At each occurrence, the action is never executed. Instead, an extra statement of the form `$value = $colors[$key];` is inserted at the beginning of the loop, changing the variable names to those used in the `foreach` statement.

PHP Alternative Syntax

One final conversion issue remains: the PHP alternative syntax for branching and looping. The use of the PHP alternative syntax varies a lot: in some PHP, it will be nearly everywhere, and in other PHP code, it will never be used. Node.js does not have an alternative syntax, so if the PHP alternative syntax is used, it needs to be converted into the normal syntax for Node.js.

This is the normal syntax for an `if…elseif…else` statement:

```
if ($a == $b) {
  print 'a is equal to b';
} elseif ($a > $b) {
  print 'a is greater than b';
} else {
  print 'a is less than b';
}
```

The alternative syntax for the same `if…elseif…else` statement removes all the right curly brackets (}) except for the last one and replaces the left curly bracket ({) with a colon (:). The last right curly bracket (}) is replaced with the `endif` keyword followed by a semicolon. Here's the alternative syntax of this example:

```
if ($a == $b):
  print 'a is equal to b';
elseif ($a > $b):
  print 'a is greater than b';
else:
  print 'a is less than b';
endif;
```

The alternative syntax can either be refactored into the normal syntax in the PHP code or only converted in the Node.js code (that is, the hybrid PHP/Node.js code in the page() function of the .njs file).

For both refactoring and converting, changing the `if` statement alternative syntax into the normal syntax takes four find-and-replace actions. In both cases—refactoring and converting—the find-and-replace actions are the same. To convert the `if` statement alternative syntax into the normal syntax, we'll need to execute four find-and-replace actions, starting with this one:

```
Operation: "Find/Replace" in Eclipse PDT
Find: ):
Replace: ) {
Options: None
Action: Find, then Replace/Find
```

At each occurrence, the replacement is done only if it is an `if` statement or an `elseif` statement using the alternative syntax. The `elseif` statement may still be using the `elseif` keyword, or if it has already been converted to Node.js, will use the Node.js `else if` statement containing whitespace.

An inline conditional is not alternative syntax. An inline conditional is an `if` and `else` statement in an abbreviated syntax using a question mark (?) and a colon (:) as part of a variable assignment. The example below shows:

```
$msg = ($a == $b)? 'a is equal to b': 'a is not equal to b';
```

A right parenthesis ( )) might be inserted as part of the "equals" value and match the find-and-replace action. So here's an example of that happening:

```
$msg = ($a == $b)? ('a is equal'+' to b'): 'a is not equal to b';
```

In both PHP and Node.js, the inline conditional syntax is the same and no conversion is needed. The find-and-replace action should not replace this instance.

After the find-and-replace action is executed, the preceding PHP example will be modified as follows:

```
if ($a == $b) {
  print 'a is equal to b';
elseif ($a > $b) {
  print 'a is greater than b';
else:
  print 'a is less than b';
endif;
```

The next find-and-replace action will add a right curly bracket (}) to the `elseif` statement. If the PHP `elseif` statement has already been converted to the Node.js `else if` statement, the `else if` text can be substituted for both the Find and the Replace fields:

```
Operation: "Find/Replace" in Eclipse PDT
Find: elseif
Replace: } elseif
Options: None
Action: Find, then Replace/Find
```

At each occurrence, it must be confirmed that a right curly bracket (}) does not already exist. After the find-and-replace action is executed, the elseif statement will have a right curly bracket (}) before it:

```
if ($a == $b) {
  print 'a is equal to b';
} elseif ($a > $b) {
  print 'a is greater than b';
else:
  print 'a is less than b';
endif;
```

The third find-and-replace action can globally replace the else: text, which can only occur as part of the if statement alternative syntax with the } else { text. Since the alternative syntax is the only way that the else: text can occur, the find-and-replace action can be executed all at once, without visiting each occurrence:

```
Operation: "Find/Replace" in Eclipse PDT
Find: else:
Replace: } else {
Options: None
Action: Replace All
```

After the third find-and-replace action, the partially converted if statement will appear similar to this example:

```
if ($a == $b) {
  print 'a is equal to b';
} elseif ($a > $b) {
  print 'a is greater than b';
} else {
  print 'a is less than b';
endif;
```

The final find-and-replace action replaces the endif; text with a right curly bracket (}). Like the third find-and-replace action, this action can be executed all at once because the endif; text is unique to the alternative syntax:

```
Operation: "Find/Replace" in Eclipse PDT
Find: endif;
Replace: }
Options: None
Action: Replace All
```

After this final action is taken, the PHP code is now in the if statement normal syntax. The alternative syntax has been removed:

```
if ($a == $b) {
  print 'a is equal to b';
} elseif ($a > $b) {
```

```
    print 'a is greater than b';
} else {
    print 'a is less than b';
}
```

Besides the if statement alternative syntax, the for, foreach, while, and switch statements also have alternative syntaxes. The rest of this chapter will briefly describe these other alternative syntaxes and how to convert them into normal syntax. These descriptions are provided for reference. If you are reading this book cover to cover, you may safely skip the remainder of this chapter, as these alternative syntaxes are obvious and unsurprising.

PHP also has a for statement alternative syntax. Here's a PHP example with the for statement normal syntax:

```
for ($key=0; $key < count($colors); ++$key) {
    print $colors[$key]."\n";
}
```

Here's the alternative syntax for this same example:

```
for ($key=0; $key < count($colors); ++$key):
    print $colors[$key]."\n";
endfor;
```

To refactor the PHP code itself or convert the PHP code to Node.js code, the following find-and-replace action will convert the opening line from the alternative syntax to the normal syntax:

```
Operation: "Find/Replace" in Eclipse PDT
Find: ):
Replace: ) {
Options: None
Action: Find, then Replace/Find
```

At each occurrence, the replacement is done only if it is a for statement using the alternative syntax.

A second find-and-replace action completes the conversion from alternative syntax to normal syntax by converting the last statement into normal syntax:

```
Operation: "Find/Replace" in Eclipse PDT
Find: endfor;
Replace: }
Options: None
Action: Replace All
```

The for statement is now in the normal syntax.

PHP has a foreach statement alternative syntax. The following is a PHP example with the foreach statement normal syntax:

```
foreach ($colors as $key => $value) {
   print $value."\n";
}
```

Here's the alternative syntax for this same example:

```
foreach ($colors as $key => $value):
   print $value."\n";
endforeach;
```

To refactor the PHP code itself or convert the PHP code to Node.js code, the following find-and-replace action will convert the opening line from the alternative syntax to the normal syntax:

```
Operation: "Find/Replace" in Eclipse PDT
Find: ):
Replace: ) {
Options: None
Action: Find, then Replace/Find
```

At each occurrence, the replacement is done only if it is a foreach statement using the alternative syntax.

A second find-and-replace action completes the conversion from alternative syntax to normal syntax by converting the last statement into normal syntax:

```
Operation: "Find/Replace" in Eclipse PDT
Find: endforeach;
Replace: }
Options: None
Action: Replace All
```

The foreach statement is now in the normal syntax.

PHP has a while statement alternative syntax. Here's a PHP example with the while statement normal syntax:

```
$key = 0;
while ($key < count($colors)) {
   print $colors[$key]."\n";
   ++$key;
}
```

And this is the alternative syntax for the same example:

```
$key = 0;
while ($key < count($colors)):
   print $colors[$key]."\n";
   ++$key;
endwhile;
```

To refactor the PHP code itself or convert the PHP code to Node.js code, the following find-and-replace action will convert the opening line from the alternative syntax to the normal syntax:

```
Operation: "Find/Replace" in Eclipse PDT
Find: ):
Replace: ) {
Options: None
Action: Find, then Replace/Find
```

At each occurrence, the replacement is done only if it is a `while` statement using the alternative syntax.

A second find-and-replace action completes the conversion from alternative syntax to normal syntax by converting the last statement into normal syntax:

```
Operation: "Find/Replace" in Eclipse PDT
Find: endwhile;
Replace: }
Options: None
Action: Replace All
```

The `while` statement is now in the normal syntax.

PHP has a `switch` statement alternative syntax. The following is a PHP example with the `switch` statement normal syntax:

```
switch ($color) {
  case 'red':
    print 'The red makes a redish hue.';
    break;
  case 'green':
    print 'The green makes a pale hue.';
    break;
  case 'blue':
    print 'The blue makes a nice tint.';
    break;
}
```

And here's the alternative syntax for this same example:

```
switch ($color):
  case 'red':
    print 'The red makes a redish hue.';
    break;
  case 'green':
    print 'The green makes a pale hue.';
    break;
  case 'blue':
    print 'The blue makes a nice tint.';
    break;
endswitch;
```

To refactor the PHP code itself or convert the PHP code to Node.js code, the following find-and-replace action will convert the opening line from the alternative syntax to the normal syntax:

```
Operation: "Find/Replace" in Eclipse PDT
Find: ):
Replace: ) {
Options: None
Action: Find, then Replace/Find
```

At each occurrence, the replacement is done only if it is a `switch` statement using the alternative syntax.

A second find-and-replace action completes the conversion from alternative syntax to normal syntax by converting the last statement into normal syntax:

```
Operation: "Find/Replace" in Eclipse PDT
Find: endswitch;
Replace: }
Options: None
Action: Replace All
```

The `switch` statement is now in the normal syntax.

Lucky for us, the differences between the PHP syntax and the Node.js syntax are relatively minor and easily addressed. Converting between PHP variables and Node.js variables is more of a challenge. In the next chapter, PHP variables, like `$a`, and PHP array variables, like `$colors`, will be converted from PHP to Node.js, which will make many of our `if` statements, `for` statements, and other conditionals and loops into pure Node.js code.

CHAPTER 7

Variables

Now that PHP syntax has been converted to Node.js in the previous chapter, we can turn our attention to variables, which are a little more interesting and complicated to convert.

In PHP, a variable name always starts with a dollar sign ($). For example, $a and $colors are PHP variable names, but a and colors are not. In Node.js, a variable name may start with a dollar sign ($), but does not have to. So, in Node.js, $a, $colors, a, and colors are all valid Node.js variable names.

However, in Node.js, even though it is perfectly legal, it is a widely accepted common practice to avoid variable names that begin with a dollar sign ($). It is so widely accepted that Node.js code that uses variable names that start with a dollar sign ($) looks very, very strange to Node.js developers. To accommodate this practice, it is recommended that PHP variable names be converted to Node.js variable names by removing the dollar sign ($). For example, the PHP variables $a and $colors should be converted to the Node.js variables, a and colors.

The allowed characters in a PHP variable name is a subset of the allowed characters in a Node.js variable name. It is recommended that variable names, excluding the initial dollar sign ($) for PHP variables, begin with an alphabetic character of either case, that is, a to z or A to Z, and have the remaining characters be zero or more characters that are alphabetic characters of any case (a to z or A to Z), underscores (_), or digits (0 to 9). The following text shows a regular expression that describes this variable naming scheme:

```
[a-zA-Z][a-zA-Z_0-9]*
```

Although Unicode characters in both languages and dollar signs ($) in Node.js may be used in creating variable names, it is not recommended. It is encouraged that PHP and Node.js codebases limit or refactor themselves to use the more narrow variable naming specification above. Find-and-replace actions can be invented to make both PHP and Node.js codebases conform.

Besides the dollar sign ($) difference, in Node.js, every variable must be declared using a `var` statement. For example, the following code declares the `a` variable and the `colors` variable:

```
var a = 4;
var colors;
```

Simple Variables

The `var` statement sets a "scope," that is, an area of source code where the variable name refers to this newly defined variable. Toward the end of this chapter, variable scopes will be covered in more detail, but for now, it can simply be noted that a `var` statement has a scope.

In PHP, variables are not declared. When they are first used, the PHP engine identifies them by the dollar sign ($) in their name at the time of their first use.

To convert a variable from PHP to Node.js, the dollar sign ($) is removed and the `var` keyword added at its first use. This find-and-replace action removes the dollar sign ($) and allows you to identify where to add the `var` keyword:

```
Operation: "Find/Replace" in Eclipse PDT
Find: $
Replace:
Options: None
Action: Find, then Replace/Find
```

At each occurrence, determine if this is the first time that variable is used. If it is, add the `var` keyword before the first use or at the beginning of the appropriate statement block. Statement blocks are defined with curly brackets ({ and }).

With the dollar sign ($) removed and `var` keyword added, the basic variable declaration and variable reference will now work in Node.js.

In PHP, a variable can be one of nine basic types. The basic type of a PHP variable can be determined by calling the PHP `gettype()` API function. The following list shows the nine strings that can be returned from a PHP `gettype()` API function call:

```
NULL
boolean
string
integer
double
```

```
array
object
resource
unknown type
```

In Node.js, a variable can be one of seven basic types. The basic type of a Node.js variable can be determined by using the Node.js typeof operator. The following list shows the seven strings that can be returned from the Node.js typeof operator:

```
null
boolean
string
number
object
function
undefined
```

The first three basic types in both lists—null, boolean, and string—are arguably the most important, and are essentially the same. The PHP integer and double basic types correspond very closely to the Node.js number basic type. Similarly, the PHP object and array basic types very closely correspond to the Node.js object basic type that encompasses both Node.js arrays and Node.js objects. The remaining basic types are somewhat obscure and largely irrelevant although the PHP unknown type basic type is a rough equivalent to the Node.js undefined basic type.

Nulls in PHP and in Node.js are the same, except that PHP is case insensitive while Node.js is case sensitive. There is only one value, null, which is of this type in both languages. To make PHP code compatible with Node.js, the following find-and-replace action will replace all uppercase and mixed case occurrences of the NULL text that might occur in PHP code with the lowercase null text, which is compatible with both PHP and Node.js:

```
Operation: "Find/Replace" in Eclipse PDT
Find: NULL
Replace: null
Options: None
Action: Replace All
```

Booleans in PHP and Node.js have two possible values, true and false. Again, PHP is case insensitive but Node.js is case sensitive. Since lowercase boolean values are accepted in both PHP and Node.js, all PHP and Node.js code should be refactored or converted to use lowercase true and lowercase false versions:

```
Operation: "Find/Replace" in Eclipse PDT
Find: TRUE
Replace: true
Options: None
Action: Replace All

Operation: "Find/Replace" in Eclipse PDT
```

```
Find: FALSE
Replace: false
Options: None
Action: Replace All
```

Strings are equivalent and interchangeable between PHP and Node.js. The differences between string literals, including single quotes (') versus double quotes ("), was described and converted in the previous chapter.

Integers and floating-point numbers, also called "doubles" in PHP, are of different types in PHP, but in Node.js, they are both considered numbers. Specific integer numbers, such as 10 or 4322, and floating-point numbers, such as 4.22 and 1033.48, are represented exactly the same in both languages and need no conversion between PHP and Node.js. Even specific numbers in scientific notation, such as the number, 14.8e3, are represented exactly the same in both PHP and Node.js. No find-and-replace actions are needed to handle differences between numbers in PHP and Node.js.

Arrays and objects are considered separate types in PHP, but in Node.js, an array is a type of object. In the previous chapter, some aspects of PHP arrays were explained to support the conversion to PHP `foreach` statements to Node.js `for…in` statements. The remaining aspects will now be explained as well as how to convert these remaining aspects from PHP to Node.js.

Array Variables

In PHP, an array is a collection of keys with associated values. The keys can either be integers, meaning the array is an indexed array, or they can be strings, meaning the array is an associative array. The keys for a PHP array can even be a mix of integers and strings, meaning it is a mix of an indexed and an associative array. The values are even more flexible. Values can be of any type.

Both indexed and associative arrays with specific values can be created using the PHP `array` keyword, which looks a lot like a PHP API function.

To create an indexed array with specific values, the PHP `array` keyword is used on a list of values, separated by commas (,), enclosed in parentheses ((and)). Here's an example of a PHP indexed array being created and assigned to the $a variable:

```
$a = array('red', 'green', 'blue');
```

Here are the contents of the $a variable of this PHP example:

```
$a[0] contains 'red'
$a[1] contains 'green'
$a[2] contains 'blue'
```

The array is created and each value is put into the array, starting at index #0. PHP arrays are zero-based, by default, and each value is placed at the next higher index.

In Node.js, exactly like PHP, indexed arrays with specific values are created by listing values, separated by commas (,). However, instead of enclosing the list in parentheses ((and)) as in PHP, the list is enclosed in square brackets ([and]) and there is no array keyword. Here's the same example of a Node.js indexed array being created and assigned to the a variable:

```
var a = ['red', 'green', 'blue'];
```

To convert all PHP indexed arrays with specific values to Node.js arrays, a simple find-and-replace action can be executed:

```
Operation: "Find/Replace" in Eclipse PDT
Find: array(
Replace: [
Options: None
Action: Find, then Replace/Find
```

At each occurrence, confirm that it is an indexed array and not an associative array. If it is, change the right parenthesis ( )) at the end of the list of values to a right square bracket ( ]) and then execute the find-and-replace action for this occurrence to convert the array(text into a left square bracket ([ ).

To create an associative array with specific values, the PHP array keyword is used on a list of keys and values, separated by commas (,), enclosed in parentheses ((and)). The keys are separated from the values using the "pair" operator, also called the "associate" operator, that is expressed as => in PHP code. Here's an example of a PHP associative array being created and assigned to the $a variable:

```
$a = array('red' => 0, 'green' => 128, 'blue' => 255);
```

The contents of the $a variable of this PHP example are as follows:

```
$a['red'] contains 0
$a['green'] contains 128
$a['blue'] contains 255
```

The array is created and each value is put into the array according to its key. If a statement loops over multiple keys (e.g., the foreach statement) and must determine which key is returned first, second, and so on, the keys are returned in the order of their insertion. So, a foreach statement will return the "red" key, then the "green" key, and finally, the "blue" key.

Node.js arrays are always indexed arrays. Instead of using Node.js arrays to somehow try to implement an associative array with specific values, a Node.js object literal is used. An object literal is a Node.js notation for creating a Node.js object, which is initialized with specific values.

In PHP, the indexes to an associative array are called *keys*, but in Node.js, the indexes to an object are called *properties* or *property names*. In Node.js, the values associated with a property name in an object are called *property values*.

Node.js object literals use the colon (:) operator to associate a property name with a property value. The property name/value pairs are separated by commas, which is the same as PHP, but the declaration is enclosed in curly brackets ({ and }) instead of using the `array` keyword and parentheses ((and)).

Here's an example showing a Node.js object literal containing the `red`, `blue`, and `green` properties with their associated values:

```
var a = {'red': 0, 'green': 128, 'blue': 255};
```

A basic Node.js object is not a pure associative array in the way that a PHP associative array is, but for the purposes of conversion, it is very effective.

To convert a PHP associative array with specific values to a Node.js object literal, two find-and-replace actions are needed: one will replace the PHP `array` keyword and its related punctuation and another will replace the pair operator (=>) with a colon (:).

Here's the first find-and-replace action, which replaces the PHP `array` keyword:

```
Operation: "Find/Replace" in Eclipse PDT
Find: array(
Replace: {
Options: None
Action: Find, then Replace/Find
```

At each occurrence, change the right parenthesis ( )) at the end of the list of values to a right curly bracket (}) and then execute the find-and-replace action for this occurrence to convert the `array(` text into a left square bracket ({).

The second find-and-replace action replaces the PHP pair operator (=>) with the Node.js colon operator (:):

```
Operation: "Find/Replace" in Eclipse PDT
Find: =>
Replace: :
Options: None
Action: Replace All
```

The PHP pair operator (=>) is only used in two places. It is used in PHP `foreach` statements and it is used here, to define specific key/value pairs for an associative array. Since PHP `foreach` statements were converted into Node.js `for...in` statements or Node.js standard `for` statements as part of the syntax conversions in Chapter 6, the pair operator (=>) should only appear as part of an associative array definition. As a result, it should be safe to global find-and-replace all pair operators (=>) without examining each occurrence.

In PHP, the value of a key in an associative array can be retrieved using the square bracket ([and]) notation. This PHP example shows how to print the value of the `green` key:

```
$a = array('red' => 0, 'green' => 128, 'blue' => 255);
print $a['green'];
```

In Node.js, a property of an object can be accessed using two different notations.

The first notation to access Node.js object properties is exactly the same as the PHP notation. The following Node.js example shows how to print the value of the green key:

```
var a = {'red': 0, 'green': 128, 'blue': 255};
console.log(a['green']);
```

The second notation to access Node.js object properties uses the dot (.) operator. For example, instead of using a['green'], the dot (.) operator is used with the undelimited name to make a.green. Here's a Node.js example using the dot (.) operator:

```
var a = {'red': 0, 'green': 128, 'blue': 255};
console.log(a.green);
```

PHP does not support the dot (.) operator for accessing values in arrays because the dot (.) operator is already used for concatenation. Node.js uses the plus (+) operator for concatenation, not the dot (.) operator, so Node.js can use the dot (.) operator for accessing values in arrays.

Since PHP only supports accessing both indexed and associative arrays using square brackets ([and]) and Node.js supports the exact same notation for both Node.js arrays and Node.js object literals, no find-and-replace actions are needed for array access when converting from PHP to Node.js. PHP does not support the dot (.) operator for array access, so it will never be used or need to be converted.

In PHP, empty arrays can be assigned to variables to indicate that they are array variables, not strings, numbers, or some other type. An empty array is created by leaving out all the values; that is, array() creates an empty array. Key/value pairs cannot be assigned to a variable until it is an array variable, even an empty one. This PHP example shows an empty array being created and assigned to the $a variable, making the $a variable an array variable:

```
$a = array();
```

An empty indexed array and an empty associative array are created the same way, using the same code: array(). The preceding $a variable could be either an indexed or an associative array. To tell the difference, we must look at how the $a variable is used.

The following PHP code shows the $a variable being used as a PHP indexed array. It is an indexed array because 0 is a number, not a string:

```
$a = array();
...
print $a[6];
```

When converted from PHP to Node.js, this code will use empty square brackets ([and]), which is an empty Node.js array. The following Node.js example shows the converted code:

```
var a = [];
...
console.log(a[6]);
```

In contrast, a PHP associative array is identified because it uses strings, not numbers, as keys. This PHP code shows the $a variable being used as a PHP associative array:

```
$a = array();
...
print $a['red'];
```

When converted from PHP to Node.js, the preceding code will use empty curly braces ({ and }), which is an empty Node.js object literal. The following Node.js example shows the converted code of the PHP associative array:

```
var a = {};
...
console.log(a['red']);
```

The following find-and-replace action converts a PHP empty array, array(), into a Node.js indexed array. By default, it converts PHP empty arrays into empty Node.js indexed arrays:

```
Operation: "Find/Replace" in Eclipse PDT
Find: array()
Replace: [ ]
Options: None
Action: Find, then Replace/Find
```

At each occurrence, examine how the array variable, such as $a in the previous examples, is being used. If it is being used as an indexed array, execute the action to replace the array() code with square brackets ([and]). If it is being used as an associative array, replace the array() code with curly braces ({ and }) to make an empty Node.js object literal.

PHP indexed arrays are zero-based, so the first index is always 0. In the following PHP example, assigning a value to $a[0] adds a value to the array, increasing the number of items in the array by one. Since the $a variable had zero values, now it has one value:

```
$a = array();
$a[0] = 'red';
```

A new value can be added by assigning a value to an index one higher than any existing index. This PHP example adds three values to an empty indexed array:

```
$a = array();
$a[0] = 'red';
$a[1] = 'green';
$a[2] = 'blue';
```

This simple PHP example is equivalent to the following PHP code:

```
$a = array('red', 'green', 'blue');
```

For PHP indexed arrays, the PHP `count()` API function can be used to retrieve the number of values in an array. Instead of using specific indexes, the PHP `count()` API function can be used to determine the index where a new value should be added. The following PHP code creates the same array as the previous two examples:

```php
$a = array();
$a[count($a)] = 'red';
$a[count($a)] = 'green';
$a[count($a)] = 'blue';
```

PHP also provides a shorthand notation for adding a value to the end of an indexed array. If empty square brackets are used, that is, [], it means to add a new value to the end of the array. In the following PHP example, the `$a[]` code works the same as the `$a[count($a)]` shown previously:

```php
$a = array();
$a[ ] = 'red';
$a[ ] = 'green';
$a[ ] = 'blue';
```

In Node.js, arrays (but not object literals) have a `push()` method. A method is a function that is attached to a Node.js object; an array is a specific kind of object. The `push()` method takes the new value to be added as an argument. This Node.js example uses the `push()` method in Node.js to accomplish the same thing that the previous four PHP examples accomplish in PHP:

```javascript
var a = [ ];
a.push('red');
a.push('green');
a.push('blue');
```

The `push()` method in Node.js works exactly like the empty square brackets ([and]) work in PHP. It finds the highest index in the indexed array, creates a new key at the highest index plus one, and stores the new value there.

The `length` property on a Node.js indexed array can also be used to add values to an array. For Node.js indexed arrays, the `length` property can be used to retrieve the number of values in the array. This Node.js example shows how to use the `length` property to add values to the end of a Node.js indexed array:

```javascript
var a = [ ];
a[a.length] = 'red';
a[a.length] = 'green';
a[a.length] = 'blue';
```

Both PHP and Node.js also support sparse arrays. A sparse array is an indexed array where the indexes are not sequential. A sparse array is not zero-based or even "anything-based." But a sparse array is always an indexed array, not an associative array.

In PHP, a sparse array can be created using the `array` keyword. This PHP example creates a sparse array called `$a`:

```
$a = array(2 => 'red', 5 => 'green', 7 => 'blue');
```

A sparse array can also be created by creating an empty array and adding values in subsequent statements. The following PHP example shows this technique:

```
$a = array();
$a[2] = 'red';
$a[5] = 'green';
$a[7] = 'blue';
```

In PHP, a sparse array only contains the values that are assigned to it. If the PHP count() API function is called on the $a variable, the number of values in the array will be 3, indicating that there are only three keys: 2, 5, and 7.

Node.js also supports sparse arrays. However, Node.js does not support initializing sparse arrays with the square bracket syntax ([and]). Instead, it only supports code similar to the second PHP example, that is, creating an empty Node.js array and adding values in subsequent statements. The following code demonstrates how to create a sparse array in Node.js:

```
var a = [ ];
a[2] = 'red';
a[5] = 'green';
a[7] = 'blue';
```

However, while calling the PHP count() API function will return 3 for the PHP sparse array, the length property on a Node.js sparse array will return 8 for the previous code. The reason is that when a sparse array is created in Node.js, key/value pairs are generated to keep the Node.js indexed array as zero-based and sequential. The generated key/value pairs are set to the undefined type. In the following, the Node.js code produces an array with the same keys as the Node.js code:

```
var a = [ ];
a[0] = undefined;
a[1] = undefined;
a[2] = 'red';
a[3] = undefined;
a[4] = undefined;
a[5] = 'green';
a[6] = undefined;
a[7] = 'blue';
```

For PHP, the array is actually sparse, but in Node.js, it is a full array with undefined values for the unassigned indexes.

Luckily, for both PHP and Node.js, adding a value to the end of a sparse array using the empty square brackets ([and]) notation in PHP and the push() method in Node.js does exactly the same thing. Both find the highest index in the sparse array, create a new key at the highest index plus one, and store the new value there.

For the two sparse arrays, $a and $b, in the following PHP code, the square bracket notation ([and]) used in the last two statements creates $a[8] and $b[8] that both have the value 'orange':

```php
$a = array(2 => 'red', 5 => 'green', 7 => 'blue');
$b = array();
$b[2] = 'red';
$b[5] = 'green';
$b[7] = 'blue';
$a[ ] = 'orange';
$b[ ] = 'orange';
```

The push() method call in the final statement of this Node.js code does the same thing to the a sparse array variable; it creates an a[8] that contains the 'orange' value:

```javascript
var a = [ ];
a[2] = 'red';
a[5] = 'green';
a[7] = 'blue';
a.push('orange');
```

For both indexed arrays and sparse indexed arrays, the only difference between PHP and Node.js in terms of how array values are assigned and retrieved is that the PHP dollar sign ($) is removed in Node.js. The dollar sign ($) was already removed in a find-and-replace action presented at the beginning of this chapter.

Also, for both indexed arrays and sparse indexed arrays, the PHP empty square bracket ([and]) notation can be replaced with the Node.js push() method call. Here's the find-and-replace action to do this:

```
Operation: "Find/Replace" in Eclipse PDT
Find: [ ]
Replace: push(
Options: None
Action: Find, then Replace/Find
```

At each occurrence, determine if the empty square brackets ([and]) are used to add a value to the end of a PHP indexed array or are used to initialize an empty Node.js array. If it not being used to add a value, skip this occurrence. If it is being used to add a value to an indexed array, create a push() method call on the array variable and move the new value to be passed as an argument to the call.

The following PHP code shows the value 'orange' being added to the end of the array:

```php
$a[ ] = 'orange';
```

Convert this PHP code into the Node.js push() method call:

```javascript
a.push('orange');
```

After this find-and-replace action, adding values to all PHP indexed arrays will be converted properly to Node.js.

For PHP normal indexed arrays, the PHP count() API function is equivalent to the length property on a Node.js array. There are several ways that the PHP count() API function can be converted to Node.js.

One way is to replace all count() function calls with an access to the length property on the same indexed array variable.

Here is some PHP code that uses the PHP count() API function call:

```
if (count($a) >= 10) {
  // do something with $a here
}
```

To convert this code to Node.js, the count() function call is replaced with an access to the length property on the array:

```
if (a.length >= 10) {
  // do something with a here
}
```

Here's the find-and-replace action to execute this conversion:

```
Operation: "Find/Replace" in Eclipse PDT
Find: count\((.*)\)
Replace: $1.length
Options: Regular expressions, Wrap search
Action: Find, then Replace/Find
```

At each occurrence, confirm that an indexed array variable, not an expression or associative array, is passed to the PHP count() API function call. If an indexed array variable is passed, execute the action. If an expression is passed, manually rewrite the code to convert the PHP count() API function call to Node.js. If an associative array is passed, skip the occurrence.

Instead of replacing all PHP count() API function calls with Node.js length property references, another way is to implement the count() function in Node.js. Here's a simple Node.js count() function:

```
function count(a) {
  return a.length;
}
```

As more PHP API functions are presented for conversion in the remaining chapters, you will often be presented with these same two conversion choices: (1) execute a find-and-replace action to replace the PHP API function call with its equivalent Node.js code inline and (2) implement the function itself in Node.js. It is mostly a matter of taste. The first way makes the Node.js code look more natural to other Node.js developers. The second is a quick-and-dirty way to just make the Node.js code work.

For sparse arrays, the PHP `count()` API function will return a different result than the Node.js `length` property shown earlier because Node.js sparse arrays are not truly sparse. Node.js sparse arrays have all the keys but the unused keys have undefined values, rather than being nonexistent.

It is recommended to remove sparse arrays from the PHP codebase, if convenient, so it becomes a nonissue when converting to Node.js. If that is not convenient, examine the PHP sparse array to determine if it ever has the PHP `count()` API function called upon it. If the number of values in the sparse array do not need to be determined or can be determined as the values are added to the sparse array, it is recommended to do that.

However, if a PHP sparse array must have its number of values determined, the following Node.js `count()` function can count the number of values in a Node.js sparse array by assuming that all undefined values are nonexistent keys. The Node.js `length` property will be avoided since it is not correct, at least in terms of how the PHP code expects the number of values to be. The following Node.js `count()` function determines the number of values in a Node.js sparse array:

```
function count(a) {
  var c = 0;
  for (var i=0; i < a.length; ++i) {
    if ((typeof a[i]) != 'undefined') {
      ++c;
    }
  }
  return c;
}
```

Since this Node.js `count()` function is complicated, it is not suitable for inlining.

As luck would have it, the Node.js `count()` function also will determine the correct number of values in a Node.js normal array as well. Node.js makes a fine distinction between a variable that exists of the undefined type and a variable that does not exist. PHP does not have that distinction; a variable of the undefined type is the same as a variable that does not exist. As a result, code converted from PHP to Node.js can ignore variables of an undefined type and treat them as if they do not exist.

Besides creating indexed arrays and adding values to indexed arrays, a third common operation is to delete a value from an indexed array.

The PHP `array_splice()` API function is used to remove values from PHP indexed arrays. The first argument is the array to modify. The second argument is the index where the modification will start. The third argument is the number of indexes to delete. The following PHP code demonstrates how to use the PHP `array_splice()` API function:

```
$a = array('red', 'orange', 'green', 'blue');
array_splice($a, 1, 1);
```

Here's the effect of the PHP `array_splice()` API function call for this example:

```
$a[0] contains 'red'
$a[1] contains 'green'
$a[2] contains 'blue'
```

The `'orange'` value has been removed and the indexes have been adjusted to keep them sequential.

The Node.js `splice()` array method is nearly the same. Instead of passing the array as the first argument, the Node.js `splice()` method is a property of the array. The two Node.js arguments are the same as the last two PHP arguments:

```
var a = ['red', 'orange', 'green', 'blue'];
a.splice(1, 1);
```

Here's the find-and-replace action that converts PHP `array_splice()` API function calls to Node.js `splice()` method calls:

```
Operation: "Find/Replace" in Eclipse PDT
Find: array_splice\((([^,]+),(.*)\)
Replace: $1.splice($2)
Options: Regular expressions, Wrap search
Action: Replace All
```

As you convert PHP to Node.js, you will discover that many PHP API functions have similar names to Node.js methods and take the same parameters minus one. In many cases, the first part of the name before the underscore (_) indicates the variable type of the first parameter; in our example, the `array_` part of the PHP name indicates that the first parameter is an array, the `$a` variable. To convert a PHP API function call to the corresponding Node.js method call, sometimes all that is needed is to move the first argument to replace the `array` text and replace the underscore (_) with a dot (.). The text `array_splice($a, …` becomes `$a.splice( … )`. Having so many PHP API functions and Node.js methods that can be mechanically converted from one to another and share the same parameters with the same definitions in the same order shows the common ancestry of both PHP and Node.js and the maturity of the language designers.

Until now, our focus has been on indexed arrays and sparse arrays, including adding, counting, and removing values from the arrays. Since Node.js associative arrays are implemented using Node.js objects, not Node.js arrays, the Node.js code for adding, counting, and removing values from associative arrays is different.

To add a value to a PHP associative array, the key (a string) is specified using the square brackets notation ([and]). Adding a value to a PHP associative array is just like accessing a value, except the expression is on the left side of an equals sign (=). In the following example, the `red`, `green`, and `blue` keys are added to the `$a` associative array variable:

```
$a = array();
$a['red'] = 0;
$a['green'] = 128;
$a['blue'] = 255;
```

In Node.js, the same square bracket notation ([and]) can be used to add properties (i.e., associative array keys) to a Node.js object:

```
var a = { };
a['red'] = 0;
a['green'] = 128;
a['blue'] = 255;
```

As you will recall, a Node.js object literal is initialized with curly brackets ({ and }), not the square brackets ([and]) used with Node.js array initialization.

Since array initialization and the removal of the dollar sign ($) were converted earlier in this chapter, adding values themselves to an associative array needs no special conversion from PHP to Node.js. No find-and-replace action is needed because PHP and Node.js notation is the same.

There is a second notation to add values to a Node.js object, using the dot (.) operator, which is based on using the dot (.) operator to retrieve Node.js object properties. The following Node.js code uses the dot (.) notation instead of the square brackets ([and]) notation in the previous example:

```
var a = { };
a.red = 0;
a.green = 128;
a.blue = 255;
```

In converting PHP code to Node.js, there is no reason to use the dot (.) notation for adding values to a Node.js object but it is a good idea to be aware that it exists.

To determine the number of values in a PHP associative array, the PHP `count()` API function is used; it works for both indexed and associative PHP arrays. The following PHP code shows the PHP `count()` API function being applied to the $a associative array variable:

```
if (count($a) >= 10) {
    // do something with "$a" here
}
```

While the PHP `count()` API function works for both kinds of PHP arrays, the Node.js code is different, depending on whether it is an indexed array or an associative array. While the `length` property exists for Node.js arrays, it does not exist for Node.js objects. Instead, all the keys in a Node.js object are retrieved using the `keys()` method on the global object named `Object`. The `keys()` method returns a Node.js array, which does have a `length` property. The following Node.js code shows the `Object.keys(a).length` code determining the number of values in the `a` associative array and, if it is greater to or equal to 10, executing some code:

```
if (Object.keys(a).length >= 10) {
  // do something with "a" here
}
```

Converting the PHP `count()` API function calls into Node.js can be done by executing the following find-and-replace action:

```
Operation: "Find/Replace" in Eclipse PDT
Find: count\((.*)\)
Replace: Object.keys($1).length
Options: Regular expressions, Wrap search
Action: Find, then Replace/Find
```

At each occurrence, confirm that an associative array variable is passed to the PHP `count()` API function call. If so, execute the find-and-replace action. Otherwise, find the next occurrence.

For Node.js associative arrays, also known as Node.js objects, a Node.js `count()` function can be implemented as a replacement for the PHP `count()` API function. The following function would handle Node.js objects only:

```
function count(a) {
  return Object.keys(a).length;
}
```

Given quick-and-dirty Node.js `count()` functions for normal indexed arrays, sparse indexed arrays, and associative arrays, these separate Node.js `count()` functions can be combined into a single Node.js `count()` function that works on all three array types as shown here:

```
function count(a) {
  var c = 0;
  if (a instanceof Array) {
    for (var i=0; i < a.length; ++i) {
      if ((typeof a[i]) != 'undefined') {
        ++c;
      }
    }
  } else {
    c = Object.keys(a).length;
  }
  return c;
}
```

The Node.js `count()` function uses the `instanceof` keyword to determine if the Node.js argument is a Node.js indexed array, or if that evaluates to `false`, assuming that the argument is an associative array implemented as a Node.js object.

No find-and-replace action is needed to convert between PHP and Node.js because the code already invokes the count() function.

To remove a value from a PHP associative array, use the PHP unset() API function. The following PHP code removes the orange key and its associated value, 64, from the $a associative array:

```
$a = array('red' => 0, 'orange' => 64, 'green' => 128, 'blue' => 255);
unset($a['orange']);
```

Here are the contents of the $a associative array as they are after the preceding PHP code is executed (the orange key and its value no longer exist):

```
$a['red'] contains 0
$a['green'] contains 128
$a['blue'] contains 255
```

In Node.js, the delete keyword can be used to remove a property from a Node.js object. A deleted property is no longer included when the keys() method of the Object object is called on the Node.js object. The delete keyword removes the orange key from the a associative array variable in this Node.js code:

```
var a = {'red': 0, 'orange': 64, 'green': 128, 'blue': 255};
delete a['orange'];
```

And here are the contents of the a associative array as they are after the previous Node.js code is executed (again, the orange key and its value no longer exist):

```
a['red'] contains 0
a['green'] contains 128
a['blue'] contains 255
```

Converting the PHP unset() API function calls into Node.js delete statements can be done by executing this find-and-replace action:

```
Operation: "Find/Replace" in Eclipse PDT
Find: unset\((.*)\)
Replace: delete $1
Options: Regular expressions, Wrap search
Action: Find, then Replace/Find
```

At each occurrence, confirm that an associative array key is passed to the PHP unset() API function call. If so, execute the find-and-replace action. Otherwise, find the next occurrence.

After executing this find-and-replace action, deleting a value from all associative arrays has been converted from PHP to Node.js.

With these techniques and find-and-replace actions, accessing, setting, adding, counting, and removing values from normal and sparse indexed arrays as well as associative arrays can be converted from PHP to Node.js.

There is one additional possibility: in PHP, an array can have both numeric and string indexes. These kinds of arrays can be referred to as *mixed key arrays*. This PHP code creates a mixed key array with three numeric indexes and one string index:

```
$a = array('red', 'green', 'blue', 'colormodel' => 'rgb');
```

Here are the contents of the $a mixed key array:

```
$a[0] contains 'red'
$a[1] contains 'green'
$a[2] contains 'blue'
$a['colormodel'] contains 'rgb'
```

It is recommended that the PHP code be refactored to replace mixed key arrays with indexed, sparse, or associative arrays. Mixed key arrays cannot be conveniently converted to Node.js.

Mixed key arrays cannot be represented by Node.js arrays. Although properties can be added to a Node.js array just like any other Node.js object, the length property of a Node.js array would only reflect the number of numeric indexes and not any string indexes. In addition, the Node.js array would not be able to distinguish the length property from a string key named "length."

Mixed key arrays cannot be represented by Node.js objects because property names can only be strings, not numbers. The square bracket notation ([and]) works for both numeric indexes (e.g., a[2]) and string indexes (e.g., a['colormodel']). However, essential array methods, such as the Node.js push() method, would be missing, severely limiting the ability of the Node.js object to effectively implement the PHP mixed key array functionality.

As a result, it is recommended that PHP mixed key arrays be refactored into PHP code that is more friendly to Node.js conversion.

PHP array variables also have one additional quirk. The PHP engine can infer some missing array keyword statements. This code is working PHP code:

```
$a = array();
$a['home']['phone'] = '333-3333';
```

The PHP engines infers that there should be an array keyword that initializes the $a['home'] array variable and compensates for it such that the PHP page works without error. Here's the PHP code that correctly initializes the $a['home'] array variable:

```
$a = array();
$a['home'] = array(); // can be inferred by the PHP engine
$a['home']['phone'] = '333-3333';
```

However, the Node.js engine does not make similar inferences. The following Node.js code will cause a stack trace with the message "Cannot set property 'home' of undefined":

```
var a = { };
a['home']['phone'] = '333-3333';
```

The correct Node.js code must have an object, even an empty object, assigned to the home property before a property can be assigned to the home object:

```
var a = { };
a['home'] = { };
a['home']['phone'] = '333-3333';
```

It is recommended that all PHP code be refactored to explicitly use the array keyword to initialize all PHP arrays, including arrays assigned to keys of other arrays and multidimensional arrays. PHP code should never rely upon the PHP engine to infer a missing array statement:

```
$a = array();
$a['home'] = array(); // always add this statement explicitly
$a['home']['phone'] = '333-3333';
```

As you can see, PHP arrays can be converted to Node.js quite naturally and accurately.

Other Variable Types

Objects, that is, PHP's class-based system, can be converted to Node.js's prototype-based system. The next chapter is devoted to converting both PHP classes to Node.js object with prototypes and PHP's use of objects into the equivalent Node.js code that will use the corresponding Node.js objects.

PHP also has a two rather obscure variable types: resources and unknown types.

A PHP resource variable is an opaque data structure, also called a handle, whose data is only accessible by PHP API functions. For example, the PHP fopen() API function returns a resource value that points to a particular file. That resource value is stored in a variable and passed to other PHP API functions, such as fread(), fwrite(), and fclose(), which know how to understand the resource variables to read, write, and close the file, respectively. With resource variables, converting the variable itself from PHP to Node.js is not important; it is only important that the effect, such as reading, writing, or closing the file, takes place. Node.js has its own APIs for reading, writing, and closing files, so those are used instead. Converting file access from PHP to Node.js is specifically handled in Chapter 9.

Besides file access, other PHP resource variables are created when compressing or decompressing files, using cURL, reading or writing to databases, reading or writing from FTP servers, creating images and documents in specific formats, reading or writing LDAP servers, and receiving or sending email. In all these cases, the resource variable itself can be ignored and the PHP API function calls replaced with the corresponding Node.js API function calls.

An "unknown type" PHP variable is very obscure and may be a PHP resource variable that has been closed and rendered unusable. A PHP "unknown type" variable does not need to be converted to Node.js.

Node.js also has two variable types that have no corresponding types in PHP: function and undefined.

A Node.js function variable is a callback variable. The following Node.js code demonstrates that the f variable is a variable of type "function":

```
var f = function() {
};
console.log('The variable, f, is of type, "'+(typeof f)+'".');
```

The output of the Node.js code shows that the f variable is of a unique function type.

As you may recall from Chapter 4, PHP 5.3 introduced callback variables to the PHP language. Here's a PHP 5.3 example of the previous Node.js code:

```
$f = function() {
};
print 'The variable, $f, is of type, "'.(gettype($f)).'".';
```

The output of the PHP 5.3 example shows that PHP does not have a unique variable type for callback functions.

The variable $f is of type "object."

PHP 5.3 callback functions are considered objects, along with other object variables that are not callback function variables. Node.js makes a distinction between functions and objects but PHP 5.3 does not.

Undefined Variables

In Node.js, a variable can be of the "undefined" type. As described before, Node.js makes a distinction between a variable that exists but is undefined and a variable that does not exist. PHP does not make such a distinction.

In a PHP to Node.js conversion, a Node.js undefined variable can be a good substitute for a PHP variable that does not exist.

Previously, the PHP unset() API function was converted to a Node.js delete keyword statement for removing values from PHP arrays. But the PHP unset() API function can also be used on ordinary, nonarray variables:

```
$a = 4;
unset($a);
print 'isset($a) returns '.(isset($a)? 'true':'false').'.';
```

The PHP isset() API function exists to test whether a variable exists or not. If a variable has never been created or the PHP unset() API function is applied to an existing variable, the variable will be removed and the PHP `isset()` API function will return `false`. If a variable exists, the PHP `isset()` API function will return `true`. The previous PHP code returns the following output, indicating that the `$a` variable does not exist after the PHP `unset()` API function is called on it:

```
isset($a) returns false.
```

The PHP `unset()` API function can be called on any variable, including array values, array variables themselves, or normal, nonarray variables. The Node.js `delete` keyword is not as flexible.

The Node.js `delete` keyword has a boolean return value. If it could delete the variable, the Node.js `delete` keyword will return `true`. If it could not delete the variable, the Node.js `delete` keyword returns `false`. Ordinary object properties, such as those properties added to a Node.js object that implements an associative array, can be deleted. That is why the Node.js `delete` keyword works as a substitute for the PHP `unset()` API function when it is applied to PHP associative arrays. However, built-in properties, such as the `length` property on Node.js indexed arrays, and ordinary variables will return `false` if the Node.js `delete` keyword is called upon them. The Node.js `delete` keyword has no effect on these other types of variables.

Built-in properties, such as the `length` property on Node.js indexed arrays, should not have the Node.js `delete` keyword called upon them. This is a coding error. There is no reason that PHP code that is converted to Node.js should try to call the PHP `unset()` API or the Node.js `delete` keyword on built-in properties of arrays or objects.

It is possible, though, that the PHP `unset()` API function could be called on an ordinary variable in well-written PHP code. In PHP, an ordinary variable is not declared; the PHP engine creates it when it is first used. But in Node.js, an ordinary variable is declared with the `var` keyword. The `var` keyword, by its use, assigns a scope to the variable and requires that the variable exist throughout that scope. As you will recall, a scope is an area of source code where the variable name refers to the specific variable created in a `var` statement. The Node.js `delete` keyword cannot work because that would violate the implied contract that the `var` keyword creates. There is no corresponding `unvar` keyword; a Node.js variable is always valid inside its scope.

Even though an ordinary variable in Node.js cannot be deleted, the variable itself can be set to the "undefined" type and its value can be the "undefined" value. The variable still exists, but the type and the value is undefined. This is the next best thing to being able to delete a Node.js variable.

It is fortuitous that Node.js itself uses this same solution for the indexes and values in sparse arrays that should not exist. In sparse arrays, the unused keys have the "undefined" type and their corresponding values take on the "undefined" value.

The following find-and-replace action will replace PHP `unset()` API function calls with a Node.js statement that sets the Node.js variable to `undefined`:

```
Operation: "Find/Replace" in Eclipse PDT
Find: unset\((.*)\)
Replace: $1 = undefined
Options: Regular expressions, Wrap search
Action: Find, then Replace/Find
```

At each occurrence, the PHP unset() API function call should only be replaced if an ordinary Node.js variable that was created using the var keyword is passed as an argument. Otherwise, the action should not be executed.

After the previous find-and-replace action and the similar find-and-replace action for associative arrays are executed, a "deleted" value or variable for any array variable or an ordinary variable will either not exist or have the "undefined" type and be set to the "undefined" value.

The PHP isset() API function determines the existence of a variable. If the variable exists, it returns true; otherwise, it returns false. The PHP isset() API function can be applied to array values or ordinary variables.

As it turns out, testing for the Node.js undefined type is equivalent to the PHP isset() API function in terms of PHP to Node.js conversion.

Whether a Node.js value is actually deleted or is set to the undefined value, the Node.js typeof operator can evaluate it and will return undefined as its type. The typeof operator does not distinguish between these two different states, even though the Node.js delete operator does.

The following Node.js code demonstrates that used and unused values in a sparse array can be distinguished using the Node.js typeof keyword:

```
var a = [ ];
a[1] = 'red';
console.log('used value in sparse array exists: '
  +((typeof a[1]) != 'undefined'));
console.log('unused value in sparse array exists: '
  +((typeof a[0]) != 'undefined'));
```

The output of the Node.js code proves that testing a Node.js sparse array key to see if it is of the undefined type is equivalent to calling the PHP isset() function on the corresponding PHP code:

```
used value in sparse array exists: true
unused value in sparse array exists: false
```

The following Node.js code demonstrates that used and unused keys in a Node.js associative array can be distinguished using the Node.js typeof keyword:

```
var a = { model: false };
console.log('known associative array key exists: '
  +((typeof a['model']) != 'undefined'));
console.log('unknown associative array key exists: '
```

```
  +((typeof a['color']) != 'undefined'));
delete a['model'];
console.log('deleted associative array key exists: '
  +((typeof a['model']) != 'undefined'));
```

The output proves that it works for Node.js objects, which is our implementation of a PHP-style associative array:

```
known associative array key exist: true
unknown associative array key exist: false
deleted associative array key exist: false
```

The following Node.js code demonstrates that Node.js ordinary variables set to the undefined value array can be distinguished using the Node.js typeof keyword as expected:

```
var a = false;
console.log('ordinary variable exists: '+((typeof a) != 'undefined'));
a = undefined;
console.log('ordinary undefined variable exists: '+((typeof a) != 'undefined'));
```

The output proves that it works for Node.js objects, which is our implementation of a PHP-style associative array:

```
ordinary variable exists: true
ordinary undefined variable exists: false
```

This Node.js test code proves that PHP isset() API function calls can always be converted into Node.js typeof keyword tests.

As a result, converting the PHP isset() API function calls into Node.js can be done by executing this find-and-replace action:

```
Operation: "Find/Replace" in Eclipse PDT
Find: isset\((.*)\)
Replace: ((typeof $1) != 'undefined')
Options: Regular expressions, Wrap search
Action: Replace All
```

As expected, a quick-and-dirty alternative is to implement the PHP isset() API function in Node.js:

```
function isset(a) {
  return ((typeof $1) != 'undefined');
}
```

The only caveat to these two ways of converting the PHP isset() API function into Node.js is that variables declared with the var keyword must be in scope. If the Node.js variable is not in scope, the Node.js server will exit with a stack trace and emit a message. The following message was emitted because of an out-of-scope v variable:

```
ReferenceError: v is not defined
```

With the variable types and various variable-related APIs converted from PHP to Node.js, there is a final issues to address: variable scoping.

Scope

In both PHP and Node.js, each variable has one in five different scopes: global scope, local scope, static scope, class scope, and function scope.

In PHP, a variable in global scope means that the variable is accessible throughout the entire PHP page. The $a variable in this PHP example is a global variable:

```php
<?php
$a = 'global variable';
?>
```

Inside PHP functions, a global variable must be redeclared as global by using the PHP global keyword in order to access it:

```php
<?php
$a = 'global variable';
function printglobal() {
  global $a;
  print $a;
}
?>
```

A Node.js global variable can be created by adding it as a property to the Node.js object named global. The following Node.js code creates an a variable that is shared globally:

```
global.a = 'global variable';
```

A Node.js global variable can be accessed from inside a function in the same way:

```
global.a = 'global variable';
function printglobal() {
  console.log(global.a);
}
```

There are other ways to create Node.js global variables, but they will not be covered here.

To convert a PHP global keyword statement into a Node.js statement that allows access to the corresponding Node.js global variable, execute this find-and-replace action:

```
Operation: "Find/Replace" in Eclipse PDT
Find: global\s++\$?([^;]++);
Replace: global\s++\$?([^;]++);
Options: Regular expressions, Wrap search
Action: Find, then Replace/Find
```

At each occurrence, determine if the global variable needs to be written to. If the Node.js global variable needs to be written to, prefix all the global variable accesses in that function with `global.` text. Also, delete the PHP `global` keyword statement. If the global variable is read-only, execute the action.

The find-and-replace action converts a PHP statement like `global $a` into a Node.js statement of the form, `var a = global.a`. Declaring a new variable in the Node.js function, which reflects the value of the global variable, will allow the function to access the global variable without updating all the global variable references.

It is recommended that global variables be avoided in both PHP and Node.js.

While global variables are few and far between, local variables are commonly used.

In PHP, a local variable is declared inside a function. Unless the `global` keyword statement is used, a local variable is, by default, a separate variable from other variables outside the function, even if they have the same name. In the following PHP example, the last statement will print "global," not "local," to illustrate that the `f()` function call had no effect on the `$a` global variable. The `$a` variable inside the `f()` function is a local variable that is completely separate from the `$a` global variable:

```
$a = 'global';
function f() {
  $a = 'local';
}
f();
print $a; // prints "global"
```

A PHP local variable exists until the function call exists or until the PHP `unset()` API function is called upon it. A PHP local variable is created when it is first referenced.

In Node.js, using the `var` keyword inside a function declares a Node.js local variable. No matter where the local variable is declared in a function, it is created by the Node.js engine before the first statement and assigned the `undefined` value.

The following Node.js example will print two lines: it will print the text "undefined" on the first line, and then print the text "red" on the second line. This example shows that the a variable is created as soon as the `f()` function begins executing:

```
function f() {
  console.log(a);
  var a = 'red';
  console.log(a);
}
f();
```

Generally, converting PHP local variables to Node.js local variables does not require any special conversion techniques beyond the general variable conversions presented earlier in this chapter.

Static variables are similar to local variables except that a single variable is shared between all calls to the function and its value is preserved between function calls. In contrast, local variables are created during each function call and are destroyed when the function call returns.

PHP supports static variables using the PHP `static` keyword. The initialization of the static variable only occurs when the static variable is created on the first call to the function. This PHP example illustrates how the `$a` static variable retains its value between calls to the `f()` function:

```
function f() {
  static $a = 0;
  print $a;
  ++$a;
}
f(); // prints 0
f(); // prints 1
f(); // prints 2
```

A static variable behaves like a global variable, but is not accessible outside the function.

Node.js does not support static variables. However, a static variable can be simulated by assigning it as a property to the function. This Node.js example shows an effective conversion of the previous PHP code:

```
function f() {
  if (f.a == undefined) f.a = 0; // initialize the simulated static variable
  console.log(f.a);
  ++f.a;
}
f(); // prints 0
f(); // prints 1
f(); // prints 2
```

The a property is assigned to the f function, which preserves it across function calls. The f.a property simulates the $a static variable from the PHP example.

Statistically, the use of static variables in PHP is rare. Many PHP pages have no static variables at all. With this in mind, the following find-and-replace action finds PHP static variables by finding the `static` keyword and relies heavily on the developer to implement the static variable appropriately in Node.js:

```
Operation: "Find/Replace" in Eclipse PDT
Find: static\s++\$?([^;\s]++)\s++(.*);
Replace: if (f.$1 == undefined) f.$1 $2;
Options: Regular expressions, Wrap search
Action: Find, then Replace/Find
```

At each occurrence, remove the `static` keyword statement and implement the static variable in Node.js, using the Node.js example above. Replace references to the PHP variable, like $a, with Node.js references to the function property, like f.a. The find-and-replace action will find PHP static variable initialization code that looks like `static $a = 0` and replace it with Node.js code that looks like `if (f.a == undefined)` `f.a = 0`. The initialization code will need to replace the text, `f`, with the name of the actual function that the static variable is contained within.

Class variables, that is, variables with class scope, will be covered in the next chapter. The next chapter is devoted to converting both PHP classes to Node.js object with prototypes and PHP's use of objects into the equivalent Node.js code that will use the corresponding Node.js objects.

Function parameters, which can be called variables with function scope, are the variables inside the function that are associated with values or variables passed from the code that calls the function. Function arguments are the actual values or variables passed from the code outside the function during a specific function call. In the following PHP example, the $a variable is a function parameter and the $b variable is a function argument:

```
function f($a) {
}
f($b);
```

By default, PHP arguments are passed by value. Pass by value means that the function argument (the $a variable in the following PHP example) will have its value copied into the function parameter, $b, of the function. When an argument is passed by value, the function parameter behaves like a local variable. Changes to the $b variable here do not change the value of $a:

```
$a = 'global';
function f($b) {
  $b = 'local';
}
f($a);
print $a; // prints "global"
```

Instead of passing by value, a function can have arguments passed by reference. An ampersand (&) is added as a prefix to any function parameter that uses pass by reference instead of pass by value. In the following PHP code, the $b function parameter is passed by reference, instead of by value:

```
$a = 'global';
function f(&$b) {
  $b = 'local';
}
f($a);
print $a; // prints "local"
```

Passing by reference means that the function parameter, the $b variable, becomes an alias for the function argument, the $a variable. Any change to the $b variable, such as assigning it a value, changes the $a variable as well. When the $a variable is passed by value, the output will be "global," but when the $a variable is passed by reference, the output will be "local."

When reading from a function parameter, passing by value and passing by reference are the same, except for some minor performance differences. It is only when writing to a function parameter that passing by value or passing by reference makes a big difference. With pass by value, the copy is changed but the original is unaffected. But with pass by reference, both the copy and the original are changed because they refer to the same variable.

Node.js arguments are only passed by value. When the a variable is passed as an argument to the f() function in the following Node.js code, it is unchanged even though the b variable is modified inside the f() function. The a variable keeps the value 'global', even though the b variable changes its own value from 'global' to 'local':

```
var a = 'global';
function f(b) {
  b = 'local';
}
f(a);
console.log(a); // prints "global"
```

Passing by reference can be simulated in Node.js. If a variable is put into a Node.js array, the array contents are shared, not copied, between the function argument and the function parameter. So, if the function modifies the contents of the array, the contents of the function argument are modified as well. The following Node.js code packs the a variable into an array, passes it to the f() function, and unpacks the a variable from the array at a[0]. During the f() function call, the b variable is now a Node.js array. It simulates pass by reference by substituting b[0] for all places that it would have used b. The net result is that the a variable contains the text "local," instead of "global," which shows that it has the same behavior as passing by reference:

```
var a = 'global';
function f(b) {
 b[0] = 'local';
}
a = [a];
f(a);
a = a[0];
console.log(a); // prints "local"
```

Using arrays in Node.js is an approximation of passing by reference in PHP. When the a variable is packed into an array using the a = [a] statement, a copy of the value of the a variable is stored, not an alias to the a variable itself. In the same vein, the value of

the a[0], not the variable itself, is copied back into the actual a variable using the a =
a[0] statement after the f() function call. This code takes advantage of the fact that
passing by value and passing by reference work the same in terms of reading from
variables.

Inside the f() function, the b variable, which is now a Node.js array, can have its values,
such as b[0], modified and those modifications will be reflected in the a array variable
passed as an argument. If the b variable is a copy of the a variable, how can a change to
the b variable affect the a variable?

Node.js copies values using shallow copying. Shallow copying means that for composite
variables such as arrays and objects, which are collections of multiple values, the language only copies the single value that points to the composite variable. It is still a copy,
though, because the variable itself can be changed to point to a different composite
object or assigned a simple value. But with a shallow copy, both the function argument
and the function parameter point to the same object.

Deep copying is the opposite of shallow copying. Deep copying means that for composite
variables such as arrays and objects, which are collections of multiple values, the language traverses the entire structure and copies all its parts. PHP copies values using deep
copying.

When the Node.js code for simulating passing by reference is converted to PHP, it does
not work:

```
$a = 'global';
function f($b) {
    $b[0] = 'local';
}
$a = array($a);
f($a);
$a = $a[0];
print $a; // prints "global"
```

The $a variable has the value 'global' instead of 'local' after the f() function call.
It does not work because, when the f() function is called, the $a variable is copied to
the $b variable using deep copying, instead of shallow copying that is used in Node.js.
The $b variable does not point to the same array that the $a variable does; it points to
a new copy of the array. Simulating passing by reference relies on shallow copying.

In a lot of code, it makes no difference that PHP does deep copying and Node.js does
shallow copying. It is still important to understand the difference, though, so that you
can address those relatively rare situations where some PHP code changes an object and
relies on deep copying to keep copies of the object unchanged. It is recommended that
these situations be eliminated using refactoring although they can also be addressed by
explicitly copying the contents of Node.js variables that would otherwise be shared.

To convert PHP functions that use passing by reference to Node.js, execute the following find-and-replace action. At each occurrence, this action heavily relies on the developer to manually find and change related Node.js code that is not addressed by the Replace field:

```
Operation: "Find/Replace" in Eclipse PDT
Find: &\$?
Replace:
Options: Regular expressions, Wrap search
Action: Find, then Replace/Find
```

At each occurrence, follow these three steps:

1. Inside the function, add a [0] suffix to each use of the function parameter passed by reference. For example, inside the f() function, replace every use of the a and c variables passed by reference with a a[0] or c[0]. Do not replace the b variable because it is passed by value:

```
function f(&a, b, &c) {
  if (a[0] > 10) { // a becomes a[0]
    a[0] += 10; // a becomes a[0]
    if (b < 3) {
      c[0] = 100; // c becomes c[0]
    } elseif (c[0] > 30) { // c becomes c[0]
      c[0] = a[0] * b;? // a becomes a[0] and c becomes c[0]
    }
  }
}
```

2. Find every function call in every page to the function where a function parameter is passed by reference. Before the function call, pack any function arguments that are passed by reference into an array. After the function call, unpack any function arguments that are passed by reference from the array. For example, the first and third function parameters are passed by value, so put the x and z variables into one-value arrays, call the f() function, then remove the x and z variables from the arrays:

```
var x = 0;
var y = 10;
var z = 100;
x = [x];
z = [z];
f(x, y, z);
x = x[0];
z = z[0];
```

3. Remove the ampersand (&), and if it still exists, the dollar sign ($) from the function parameters. For example, the f() function still uses the ampersand (&) for the a and c variables:

```
function f(&a, b, &c) {
...
}
```

Remove the ampersand (&) from the a and c variables so all variables are passed by value:

```
function f(a, b, c) {
    ...
}
```

Although PHP function parameters are not often passed by reference, it is useful to know how to convert them to Node.js.

PHP functions are more sophisticated than Node.js functions. Besides building in support for passing by reference for parameters into the language, PHP also provides specific support for default argument values.

A default argument value is the value that the parameter takes if the function call does not provide one. For example, the $c function parameter will take the value 'too little' if a function call is made with two arguments, instead of three:

```
function f($a, $b, $c = 'too little') {
    ...
}
f(10, 100, 'too much'); // 3 arguments so default argument value not used
f(5, 50); // 2 arguments so $c takes the 'too little' value
```

Unlike PHP, Node.js does not provide specific support for default argument values. However, Node.js does allow that function calls have a different number of arguments than the number of function parameters. If fewer arguments are provided than function parameters, the extra parameters take on the undefined type with the undefined value. If more arguments are provided than function parameters, the extra arguments are ignored.

The missing arguments can be detected by testing for the undefined type and then resetting the value of the argument to the desired default value. The following Node.js code implements the f() function from the previous PHP code, including the c default argument value:

```
function f(a, b, c) {
    c - ((typeof c) != 'undefined')? c: 'too little');
    ...
}
f(10, 100, 'too much'); // 3 arguments so c is set to 'too much'
f(5, 50); // only 2 arguments so c is set to 'too little'
```

The use of the typeof operator to implement default operators is very accurate, but there is a more common Node.js idiom that is not as accurate. The following Node.js code is more common:

```
function f(a, b, c) {
    c = c || 'too little';
    ...
}
```

The "or" operator (||) returns the left value, if the left value evaluates to true; otherwise, it returns the right value. Most values evaluate to true; only a few values evaluate to false. Besides the boolean value (false), other values that evaluate to false are the undefined value of the undefined type, zero, the empty string, null, and NaN ("Not a Number").

The difference between implementing the default argument value using the typeof keyword and using the "or" operator (||) idiom is that the "or" operator (||) would replace the empty string into the 'too little' default argument value. This Node.js example illustrates the difference:

```
var d = '';
f(5, 50, d);
```

If the typeof keyword is used, the c function parameter would be kept as the empty string. If the "or" operator (||) approach is used, the c function parameter would be reset to the 'too little' value. In many cases, both approaches would do the same thing. As long as a zero, the empty string, a null, or a NaN is never passed as a function argument to a function parameter that had a different default argument value, both approaches would work just as well.

To convert default argument values from PHP to Node.js, use the following find-and-replace action to visit all functions:

```
Operation: "Find/Replace" in Eclipse PDT
Find: function
Replace:
Options: Wrap search
Action: Find, then Replace/Find
```

At each occurrence, identify any default argument values and add a statement similar to the following, but replace 'param' with the actual name of the function parameter and replace the empty string with the actual default value:

```
param = ((typeof param) != 'undefined')? param: '');
```

Remove the default argument value from the function parameters in the parameters declaration.

If a PHP default argument value is left in the code, Node.js will exit with a stack trace. A stack trace is also a good way to detect unconverted default argument values.

This chapter described how to convert simple variables, like strings and arrays, with their most common manipulations and in their most common contexts from PHP into Node.js. PHP also supports complex variables that are created from PHP classes. The next chapter is devoted to explaining how to convert PHP classes into the equivalent Node.js code.

CHAPTER 8

Classes

All languages, including PHP and Node.js, have a set of fundamental variable types, such as booleans, numbers, and strings. For PHP and Node.js, these fundamental types were described in detail in the previous chapter. Variables can be created of these fundamental types. Many languages, including PHP and Node.js, also allow variables and functions to be combined together into a single more complex variable.

PHP uses what is called a traditional class-based object system. In the PHP class-based object system, a PHP class is a type that is defined by the user. Like a fundamental type, such as a boolean or a number, a type is not an actual variable; it is a kind of variable. A PHP object is an actual variable that was created from a PHP class.

Node.js does not use a traditional class-based object system; it uses a prototype-based system. In a prototype-based system, objects share a common object, called a prototype, which can provide variables and functions to be used by all objects that use that prototype. A Node.js object is an actual variable. A Node.js prototype object, or just called a "prototype," is a Node.js object shared by multiple Node.js variables.

Encapsulation

To learn how to convert a PHP class to Node.js, let's begin with a simple PHP class.

The following PHP code creates a simple class called Format, which holds a format string, like Error #{$1}: {$2}. The format string contains literal text and macros. Macros are contained in curly braces ({ and }) and indicate that some sort of substitution should be done. An array, such as array('30', 'User not found'), can be passed to the apply() method to return a string like Error #30: User not found:

```
class Format {
  function Format($s) {
    $this->source = $s;
```

```
    }

    function apply($a) {
      $ret = $this->source;
      for ($i=1; $i <= count($a); ++$i) {
        $ret = str_replace('{'.$i.'}', $a[$i-1], $ret);
      }
      return $ret;
    }
  }
```

A PHP class is created using the PHP `class` keyword. The PHP `class` keyword is followed by the name of the class. After the class name, a block containing the class definition is enclosed in curly brackets ({ and }):

```
class Format {
  ...
}
```

Node.js does not have a `class` keyword. In Node.js, a normal function takes the place of the PHP `class` keyword. So, the PHP `class` keyword is replaced with the Node.js `function` keyword, as follows. All Node.js functions require parentheses ((and)) so an empty pair has been added here:

```
function Format() {
  ...
}
```

Inside a PHP class, there is a special function that has the same name as the class. This special function is called a constructor. A constructor is a function that is automatically called on an object as soon as it is created. When an object of the PHP `Format` class is created, the `Format` class function, its constructor, will be called automatically. Here's the PHP `Format` constructor:

```
class Format {
  function Format($s) {
    $this->source = $s;
  }
  ...
}
```

A PHP class can have variables as well as functions. In PHP, the `$this` variable is a special variable that refers to the object itself. To access variables and functions attached to the `$this` variable, the PHP pointer operator (->) is used. Previously, the `$this` variable was used to create a `source` variable inside the newly created object. The single statement in the PHP `Format` class saves the `$s` argument passed to the constructor in the source variable inside the newly created object.

As described before, Node.js uses a normal function to define a class. In Node.js, that function takes the place of both the PHP class and the PHP constructor. A Node.js function is both the class and its constructor. The following Node.js function indicates that there is a Node.js `Format` class (that is, a new Node.js complex type) and it contains the Node.js code to construct it:

```
function Format(s) {
   this.source = s;
}
```

Like the PHP `$this` special variable, Node.js has a special variable called `this`. Instead of using the PHP pointer operator, the Node.js dot operator (.) is used to access variables and functions attached to the `this` variable. The `s` parameter is added to the Node.js `Format` function and stored in the `source` variable attached to the newly created object.

In PHP, variables are stored in the object simply by accessing the `$this` variable but class functions are explicitly defined in class definition blocks. In a way, a PHP class can be viewed as just a collection of related functions with the option to share class data using the `$this` variable. Besides a constructor function, a class can have any number of other class functions. The PHP `Format` class has one other function—the `apply()` function:

```
function apply($a) {
   $ret = $this->source;
   for ($i=1; $i <= count($a); ++$i) {
     $ret = str_replace('{'.$i.'}', $a[$i-1], $ret);
   }
   return $ret;
}
```

The PHP `apply()` function returns a string based on the `source` format string and the `$a` array argument, which contains specific strings to be substituted for the macros, such as {$1} and {$2} and so on. Its PHP code first makes a copy of the format string, `source`, and then loops over each string in the array and substitutes the array string for its corresponding macro. The now-formatted string in the `$ret` variable is returned.

In Node.js, every object created using a Node.js constructor function shares a special object called the "prototype" or the "prototype object." The prototype object is automatically created once per function and stored in the `prototype` property of each Node.js function. By assigning a function (such as the Node.js `apply()` function) to the shared prototype object, any objects created with the corresponding constructor function will have access to the functions in the shared prototype as well:

```
Format.prototype.apply = function(a) {
   var ret = this.source;
   for (var i=1; i <= a.length; ++i) {
     var ff, f = '{$'+i+'}';
     while ((ff = ret.indexOf(f)) !== -1) {
       ret = ret.substring(0, ff) + a[i-1] + ret.substring(ff + f.length);
```

```
      }
    }
    return ret;
};
```

This Node.js code creates an `apply` property on the `prototype` object of the Node.js `Format()` constructor function. A function is assigned to the `apply` property that is a straightforward Node.js conversion of the PHP `apply()` method. As a side note, the three statements inside the `for` statement are a Node.js implementation of the PHP `str_replace()` API function.

The Node.js `Format` constructor function plus the `Format.prototype.apply()` function make a working Node.js version of the PHP `Format` class. The entire Node.js `Format` code is as follows:

```
function Format(s) {
  this.source = s;
}

Format.prototype.apply = function(a) {
  var ret = this.source;
  for (var i=1; i <= a.length; ++i) {
    var ff, f = '{$'+i+'}';
    while ((ff = ret.indexOf(f)) !== -1) {
      ret = ret.substring(0, ff) + a[i-1] + ret.substring(ff + f.length);
    }
  }
  return ret;
};
```

To convert a PHP class to Node.js, execute the following find-and-replace action:

```
Operation: "Find/Replace" in Eclipse PDT
Find: class
Replace:
Options: None
Action: Find, then Replace/Find
```

At each occurrence, remove the `class Format {` text that begins the class and remove the right curly bracket (}) that ends the class. For each function in the class except for the constructor, rewrite the function definition to start with `classname.proto type.methodname = function` in place of `function methodname` where the "classname" text is replaced with the actual class name, such as "Format," and the "methodname" text is replaced with the actual method name, such as "apply." For these same functions, add a semicolon (;) after the right curly bracket (}) that ends the function. Assigning a function to the `classname.prototype.methodname` is a statement and all Node.js statements must end with a semicolon (;).

To convert the code inside each PHP method to Node.js, the PHP `$this` variable needs to be converted to the Node.js `this` variable. A find-and-replace action will work in many cases, but unfortunately, will not work in all cases.

Every Node.js function, including callback functions, have their own `this` variable, which is different than the function that it is contained in. The `write()` function attempts to write the data in the `data` property of the `this` variable of the Node.js `File Writer` class. However, `this.data` actually refers to the `this` variable of the callback function that is passed as the fourth argument to the `fs.open()` call:

```
FileWriter.prototype.write = function() {
    fs.open(this.filename, "w", 0666, function(error, fp) {
        // the "this.data" below refers to this callback, not the write function
        fs.write(fp, this.data, null, "utf-8", function() {
            ...
        });
    });
};
```

To make the issue plainer, let's rewrite the Node.js `write()` function to assign the callback to a function variable. This Node.js code defines the `fsopencb()` function first and then passes it as the callback argument to the `fs.open()` function call:

```
FileWriter.prototype.write = function() {
    var fsopencb = function(error, fp) {
        // the "this.data" below refers to the fsopencb function
        fs.write(fp, this.data, null, "utf-8", function() {
            ...
        });
    };
    fs.open(this.filename, "w", 0666, fsopencb);
};
```

In Node.js, both the `write()` and `fsopencb()` functions have separate, unrelated `this` variables. When the `this` variable is used inside the `fsopencb()` function, it refers to the one associated with the `fsopencb()` function; for example, the `this` `.data` variable passed to the `fs.write()` function call refers to the `this` variable of the `fsopencb()` function. Only when the `this` variable is used inside the `write()` function directly does the `this` variable refer to `FileWriter` objects and all other objects that share the same prototype object.

To address this issue, the `this` variable can be assigned to a local variable. As you will recall from the discussion of shallow copying versus deep copying in a previous chapter, Node.js only does shallow copying for composite Node.js objects, including the `this` variable. So, both reading and writing properties on the local variable will read and write the actual `this` variable.

In the following Node.js code, the `this` variable of the `write()` function is assigned to the `that` local variable. Instead of using the `this` variable, properties are accessed using the `that` local variable:

```
FileWriter.prototype.write = function() {
  var that = this;
  fs.open(that.filename, "w", 0666, function(error, fp) {
    fs.write(fp, that.data, null, "utf-8", function() {
      ...
    });
  });
};
```

Unlike the `this` variable, which refers to different variables depending on the context, local variables refer to only one consistent variable and one value, regardless of the context. As long as the `that` local variable is accessible, the `that.filename` and `that.data` variables, even if they are used inside callbacks or other functions, will still refer to the `filename` and `data` properties on the `this` variable of the `write()` function.

To safely convert PHP `$this` references to Node.js, the following find-and-replace function replaces `$this->` with `that.` instead of `this`:

```
Operation: "Find/Replace" in Eclipse PDT
Find: $this->
Replace: that.
Options: None
Action: Find, then Replace/Find
```

At each occurrence, a `that` local variable should be defined as the first statement of the correct function that the PHP `$this` variable expects to refer to. The following Node.js statement shows how the `that` local variable should be defined:

```
var that = this;
```

Converting the PHP constructor, the PHP methods, and the PHP `$this` variable to their Node.js equivalents are the only extra conversion steps needed for PHP classes. Converting the PHP code inside the functions, including the syntax, variables, and function calls, is handled in other chapters and needs no special treatment.

Until this point, the focus has been on converting the PHP classes to Node.js. PHP classes are used to create PHP objects. Now, the focus will be shifted to converting the PHP code that uses PHP classes to create PHP objects.

A PHP object is created by using the PHP `new` keyword and calling the class constructor. The following PHP code creates a `Format` object and assigns it to the `$fmt` variable:

```
$fmt = new Format('Error #{$1}: {$2}');
```

A Node.js object is created with nearly the same code as a PHP object. A Node.js object is created by using the Node.js `new` keyword and calling the Node.js constructor function. The following Node.js code creates a Format object and assigns it the `fmt` variable:

```
var fmt = new Format('Error #{$1}: {$2}');
```

Since both PHP and Node.js use the new keyword and use it in the same way, no special conversion is needed to convert PHP object creation to Node.js.

PHP can only create objects in one way: using a PHP class and the PHP new keyword. Node.js objects can be created in three ways: using the new keyword and a constructor function, as an object literal, and using the Object.create() function.

In this chapter, the new keyword and a constructor function have been used as a way to convert PHP classes to Node.js. When a Node.js object is created using a constructor function, the newly created object knows the name of the constructor function used to create it. The constructor function can be considered its class. The following Node.js code prints the class name of the fmt object:

```
console.log(fmt.constructor.name);
```

The constructor property is automatically created for any object that is created using a constructor function.

Classless Node.js objects can also be created. In previous chapters, the Node.js object literal notation, which uses curly brackets ({ and }), was used extensively. Objects created using the object literal notation have a constructor property, but its name is just "Object," so it is essentially classless. The following Node.js code creates an object using the object literal notation and prints its constructor name:

```
var obj = { source: 'Error #{$1}: {$2}' };
console.log(obj.constructor.name); // Object
```

Every object, including fmt and obj, has a __proto__ property that points to the prototype object associated with the object. Functions are objects, too, and have a __proto__ property as well but it is uninteresting. Besides a __proto__ property, functions also have a prototype property that is the object that is assigned as the __proto__ property to newly created objects when the new keyword is used with a call to the function. The __proto__ property is the prototype of an object; the prototype property is the prototype that is assigned to new objects. It is widely considered bad form to write Node.js code that uses the __proto__ property. The __proto__ property is considered for internal use only and is not recommended for general use. Furthermore, the __proto__ property is deprecated.

For objects created with either the new keyword and object literals, their prototype object is an empty object literal. This empty object literal can have properties (including functions) assigned to it, but by default it is empty. The following Node.js code demonstrates the apply() function being added to the empty object of the prototype property for the Format function:

```
Format.prototype.apply = function(a) {
    ...
};
```

After this Node.js code executes, the object will not be empty. It will have one property: the `apply` property.

This discussion of prototypes, the `prototype` property, and the `__proto__` property leads us to the third way to create a Node.js object: using the `Object.create()` function.

The Node.js `Object.create()` function creates a new object using an existing object as a prototype object. The first argument is the object to use as a prototype. If `null` is passed, the prototype is `null`. The second argument is an object that specifies the attributes of the new object to create.

The following Node.js code creates an `errlist` object using the `fmt` object from earlier in this chapter as a prototype. The `fmt` object already has a `source` variable (which is set to `Error #{$1}: {$2}`) and an `apply()` function. The newly created `errlist` object can access these properties in its prototype and adds its own `log` array variable to keep a list of error messages and an `err()` function, which will format an error message, save it to the log, and show it on the console:

```
var errlist = Object.create(fmt, {
  'log': {
    value: [ ],
    enumerable: true
  },
  'err': {
    value: function(a) {
      var msg = this.apply(a);
      this.log.push(msg);
      console.log(msg);
    }
  }
});
```

If you look carefully, the second argument is not the new object itself but is an object that describes the properties of the new object. Each property is the name of a property of the new object with a set of attributes, including its value and the `enumerable` attribute (optional).

If the `enumerable` attribute is set to `true`, the property will be included if a `for...in` statement is used on the object; otherwise, it will not be included. In the previous Node.js code, the `log` property will be included in a `for...in` statement, but since the `enumerable` attribute defaults to `false`, the `err` property will not.

There are additional optional attributes that are used, too.

The `writable` attribute allows the value to be replaced; it defaults to `false`. In the example above, the `push()` method still works on the `log` property even though the `writable` attribute has defaulted to `false` because it modifies the array that the `log` property points to; it does not try to point the `log` property to a different array or change it into a different type.

The configurable attribute allows the property to be deleted; it defaults to false.

The get attribute and the set attribute specify functions to retrieve the property value and set the property value, respectively. Node.js code can override how a property is retrieved and set.

Once the object is created, its variables can be accessed and its functions can be called.

In PHP, the object can be accessed, including calling its functions, using the PHP pointer operator (->). If the PHP pointer operator (->) is used, only the object itself requires a dollar sign ($); the variables or functions inside the object are specified without a dollar sign ($). The following PHP code calls the apply() function in the $fmt variable to print Error #30: User not found:

```
print $fmt->apply(array('30', 'User not found'));
```

A Node.js object is accessed using the Node.js dot (.) operator in place of the PHP pointer operator (->). The following Node.js code calls the apply() function on the Node.js fmt object and prints Error #30: User not found:

```
console.log(fmt.apply(['30', 'User not found']));
```

For this statement, the rest of the PHP to Node.js conversion, including converting arrays and variables, is covered in previous chapters.

To sum up, creating a new PHP object and then executing an object function is demonstrated here:

```
$fmt = new Format('Error #{$1}: {$2}');
print $fmt->apply(array('30', 'User not found'));
```

This PHP code is converted into the following Node.js code:

```
var fmt = new Format('Error #{$1}: {$2}');
console.log(fmt.apply(['30', 'User not found']));
```

The following find-and-replace action replaces PHP pointer operators (->) with the Node.js dot (.) operators. Node.js does not have a pointer operator (->), and in PHP, the pointer operator (->) only has one purpose, so the action can be executed globally without visiting each occurrence:

```
Operation: "Find/Replace" in Eclipse PDT
Find: ->
Replace:.
Options: None
Action: Replace All
```

Storing variables and functions in a single object is sometimes called encapsulation. Both PHP and Node.js support encapsulation.

Inheritance

PHP, like other traditional class-based objects systems, supports inheritance. In PHP, one class can define itself as having all the variables and functions of another class as well as adding its own variables and functions. The original class is called the "base class" and the other class is called the "derived class." The derived class is said to inherit or extend the base class.

A useful example of inheritance is a collection of classes for showing the correct web pages to each user that logs in. A simple website might have two kinds of users: many ordinary users, and a single administrator user, probably the owner, who uses the website but also maintains it and keeps it running.

The following PHP page shows a simple PHP class called "User." The User class has a getName() function, which simply returns the name of the user. The User class also has a homePage() function, which returns the HTML for an ordinary user's home page:

```php
<?php
class User {
  function User($name) {
    $this->name = $name;
  }

  function getName() {
    return $this->name;
  }

  function homePage() {
    $msg = 'Welcome '.$this->name;
    return '<html><head><title>'.$msg.'</title></head><body>'
      .$msg.'</body></html>';
  }
}
$me = new User('guest');
print $me->homePage();
?>
```

At the end of the page, a new User object is created with the PHP new keyword and the home page is printed out to create a complete, albeit very simple, HTML page.

Similarly, the name of the user can be shown using the getName() function in the following PHP code fragment:

```php
$me = new User('guest');
print 'My username is '.$me->getName();
```

Using conversion techniques explained earlier in this chapter, the PHP User class can be converted to the following Node.js code:

```javascript
function User(name) {
  this.name = name;
```

```
}

User.prototype.getName = function() {
  return this.name;
};

User.prototype.homePage = function() {
  var msg = 'Welcome '+this.name;
  return '<html><head><title>'+msg+'</title></head><body>'+msg+'</body></html>';
}

var me = new User('guest');
console.log(me.homePage());
```

Similarly, the PHP code that uses the getName() function can be converted to Node.js:

```
var me = new User('guest');
console.log('My username is '+me.getName();
```

Now, for administrators, the following PHP code extends the User class to make a PHP derived class called "Admin." The PHP User class is now a base class but it does not need to be changed in any way. The derived class, the Admin class, uses the PHP extends keyword to show that it is derived from the User class. The Admin class contains all the data and functions of an ordinary user as well as an extra function. The logPage() function takes an array of log messages and returns the HTML for a System Log page:

```
class Admin extends User {
  function Admin($name) {
    $this->name = $name;
  }

  function homePage() {
    $msg = 'Welcome '.$this->name.' (administrator)';
    return '<html><head><title>'.$msg.'</title></head><body>'
      .$msg.'</body></html>';
  }

  function logPage($log) {
    $loghtml = '';
    for ($l=0; $l < count($log); ++$l) {
      $loghtml .= $log[$l].'<br />';
    }
    return
      '<html><head><title>System Log</title></head><body>'
        .$loghtml.'</body></html>';
  }
}
```

The Admin class actually contains four functions, even though three are listed. It contains the getName() function that it inherited from the User base class. The following PHP code creates an Admin object but uses the getName() function from the User class to get 'admin', the name of this user:

```
$me = new Admin('admin');
print 'My username is '.$me->getName();
```

This PHP code prints "My username is admin." If the Admin class did not derive from the User class, the PHP code would show an error because the Admin class does not define its own getName() function.

When the Admin class is used, the homePage() function in the Admin class overrides the homePage() function from the User class. The word "overrides" means that, when there are multiple possible functions, the overriding function will be called. All functions derived classes override any functions in the base class with the same function name.

The following PHP code will call the homePage() function in the Admin class instead of the User class because all functions in the Admin class override functions in the User class with the same name:

```
$me = new Admin('admin');
print $me->homePage();
```

The PHP code above will print "Welcome admin (administrator)" in the page instead of "Welcome admin" because the homePage() function from the Admin class is called.

The Admin class also defines a logPage() function. The log page makes a System Log HTML page. Since this page should only be available to administrators, it is only in the Admin class. The following PHP code shows the System Log page:

```
$log = array('Error #30: User not found', 'Error #31: Invalid password');
$me = new Admin('admin');
print $me->logPage($log);
```

If the logPage() function called on User objects, the PHP page will show an error:

```
$log = array('Error #30: User not found', 'Error #31: Invalid password');
$me = new User('guest');
print $me->logPage($log); // PHP error because it is a User, not an Admin object
```

Even though PHP classes are types, there is an unmistakable similarity between class inheritance in PHP and Node.js object prototypes. In PHP, if a function such as the getName() function is not found in the derived class, it will automatically try to find the function in the base class. Similarly, in Node.js, if a function is not found in the object itself, it will automatically try to find the function in the object's prototype. Also, if a function exists in both a PHP base class and a PHP derived class, such as the home Page() function, the PHP derived class function will override the base class function in the same way that a Node.js object function will override the same function in the Node.js object's prototype. And, lastly, if the code tries to call a function that does not exist in a PHP class hierarchy or a Node.js prototype chain, like trying to call the log Page() function on a User object, an error will occur.

To implement PHP class inheritance in Node.js using object prototypes, the PHP class structure needs to be converted to a Node.js object structure. When the PHP new keyword is used, the PHP engine does that very thing: it follows the PHP `extends` keyword to find the PHP base class, then it creates a PHP base class object, then it creates a PHP derived class object to wrap around that PHP base class object. In PHP, it is automatic, but in Node.js, it must be explicit.

The following PHP code shows the PHP `Admin` class using the PHP `extends` keyword to inherit from the PHP `User` class:

```
class Admin extends User {
  function Admin($name) {
    $this->name = $name;
  }
  ...
}
```

For simplicity's sake, when PHP classes that extend other classes are converted to Node.js, they will use the Node.js `new` keyword, instead of object literals or the `Object.create()` function. Like a PHP class that does not use the PHP `extends` keyword, the PHP `Admin` constructor is converted using the previously presented techniques into a Node.js constructor function:

```
function Admin(name) {
  // the "extends" keyword not converted yet
  this.name = name;
}
```

Also, ignoring the PHP `extends` keyword and its implications, the rest of the PHP derived class functions are converted to Node.js using the previously presented techniques. Here, the `homePage()` function is converted to Node.js by adding it to the `Admin`'s pro totype property:

```
Admin.prototype.homePage = function() {
  var msg = 'Welcome '+this.name+' (administrator)';
  return '<html><head><title>'+msg+'</title></head><body>'+msg+'</body></html>';
}
```

The PHP `logPage()` class function is converted to Node.js in the same way:

```
Admin.prototype.logPage = function(log) {
  var loghtml = '';
  for (var l=0; l < count(log); ++l) {
    loghtml += log[l]+'<br />';
  }
  return '<html><head><title>System Log</title></head><body>'
    +loghtml+'</body></html>';
}
```

After the PHP class functions are converted to Node.js, the PHP `extends` keyword can be converted to Node.js by implementing a chain of prototype objects in the Node.js constructor function. If the chain of Node.js prototype objects is properly set up, any attempt to access an object property, no matter where the attempt is, will cause the

Node.js system to start searching for the property in the derived class object first and then the base class object afterward. Regardless of whether the property access is for a variable or a function, properties will always be searched along the chain of Node.js prototype objects. Regardless of whether the property access is from a function in the base class object, in the derived class object, or from code external to the object, properties will always be searched along the chain of Node.js prototype objects. If the Node.js chain of prototype objects is correctly set up, the Node.js class object will access variables and functions in the same way that the PHP traditional class-based system does.

Here is the `Admin` constructor function as it currently stands:

```
function Admin(name) {
  // the "extends" keyword not converted yet
  this.name = name;
}
```

To implement the PHP `extends` keyword, a base class object is needed. The Node.js base class object is created using the Node.js `new` keyword:

```
new User(name)
```

Next, the new Node.js base class object becomes the prototype object of a new empty object that is created using the Node.js `Object.create()` function. The empty object will eventually be made into a copy of the current derived class prototype object:

```
var p = Object.create(new User(name), { });
```

The Node.js `Object.create()` function is used to conveniently create an empty Node.js object using the newly created `User` object as its prototype. Remember that the second argument to the `Object.create()` function is a description of the object to be created, including attributes such as `value` and `enumerable`, and not the object literal itself.

The Node.js `Object.create()` function call is inserted as the first statement of the `Admin` constructor function:

```
function Admin(name) {
  var p = Object.create(new User(name), { });
  // the "extends" keyword not fully converted yet
  this.name = name;
}
```

Even though the newly created `Admin` object will have a `User` object as a prototype, it already has a prototype. The existing prototype, the `Admin.prototype` object, already has properties, like the `homePage()` and `logPage()` functions. Unlike a simple PHP class where functions are attached to the PHP object itself, a simple Node.js object still shares all its functions via a prototype object with all the other simple Node.js objects created the same way, even if it is not derived from any other object. This prototype has to be preserved in the chain of Node.js prototype objects.

All the properties of the shared prototype object must be copied to the private prototype object of the Node.js Admin object. The properties are copied between Node.js objects using a for...in statement. The constructor property is copied explicitly because the constructor property has its enumerable attribute set to false:

```
for (var pp in this.constructor.prototype) {
  p[pp] = this.constructor.prototype[pp];
}
p.constructor = this.constructor;
```

Each Admin object must have its own private copy of the shared Admin.prototype object because there is only one Admin.prototype object. If the Admin.prototype object was changed to point its own prototype to a single User object, that single User object would be shared among all Admin objects. That would work for functions in the single User object, but for variables, each Admin object needs its own separate User object. Since each Admin object needs to be able to set the prototype of its prototype to a particular User object, the prototype cannot be shared and a copy must be made.

The Node.js for...in statement is added after the Object.create() function call in the Admin constructor function:

```
function Admin(name) {
  var p = Object.create(new User(name), { });
  for (var pp in this.constructor.prototype) {
    p[pp] = this.constructor.prototype[pp];
  }
  p.constructor = this.constructor;
  // the "extends" keyword not fully converted yet
  this.name = name;
}
```

Finally, the chain of Node.js prototype objects, including the Admin.prototype private copy and the User base class object as well as any chain of Node.js prototype objects that the User base class object points to, is assigned as the prototype object for this specific Node.js Admin object instance. The newly created Admin object no longer uses the shared Admin.prototype object as its prototype; it uses the new chain of prototypes:

```
this.__proto__ = p;
```

As described previously, the __proto__ property is the prototype of this object. The prototype property is the object assigned to the __proto__ property of newly created objects that were created using the new keyword with this constructor function. Even though the __proto__ property is for internal use only, it is unavoidable for this scenario in a PHP to Node.js conversion and must be used in this limited case.

Since the __proto__ property is deprecated, it may be removed from future Node.js versions. If it is, you will need to refactor your PHP class hierarchy to use base classes in a more prototypical style or remove PHP base classes all together. But, for the time being, you can use it to simulate class-based inheritance in Node.js.

The complete Node.js `Admin` constructor function that implements traditional class-based inheritance is shown next. For Node.js, only the `Admin` constructor function needs to be modified if `Admin` objects inherit from `User` objects:

```
function Admin(name) {
  var p = Object.create(new User(name), { });
  for (var pp in this.constructor.prototype) {
    p[pp] = this.constructor.prototype[pp];
  }
  p.constructor = this.constructor;
  this.__proto__ = p;
  this.name = name;
}
```

Both wide and deep PHP class hierarchies can be converted to Node.js by using this modification to the Node.js derived object constructor function. This Node.js conversion technique will work for multiple PHP derived classes that inherit from a single PHP base class as well as a PHP class that inherits from another PHP class that inherits from another PHP, and so on, to any arbitrary length.

The following find-and-replace action locates the PHP `extends` keyword and guides its conversion to Node.js:

```
Operation: "Find/Replace" in Eclipse PDT
Find: extends
Replace:
Options: None
Action: Find, then Replace/Find
```

At each occurrence, add the following statement to the Node.js derived class object constructor function that calls the Node.js base class object constructor function with the new keyword. That is, change new `User(name)` in the following statement to call the PHP base class with the correct arguments and add the following statement to derived class constructor:

```
var p = Object.create(new User(name), { });
```

Next, add the following statements after the statement that was just added. These statements need no modification:

```
for (var pp in this.constructor.prototype) {
  p[pp] = this.constructor.prototype[pp];
}
p.constructor = this.constructor;
this.__proto__ = p;
```

Once the PHP `extends` keyword has been replaced by the find-and-replace action, the PHP class hierarchy has been converted to the corresponding Node.js code.

PHP parent and static Keywords

For classes, PHP also has the PHP parent keyword. The PHP parent keyword refers to the PHP base class that a PHP derived class is directly derived from and can be seen as a sort of alias.

The PHP parent keyword is used with the PHP scope resolution operator (::) to access data or methods in the PHP base class that are overridden in the PHP derived class. The PHP parent keyword allows the PHP derived class to refer to its PHP base class without using its name, just in case the PHP base class is renamed or the PHP class hierarchy is reorganized. The PHP scope resolution operator (::) allows PHP code to access overridden parts of the PHP base class and avoid having to copy and paste now-inaccessible PHP base class code.

The following PHP code demonstrates the PHP parent keyword, used in a stripped-down version of the PHP User base class and the PHP Admin derived class:

```
class User {
  function User($name) {
    $this->name = $name;
  }

  function getActions() {
    return array('login', 'logout', 'setHomePage');
  }
}

class Admin extends User {
  function Admin($name) {
    $this->name = $name;
  }

  function getActions() {
    $a = array('showSystemLog', 'showLoggedInUsers');
    $u = parent::getActions(); // use the "parent" keyword
    return array_merge($a, $u);
  }
}

$me = new Admin('admin');
$actions = $me->getActions();
for ($a=0; $a < count($actions); ++$a) {
  print $actions[$a].'<br />';
}
```

The PHP parent keyword is used in the getActions() function of the PHP Admin derived class. The following PHP code shows the getActions() function of the PHP Admin class where the PHP parent keyword is used:

```
function getActions() {
    $a = array('showSystemLog', 'showLoggedInUsers');
    $u = parent::getActions(); // use the PHP "parent" keyword
    return array_merge($a, $u);
}
```

Together, PHP parent keyword and the PHP scope resolution operator (::), that is, the parent:: text, can be converted to the Node.js code, this.__proto__.__proto__.. As you may recall, the prototype object of a Node.js Admin object contains its private copy of the previously shared Node.js Admin functions. In Node.js, the prototype of that prototype is the User object contained within the Admin object. The __proto__ property skips the Node.js Admin functions and provides access to the overridden User functions. The following Node.js code shows the Node.js implementation of the PHP get Actions() function of the PHP Admin class:

```
Admin.prototype.getActions = function() {
    var a = ['showSystemLog', 'showLoggedInUsers'];
    var u = this.__proto__.__proto__.getActions(); // PHP "parent" keyword
    return a.concat(u);
}
```

Here's the complete Node.js conversion of the PHP parent keyword example code:

```
function User(name) {
    this.name = name;
}

User.prototype.getActions = function() {
    return ['login', 'logout', 'setHomePage'];
}

function Admin(name) {
    var p = Object.create(new User(name), { });
    for (var pp in this.constructor.prototype) {
        p[pp] = this.constructor.prototype[pp];
    }
    p.constructor = this.constructor;
    this.__proto__ = p;
    this.name = name;
}

Admin.prototype.getActions = function() {
    var a = ['showSystemLog', 'showLoggedInUsers'];
    var u = this.__proto__.__proto__.getActions();
    return a.concat(u);
}

var me = new Admin('admin');
var actions = me.getActions();
for (var a=0; a < actions.length; ++a) {
    console.log(actions[a]);
}
```

The following find-and-replace action converts the PHP `parent` keyword into the corresponding Node.js access to the overridden variable or function:

```
Operation: "Find/Replace" in Eclipse PDT
Find: parent::
Replace: this.__proto__.__proto__.
Options: None
Action: Replace All
```

The find-and-replace action can be run globally without visiting each occurrence because the PHP `parent` keyword serves one specific purpose and is only used in one specific way.

Besides the PHP `parent` keyword, the PHP scope resolution operator (::) is used in other contexts. It can be used to access static variables in PHP classes. A PHP static class variable is a single variable that is shared by all objects of a PHP class, unlike a nonstatic class variable where each PHP object has its own variable.

The PHP `static` keyword is used to declare a static class variable. Unlike a nonstatic variable, a PHP static class variable must be declared. The class name and the PHP scope resolution operator (::) are used to access the static class variable.

The following PHP page declares the `$num` static variable in the PHP `User` class, which tracks the number of PHP `User` objects that are created. The PHP page then makes three PHP `User` objects and uses the `User::$num` variable to print out "The number of User objects is 3":

```php
<?php
class User {
  static $num = 0;   // declare the static variable

  function User($name) {
    $this->name = $name;
    ++User::$num; // use the static variable
  }
}
$gilly = new User('gilly');
$ardo = new User('ardo');
$hoss = new User('hoss');
// use the static variable again
print 'The number of User objects is '.User::$num;
?>
```

In Node.js, the prototype object of a constructor function is shared. Functions are routinely added to the Node.js prototype so they can be shared between multiple objects. Similarly, a variable can be shared between multiple objects by adding it to the class constructor prototype.

The previous PHP static class variable example is converted to the following Node.js code. The PHP `User::$` text is replaced with the Node.js `User.prototype.` text:

```
function User(name) {
  this.name = name;
  ++User.prototype.num; // use the static variable
}

User.prototype.num = 0;  // declare the static variable

$gilly = new User('gilly');
$ardo = new User('ardo');
$hoss = new User('hoss');
// use the static variable again
console.log('The number of User objects is '+User.prototype.num);
```

Previously, when converting PHP class inheritance to Node.js, the shared prototype was copied and removed from the chain of Node.js prototypes for the derived class objects. However, the shared prototype object still exists and still can be accessed directly. Converting inheritance from PHP to Node.js does not affect how the static class variables are implemented in Node.js. The following find-and-replace action will find where PHP static class variables are defined:

```
Operation: "Find/Replace" in Eclipse PDT
Find: static $
Replace: classname.prototype.
Options: None
Action: Find, then Replace/Find
```

At each occurrence, replace `classname` in the Replace field with the actual class name that the PHP static class variable is contained in. Keep a list of the names of the classes that contain static class variables for the second find-and-replace action that follows.

A second find-and-replace action will convert any reference to a specific PHP static class variable to Node.js. In this find-and-replace action, replace `classname` with a class name from the list of PHP classes that contain static class variables:

```
Operation: "Find/Replace" in Eclipse PDT
Find: classname::$
Replace: classname.prototype.
Options: None
Action: Replace All
```

The find-and-replace action should be run globally without visiting each occurrence for every PHP class that contains a static class variable. After every PHP class has been addressed, PHP static class variables will be completely converted to Node.js.

This chapter described how to convert PHP classes in all their variations to Node.js. Together with the previous two chapters, these three chapters have shown how to convert the three major elements of the PHP language into Node.js: syntax, variables, and classes. In the remaining chapters, the focus will be narrowed to more specific areas, including converting, reading, and writing files; database access; and the JSON format.

CHAPTER 9

File Access

Reading and writing files is common in PHP applications. Configuration and template files provide a way to customize a web application, and in order for these files to have their intended effect, a PHP application needs to read and write these files.

Reading and Writing Files

The PHP `file_get_contents()` API function is one of the easiest and most common ways to read a file. It was added in PHP 4.3.0 and was immediately popular so only very old PHP 4 code does not use it. The following PHP code reads the file named *data.txt* from the same folder that the PHP file is in. The file is read as a long string that is assigned to the $contents variable:

```
$contents = file_get_contents('data.txt');
print $contents;
```

If a file named *data.txt* does not exist, a `false` boolean value is assigned to the $con tents variable. So, if the *data.txt* file exists and is readable, a string is returned, but if the *data.txt* file does not exist or is not readable, a boolean is returned.

As discussed previously, PHP API functions, including `file_get_contents()`, block until they return. The PHP code after the PHP `file_get_contents()` API function call does not get executed until the PHP `file_get_contents()` API function call either completely succeeds or completely fails. There is no callback mechanism for this PHP API.

The previous PHP statement is converted in the following Node.js code. The `readFile Sync()` API function in the `fs` module is the closest Node.js equivalent to the PHP `file_get_contents()` API function:

```
var fs = require('fs');

var contents = false;
try {
  contents = fs.readFileSync(__dirname+'/'+'data.txt', 'utf8');
} catch (err) {
  // do nothing
}
console.log(contents);
```

Many Node.js API functions come in two forms: an asynchronous and a synchronous version. The asynchronous version is the default, unadorned name. The synchronous version has the word "Sync" appended to the end of the asynchronous name. In this case, the Node.js `fs.readFile()` API function is the asynchronous version and the Node.js `fs.readFileSync()` API function is the synchronous version.

The asynchronous version does not block and relies on callbacks to handle the results of the Node.js API function call. The synchronous version actually does block, just like PHP does, and Node.js code after the API function does not execute until the API function call either completely succeeds or completely fails. No callback mechanism is used for the synchronous version: it is not needed.

For the Node.js `fs.readFileSync()` API function, the first argument is the filename to read and the second argument is the encoding to use. By default, the second argument does no encoding, which causes the function to return a raw buffer of bytes instead of a string. Instead, the `'utf8'` string (for UTF-8 encoding) is passed as the second argument to cause the function to return a string.

The first Node.js argument prepends the *data.txt* filename with the `__dirname` variable and a path separator, a forward slash (/). In Node.js, the `__dirname` variable contains the directory name of where the current Node.js source file, the *.njs* file, is located. Node.js can use both a forward slash (/) or a backward slash (\) as a directory name separator. In a string, a literal backward slash has to be delimited by another backward slash (\) to make a double backward slash (\\) because a backward slash is a delimiter for other things such as a newline (\n).

In PHP, a relative filename corresponds to the directory that the PHP file is in. For example, if the *index.php* file is in the *common* directory and the PHP `file_get_con tents()` API function is invoked in the *index.php* file with the argument *data.txt*, the *data.txt* file will be searched for in the *common* directory. However, in Node.js, a relative filename corresponds to the directory where the Node.js executable was run. So, regardless of where an *index.njs* file is located that calls the Node.js `fs.readFileSync()` API function, it will always look in the directory where the Node.js server was started. To access the *data.txt* file in the same directory as the *.njs* file, the `__dirname` variable and the forward slash (/) path separator must be prepended.

For the synchronous versions of the Node.js API functions, including the `fs.read FileSync()` API function, Node.js exceptions are used. The Node.js `try` keyword and the Node.js `catch` keyword are used to handle exceptions. The Node.js `try` keyword and the "try block" wrap Node.js code that will always be executed but where a Node.js exception might occur and be thrown. If a Node.js exception does occur while the Node.js "try block" is executing, the Node.js "try block" will immediately stop executing and the Node.js `catch` keyword and the "catch block" will start to be executed. If a Node.js exception does not occur, the Node.js `catch` keyword and the "catch block" will be ignored and never executed.

PHP 5 supports exceptions but they are rarely used. Very few of the PHP API functions use PHP exceptions. PHP 4 does not support PHP exceptions.

In the example that uses the Node.js `fs.readFileSync()` API function, the `contents` variable is initialized to `false` and remains false when a Node.js exception is thrown. The PHP `file_get_contents()` API function returns `false`, so both the PHP and Node.js code perform the same when there is an error.

While replacing the PHP `file_get_contents()` API function with the Node.js `fs.read FileSync()` API function is convenient, the Node.js `fs.readFile()` API function is preferable. When a synchronous API is invoked in Node.js, the entire Node.js server blocks and waits for the synchronous API call to complete. During that time, the Node.js server is frozen when it could be handling new requests or doing some other useful work.

The following code uses the asynchronous Node.js `fs.readFile()` API function:

```
var fs = require('fs');

var contents = false;
fs.readFile(__dirname+'/'+'data.txt', 'utf8', function(err, data) {
  if (!err) {
    contents = data;
  }
  console.log(contents);
});
```

The synchronous Node.js `fs.readFileSync()` API function returns the data as the return value and uses the Node.js `try` keyword and the Node.js `catch` keyword to indicate an error. The asynchronous Node.js `fs.readFile()` API function forgoes those mechanisms and, instead, accepts a third argument, a callback function, to both return the data and indicate an error.

In earlier chapters, the concept of linearity was introduced to encourage PHP code to be refactored to be more linear. If the PHP code is made linear, the asynchronous Node.js APIs, like the Node.js `fs.readFile()` API function, is nearly as easy to use as the synchronous Node.js APIs.

The original PHP code is fully linear because only a single PHP `print` statement exists after the blocking PHP `file_get_contents()` API function call. When this PHP code is converted to Node.js, this PHP `print` statement can be moved into the callback function of the Node.js `fs.readFile()` API function.

To convert the PHP `file_get_contents()` API function into Node.js, first insert a Node.js `require()` API function call near the top of the *.njs* file. The following Node.js code loads the `fs` built-in module, "fs" being short for "filesystem":

```
var fs = require('fs');
```

Next, execute the following find-and-replace action to convert the PHP `file_get_contents()` API function calls into Node.js `fs.readFile()` API function calls:

```
Operation: "Find/Replace" in Eclipse PDT
Find: file_get_contents(
Replace: fs.readFile(
Options: None
Action: Find, then Replace/Find
```

At each occurrence, apply the linearity concepts from previous chapters to correctly implement the Node.js callback function that replaces the PHP return value. For the previous example, the PHP `$contents` variable that is assigned the return value is converted to the Node.js `contents` variable that is used in the callback function passed as the third argument to the Node.js `fs.readFile()` API function call. Also, insert the `__dirname` constant before the first Node.js argument, if required.

There is a third way to read a file in Node.js, although it has no corresponding PHP feature. A Node.js stream can be created to read a file. Events, such as the `data`, `close`, and `error` events, are sent while the stream is read. Event handlers can be set up to handle these events.

The following code creates a Node.js stream for reading:

```
var fs = require('fs');

var stream = fs.createReadStream(__dirname+'/'+'data.txt', {
  'encoding': 'utf8'
});
```

The filename is passed as the first argument to the Node.js `fs.createReadStream()` API function. The second argument is a Node.js object that specifies the options, like `encoding`, `flags`, `mode`, and `bufferSize`.

Subsequent Node.js code creates a `contents` variable and the `cb` callback function. The default value of the `contents` variable is `false`, which will be the value returned if the file cannot be read. The callback function contains the Node.js code to run after the stream is read:

```
var contents = false;
var cb = function() {
  console.log(contents);
};
```

Next, the Node.js stream error event is attached to a function that calls the Node.js cb callback function. The Node.js contents variable will be reset to false in case it has been changed:

```
stream.on('error', function(err) {
  contents = false;
  cb();
});
```

Then, the following Node.js code attaches a function to the Node.js stream data event. Multiple Node.js stream data events may be sent. Each Node.js stream data event will contain the next portion or the reminder of the file in the chunk variable:

```
stream.on('data', function(chunk) {
  if (contents === false) {
    contents = '';
  }
  contents += chunk;
});
```

Each "chunk" is added to the contents variable. When the last Node.js data event is received, the contents variable will contain the entire contents of the file.

Finally, the Node.js stream close event is caught and the cb callback function is called when the file is closed:

```
stream.on('close', function() {
  cb();
});
```

The Node.js stream close event code can be rewritten to call the cb callback directly by passing the cb callback function as the second argument:

```
stream.on('close', cb);
```

PHP does not have any equivalent to the Node.js fs.createReadStream() API function.

The PHP file_put_contents() API function complements the PHP file_get_con tents() API function. It writes data to a file just as the PHP file_get_contents() API function reads data from a file. Even though the PHP file_get_contents() API function was introduced in PHP 4.3.0, the PHP file_put_contents() API function was added in PHP 5:

```
$s = 'the quick brown fox jumped over the lazy dog'.PHP_EOL;
file_put_contents('fox.txt', $s);
print 'File written.';
```

The PHP_EOL constant is the end-of-line marker for the operating system that the web server is running on.

The Node.js fs.writeFileSync() API function is almost a drop-in conversion for the PHP file_put_contents() API function. However, as with the reading files, it is preferable to use the nonblocking version, the Node.js fs.writeFile() API function.

The following code uses the asynchronous Node.js fs.writeFile() API function:

```
var fs = require('fs');
var os = require('os');

var s = 'the quick brown fox jumped over the lazy dog'+os.EOL;
fs.writeFile(__dirname+'/'+'fox.txt', s, function(err) {
  console.log('File written.');
});
```

The Node.js os built-in module contains an EOL constant that serves the same purpose as the PHP_EOL constant.

To convert PHP_EOL to Node.js, first insert the Node.js require() API function call to include the os built-in module, "os" being short for "operating system":

```
var os = require('os');
```

Next, execute the following find-and-replace action to replace all PHP_EOL text with the Node.js os.EOL text:

```
Operation: "Find/Replace" in Eclipse PDT
Find: PHP_EOL
Replace: os.EOL
Options: None
Action: Replace All
```

Next, execute the following find-and-replace action to convert the PHP file_put_contents() API function calls into Node.js fs.writeFile() API function calls:

```
Operation: "Find/Replace" in Eclipse PDT
Find: file_put_contents(
Replace: fs.writeFile(
Options: None
Action: Find, then Replace/Find
```

At each occurrence, apply the linearity concepts from previous chapters to correctly implement the Node.js callback function. The subsequent PHP code that relies on a blocking API must be moved into the Node.js callback function, which is executed after the file is written and closed in Node.js. Also, insert the __dirname constant before the first Node.js argument, if required.

PHP file() API Function

The PHP file() API function dates back to the first release of PHP 4. The PHP file_get_contents() API function arrived later, in PHP 4.3.0, but there is still older PHP code that uses the PHP file() API function.

The PHP file() API function returns an indexed array. Each value in the array contains a single line of the file. The following PHP code prints the first line of the *data.txt* file, including the EOL character sequence at the end of the line:

```
$a = file('data.txt');
print $a[0];
```

In PHP 5, an optional second parameter was added, the flags parameter. The flags had three options that could be combined using the bitwise OR operator (|):

```
FILE_IGNORE_NEW_LINES
FILE_USE_INCLUDE_PATH
FILE_SKIP_EMPTY_LINES
```

The first one, FILE_IGNORE_NEW_LINES, is the most commonly used. It instructs the PHP file() API function to remove EOL characters from the end of each line.

The following PHP code prints the first line of the *data.txt* file but does not include the EOL character sequence at the end of each value in the array:

```
$a = file('data.txt', FILE_IGNORE_NEW_LINES);
print $a[0];
```

The Node.js conversion for the PHP file() API function is somewhat more complicated than the Node.js conversion for the PHP file_get_contents() API function:

```
var fs = require('fs');
var FILE_IGNORE_NEW_LINES = 0x2;

var a = false;
var flags = FILE_IGNORE_NEW_LINES;
fs.readFile(__dirname+'/'+'data.txt', 'utf8', function(err, data) {
  if (!err) {
    a = data.replace(/\r\n?/g,'\n');
    a = a.split('\n');
    a.neol = a.length - 1;
    if ((a.length > 0) && (a[a.length-1] === '')) {
      a.splice(a.length-1, 1);
    }
    if ((flags & FILE_IGNORE_NEW_LINES) === 0) {
      for (var i=0; i < a.neol; ++i) {
        a[i] += '\n';
      }
    }
  }
```

```
      delete a.neol;
    }
    console.log(a[0]);
  });
```

The `if` statement with the `!err` condition is where things get complicated.

The first Node.js statement converts EOL characters for Windows, Mac, and Linux text files into the `\n` end-of-line character for the operating system that the Node.js server is running on:

```
a = data.replace(/\r\n?/g,'\n');
```

The second Node.js statement converts the string to an array of lines that conforms to the PHP `file()` API function specification:

```
a = a.split('\n');
```

The following Node.js statements handle the last line of the file. The PHP implementation has quirky handling for the last line of a file:

```
a.neol = a.length - 1;
if ((a.length > 0) && (a[a.length-1] === '')) {
  a.splice(a.length-1, 1);
}
```

Finally, if the `FILE_IGNORE_NEW_LINES` is not specified, EOL characters are added to the end of the lines. To conform to the PHP implementation, the last line may or may not have an EOL character appended to it:

```
if ((flags & FILE_IGNORE_NEW_LINES) === 0) {
  for (var i=0; i < a.neol; ++i) {
    a[i] += '\n';
  }
}
```

Due to the length of the converted Node.js code, it is recommended that the PHP `file()` API function be implemented using the quick-and-dirty technique of creating a Node.js `file()` function to match the specification of the PHP `file()` API function as close as possible.

The following Node.js `file()` function demonstrates how to implement a Node.js `file()` function with similar parameters to the PHP `file()` API function, plus an additional callback function parameter:

```
var fs = require('fs');
var FILE_IGNORE_NEW_LINES = 0x2;

function file(filename, flags, callback) {
  if (!callback) {
    callback = flags;
    flags = 0;
  }
```

```
    fs.readFile(filename, 'utf8', function(err, data) {
      if (err) {
        data = false;
      } else {
        data = data.replace(/\r\n?/g,'\n');
        data  = data.split('\n');
        data.neol = data.length - 1;
        if ((data.length > 0) && (data[data.length-1] === '')) {
          data.splice(data.length-1, 1);
        }
        if ((flags & FILE_IGNORE_NEW_LINES) === 0) {
          for (var i=0; i < data.neol; ++i) {
            data[i] += '\n';
          }
        }
        delete data.neol;
      }
      callback(data);
    });
  }
```

The Node.js `file()` function would be called using the following code:

```
file(__dirname+'/'+'data.txt', FILE_IGNORE_NEW_LINES, function(data) {
  var a = data; // for clarity
  console.log(a[0]);
});
```

Similar to the PHP `file()` API function, the second argument, `flags`, is optional. The `FILE_IGNORE_NEW_LINES` flag could be omitted. The callback function would be passed as the second argument instead of the third:

```
file(__dirname+'/'+'data.txt', function(data) {
  var a = data; // for clarity
  console.log(a[0]);
});
```

The following find-and-replace action will convert the PHP `file()` API function to the Node.js `file()` function. But, before executing the action, copy the Node.js `file()` function implementation into the *.njs* file:

```
Operation: "Find/Replace" in Eclipse PDT
Find: file(
Replace:
Options: None
Action: Find, then Replace/Find
```

At each occurrence, apply the linearity concepts from previous chapters to correctly implement the Node.js callback function that replaces the PHP return value. Also, insert the __dirname constant before the first Node.js argument, if required.

Beneath the commonly used PHP `file_get_contents()` API function and the older PHP `file()` API function, PHP has a core set of file handling APIs. These APIs are used to implement the more convenient higher level APIs. Node.js also has a core set of file handling API functions.

Low-Level File Handling

Both PHP and Node.js modeled their core sets of file handling API functions on the original C language file handling API functions.

The PHP `fopen()` API function opens a file. The equivalent is the Node.js `fs.open()` API function. Both these API functions are modeled on the `fopen()` function from the C programming language. A file can be opened in a variety of modes, including reading, writing, and appending.

The following PHP code demonstrates how to open the *data.txt* file for reading:

```
$fp = fopen('data.txt', 'r');
```

In Node.js, the same *data.txt* file is opened using the Node.js `fs.open()` API function:

```
var fs = require('fs');

fs.open(__dirname+'/'+'data.txt', 'r', function(err, fd) {
  // callback function
});
```

To convert the PHP `fopen()` API function calls to Node.js, execute the following find-and-replace action:

```
Operation: "Find/Replace" in Eclipse PDT
Find: fopen(
Replace: fs.open(
Options: None
Action: Find, then Replace/Find
```

At each occurrence, apply the linearity concepts from previous chapters to correctly implement the Node.js callback function that replaces the PHP return value. Also, insert the `__dirname` constant before the first Node.js argument, if required.

In PHP, once a file is open, it can be read from using the PHP `fread()` API function.

When the file is no longer needed, the PHP `fclose()` API function should be called on the file.

The following PHP code reads the first 1,000 bytes of a file. If the file is less than 1,000 bytes long, it reads the entire file:

```
$fp = fopen('data.txt', 'r');
$contents = fread($fp, 1000);
fclose($fp);
```

In Node.js, the Node.js fs.read() API function reads from a file. The Node.js fs.read() API function uses the buffer built-in module. Buffers hold an ordered collection of bytes.

Similar to PHP, the Node.js fs.close() API function closes a file.

The following Node.js code reads the first 1,000 bytes of a file. If the file is less than 1,000 bytes long, it reads the entire file. The three lines of PHP code convert into 13 lines of Node.js code:

```
var fs = require('fs');
var Buffer = require('buffer').Buffer;

fs.open(__dirname+'/'+'data.txt', 'r', function(err, fd) {
  var contents = '';
  var raw = new Buffer(1000);
  fs.read(fd, raw, 0, raw.length, null, function(err, bytesRead, buffer) {
    var buf = buffer.slice(0, bytesRead);
    contents += buf.toString();
    fs.close(fd, function() {
      console.log(contents);
    });
  });
});
```

Besides the familiar callback functions needed in Node.js, the buffer variables, that is, the raw variable and the buf variable, add some complexity to the Node.js code. The raw variable is created to hold the data that read from the Node.js fs.read() API function. The buf variable is created to only contain the actual bytes read, essentially cutting off the unused bytes of the raw variable. The buffer argument is an alias for the raw variable; the callback assigns whatever buffer was passed as its second argument to the buffer parameter in its callback function.

In both PHP and Node.js, a file pointer is maintained that indicates the next bytes that will be read from the file. The end of the file can be tested using the PHP feof() API function. To read an entire file, the following PHP code uses the PHP feof() API function to test for the end of the file:

```
$fp = fopen('data.txt', 'r');
$contents = '';
while (!feof($fp)) {
  $contents .= fread($fp, 1000);
}
fclose($fp);
print $contents;
```

In Node.js, there is no equivalent to the PHP `feof()` API function. Instead, the `bytesRead` argument to the callback function is compared with the number of bytes requested that is passed as the fourth argument to the Node.js `fs.read()` API function. The `eof` variable in the following Node.js code illustrates where the equivalent PHP `feof()` API function call would go:

```
var fs = require('fs');
var Buffer = require('buffer').Buffer;

fs.open(__dirname+'/'+'data.txt', 'r', function(err, fd) {
  var contents = '';
  var raw = new Buffer(1000);
  var fread = function() {
    fs.read(fd, raw, 0, raw.length, null, function(err, bytesRead, buffer) {
      var eof = (bytesRead != raw.length);
      if (!eof) {
        contents += buffer.toString();
        fread();
      } else {
        if (bytesRead > 0) {
          var buf = buffer.slice(0, bytesRead);
          contents += buf.toString();
        }
        fs.close(fd, function() {
          console.log(contents);
        });
      }
    });
  };
  fread();
});
```

Due to the nature of callbacks in Node.js, the `fread` function variable must be defined such that it can be called recursively if the file is longer than the `raw` buffer variable. The `fread` function variable is called continuously until the end of the file is reached. The `fread` function variable must be called explicitly to read the first buffer of data from the file, too.

At the end of the file, the partially filled buffer is processed, then the Node.js `fs.close()` API function is called. Using the linearity concepts, the Node.js `console.log()` API function call is placed in the callback of the Node.js `fs.close()` API function.

Besides the PHP `fread()` API function, there are also the PHP `fgets()` and `fgetss()` API functions. The PHP `fgets()` API function reads a single line from a file. The PHP `fgetss()` API function reads a single line from a file and removes all the PHP tags, HTML tags, and ASCII 0 (zero) bytes from the line.

Node.js does not have a corresponding API function to either the PHP `fgets()` or `fgetss()` API functions. With a little effort, it is possible to emulate these functions in Node.js, but instead, it is recommended that the PHP code be reexamined, and possibly, refactored to use the PHP `file_get_contents()` or `file()` API functions. In many cases, the decision to use the PHP `fgets()`, `fgetss()`, or even `fread()` API functions was arbitrary, and refactoring the PHP code to use a more easily converted PHP file handling API function would work just as well.

For the rare occasions where line-by-line reading is necessary, it is recommended that the Node.js code uses the Node.js `lazy` npm package, which must be downloaded and installed. The following Node.js code uses the `lazy` package with the Node.js `fs` `.createReadStream()` API function to read the *data.txt* file line by line, similar to the way that a PHP `fgets()` function call would be used:

```
var fs  = require("fs");
var lazy = require("lazy");

var stream = fs.createReadStream(__dirname+'/'+'data.txt');
new lazy(stream).lines.forEach(function(buffer) {
  var line = buffer.toString();
  console.log(line);
});
```

Due to the disparity between the PHP `fread()` API function, the PHP `fgets()` API function, the PHP `fgetss()` API function, the Node.js `fs.read()` API function, the Node.js `lazy` package, and the Node.js `fs.createReadStream()` API function, no find-and-replace actions are offered to help convert these PHP API functions to Node.js API functions. It is recommended that the previous information be used to convert the PHP code to Node.js code on a case-by-case basis, rather than try to apply a uniform find-and-replace action.

In both PHP and Node.js, the core sets of file handling APIs can also be used to write files, not just read them. The core sets of file handling APIs in both languages are simpler than the ones for reading.

The following PHP code writes a string to a file. The second argument to the PHP `fopen()` API function call is "w" for writing, instead of "r" for reading:

```
$fp = fopen('data.txt', 'w');
$contents = 'The quick brown fox jumped over the lazy dog.';
fwrite($fp, $contents);
fclose($fp);
print 'File written.';
```

There is also a PHP `fputs()` API function. It works exactly like the PHP `fwrite()` API function. The PHP `fwrite()` and `fputs()` API functions are aliases for each other and can be used as direct substitutes for each other.

To eliminate confusion and increase consistency, execute the following find-and-replace action on all PHP code to convert all PHP `fputs()` API function calls to PHP `fwrite()` API function calls:

```
Operation: "Find/Replace" in Eclipse PDT
Find: fputs(
Replace: fwrite(
Options: None
Action: Replace All
```

In Node.js, the Node.js `fs.write()` API function writes a buffer to a file. The following
Node.js code writes a string using the `raw` buffer variable, which is initialized with a
string and the UTF-8 encoding:

```
var fs = require('fs');
var Buffer = require('buffer').Buffer;

fs.open(__dirname+'/'+'data.txt', 'w', function(err, fd) {
  var contents = 'The quick brown fox jumped over the lazy dog.';
  var raw = new Buffer(contents, 'utf8');
  fs.write(fd, raw, 0, raw.length, null, function(err, written, buffer) {
    fs.close(fd, function() {
      console.log('File written.');
    });
  });
});
```

Just like with reading, the Node.js `fs.close()` API function is called when the code is
done writing to the file.

In PHP, file handling API functions are buffered, whereas in Node.js, they are unbuf-
fered. Buffered data is held in memory until a later time when it is more convenient to
write to the actual file. The buffering process happens seamlessly and transparently so
the code almost never needs to concern itself with the buffering process.

Still, the PHP `fflush()` API function is provided to "flush" buffers, that is, write any
buffered data to the file immediately. Usually, calling the PHP `fflush()` API function
is unnecessary. However, there are rare situations where the file needs to be updated
immediately, usually because an outside program or service is monitoring the file. For
example, the PHP code may open and write to a log file that an outside program, like
the Linux `tail` program, is displaying in real time. For the outside program to see the
newly written data, the PHP code will need to call the PHP `fflush()` API function to
ensure that log entries are written immediately and not "stuck" in a buffer, waiting to
be written.

The following PHP code demonstrates the PHP `fflush()` API function, even though
flushing the buffer is not needed. A real-world example is too complicated to show here
and is beyond the scope of this book:

```
$fp = fopen('data.txt', 'w');
$contents = 'The quick brown fox jumped over the lazy dog.';
```

```
fwrite($fp, $contents);
fflush($fp); // flush buffers
fclose($fp);
print 'File written.';
```

If the PHP page was a long running page and the PHP `fwrite()` API function was called occasionally and an outside program was monitoring the file that the PHP page was writing, each PHP `fwrite()` API function call might need to be followed with a PHP `fflush()` API function call so that the outside program would get the new data for each write, instead of as a batch when the PHP engine decided to write the entire buffer.

As a final note, with all PHP file handling code, it is a good idea to examine what the particular PHP code is trying to accomplish, and convert it holistically, instead of line by line or API by API. Often, when a file is read, only the entire contents of the file is relevant and dividing it into parts, such as by line, is incidental and irrelevant. In that case, converting the PHP file handling code as a whole is easier and more effective.

Filenames

Besides reading and writing files, PHP code also provides four APIs for identifying what a filename points to on the filesystem: the PHP `file_exists()`, `is_file()`, `is_dir()`, and `stat()` API functions.

The PHP `file_exists()` API function determines whether a filename points to a file or directory or other filesystem object or is unused:

```
$exists = file_exists('data.txt');
print 'The file or directory '.($exists? 'exists': 'does not exist').'.';
```

The PHP `file_exists()` API function can be converted to the Node.js `fs.exists()` API function:

```
var fs = require('fs');

fs.exists(__dirname+'/'+'data.txt', function(exists) {
 console.log('The file '+(exists? 'exists': 'does not exist')+'.');
});
```

The following find-and-replace action converts PHP `file_exists()` API function calls into Node.js `fs.exists()` API function calls:

```
Operation: "Find/Replace" in Eclipse PDT
Find: file_exists(
Replace: fs.exists(
Options: None
Action: Find, then Replace/Find
```

At each occurrence, apply the linearity concepts from previous chapters to correctly implement the Node.js callback function that replaces the PHP return value. Also, insert the `__dirname` constant before the first Node.js argument, if required.

If a filesystem object exists, the PHP `is_file()` API function is used to determine whether a filename points to an ordinary file or not. Similarly, the PHP `is_dir()` API function is used to determine whether a filename points to a directory or not:

```
$isfile = is_file('data.txt');
$isdir = is_dir('data.txt');
print 'The filename '.($isfile? 'points': 'does not point').' to a file.';
print 'The filename '.($isdir? 'points': 'does not point').' to a directory.';
```

Additionally, the PHP `stat()` API function can retrieve information about a filesystem object that a filename points to. It can retrieve the device number, the inode number, inode protection mode, the number of links, the user ID of the owner, the group ID of the owner, the device type, the size of the object, the last access time, the last modification time, the last inode change time, the block size of the filesystem I/O, and the number of blocks used.

The PHP `is_file()`, `is_dir()`, and `stat()` API functions can be converted to the Node.js `fs.stat()` API function:

```
var fs = require('fs');

fs.stat(__dirname+'/'+'data.txt', function(err, stats) {
  var isfile = stats.isFile();
  var isdir = stats.isDirectory();
  print 'The filename '+(isfile? 'points': 'does not point')+' to a file.';
  print 'The filename '+(isdir? 'points': 'does not point')+' to a directory.';
});
```

In Node.js, the `stats` variable not only supports the `isFile()` and `isDirectory()` methods, it also supports the `isBlockDevice()`, `isCharacterDevice()`, `isSymbolic Link()`, `isFIFO()`, and `isSocket()` methods, as well as a collection of properties that very closely matches the information retrieved by the PHP `stat()` API function.

To convert the PHP `is_file()` API function to the Node.js `fs.stat()` API function, execute the following find-and-replace action:

```
Operation: "Find/Replace" in Eclipse PDT
Find: is_file(
Replace: fs.stat(
Options: None
Action: Find, then Replace/Find
```

At each occurrence, apply the linearity concepts from previous chapters to correctly implement the Node.js callback function that replaces the PHP return value. Use the Node.js `stats.isFile()` method in the code where the PHP return value was used. Also, insert the `__dirname` constant before the first Node.js argument, if required.

Converting the PHP `is_dir()` API function is very similar to converting the PHP `is_file()` API function. To convert the PHP `is_dir()` API function to the Node.js `fs.stat()` API function, execute the following find-and-replace action:

```
Operation: "Find/Replace" in Eclipse PDT
Find: is_dir(
Replace: fs.stat(
Options: None
Action: Find, then Replace/Find
```

At each occurrence, apply the linearity concepts from previous chapters to correctly implement the Node.js callback function that replaces the PHP return value. Use the Node.js stats.isDirectory() method in the code where the PHP return value was used. Also, insert the __dirname constant before the first Node.js argument, if required.

Finally, the PHP stat() API function can be converted to Node.js as the Node.js fs.stat() API function. Execute the following find-and-replace action:

```
Operation: "Find/Replace" in Eclipse PDT
Find: stat(
Replace: fs.stat(
Options: None
Action: Find, then Replace/Find
```

At each occurrence, apply the linearity concepts from previous chapters to correctly implement the Node.js callback function that replaces the PHP return value. Use the Node.js stats argument to the callback function to access information about the filesystem object. Also, insert the __dirname constant before the first Node.js argument, if required.

Even though this chapter has provided constant reminders, it is important to remember that a PHP path is relative to the location of the .php file, whereas a Node.js path is relative to the current working directory when the Node.js server was started. When converting PHP code to Node.js code, the PHP assumption must be compensated for in Node.js.

A filename itself may be a relative pathname and perhaps use the dot-dot (..) parent directory specifier in its path. In PHP, the absolute path for a filename with a relative path can be found by calling the PHP realpath() API function.

The following PHP code gets the absolute path for the parent directory of the directory where the .php file is located:

```
$parentdir = realpath('..');
print 'The parent directory of this file is '.$parentdir.'.';
```

The PHP realpath() API function is converted into the Node.js fs.realpath() API function that requires a callback:

```
var fs = require('fs');

fs.realpath(__dirname+'/'+'..', function(err, resolvedPath) {
  var parentdir = resolvedPath;
  console.log('The parent directory of this file is '+parentdir+'.');
});
```

Execute the following find-and-replace action to convert the PHP `realpath()` API function to Node.js:

```
Operation: "Find/Replace" in Eclipse PDT
Find: realpath(
Replace: fs.realpath(
Options: None
Action: Find, then Replace/Find
```

At each occurrence, apply the linearity concepts from previous chapters to correctly implement the Node.js callback function that replaces the PHP return value. Also, insert the `__dirname` constant before the first Node.js argument, if required.

If pathnames and filenames need to be analyzed, there is the PHP `dirname()`, `basename()`, and `pathinfo()` API functions.

For a Windows filename, such as *C:\Program Files\Apache2\htdocs\data.txt*, the PHP `dirname()` API function will return *C:\Program Files\Apache2\htdocs*. The PHP `basename()` API function will return *data.txt*.

For a Linux or other filename, such as */var/www/html/data.txt*, the PHP `dirname()` API function will return */var/www/html*. The PHP `basename()` API function will return *data.txt*.

In Node.js, the `path` built-in module contains similar functionality. The Node.js `path.dirname()` API function corresponds to the PHP `dirname()` API function. The Node.js `path.basename()` API can provide values that correspond to both a PHP `basename` and `filename` value. The Node.js `path.extname()` API function corresponds to the PHP `extension` value.

To convert the PHP `dirname()` API function to Node.js, add a Node.js `require()` API function call to the top of the file to import the `path` built-in module. Then, execute the find-and-replace action:

```
Operation: "Find/Replace" in Eclipse PDT
Find: dirname(
Replace: path.dirname(
Options: None
Action: Replace All
```

To convert the PHP `basename()` API function to Node.js, add a Node.js `require()` API function call to the top of the file to import the `path` built-in module. Then, execute the find-and-replace action:

```
Operation: "Find/Replace" in Eclipse PDT
Find: basename(
Replace: path.basename(
Options: None
Action: Replace All
```

The PHP `pathinfo()` API function returns an array with the following keys: `dirname`, `basename`, `extension`, and—as of PHP 5.2.0—`filename`. The `dirname` and `basename` indexes contain the same values as the PHP `dirname()` and `basename()` API functions, respectively. The `extension` and `filename` values are straightforward; for the *data.txt* example, the value of `extension` is "txt" and the value of `filename` is "data."

The following PHP code uses the PHP `pathinfo()` API function to analyze the path. The PHP `pathinfo()` API function will not work on relative paths so the PHP `real path()` API function is needed to find the absolute path:

```php
$path = realpath('data.txt');
$p = pathinfo($path);
print 'The dirname is '.$p['dirname'];
print 'The basename is '.$p['basename'];
print 'The extension is '.$p['extension'];
print 'The filename is '.$p['filename'];
```

The corresponding Node.js code requires an absolute path as well. In this case, however, the Node.js `path.realpath()` API function call is redundant since the `__dirname` constant used to locate the correct file causes the first argument to be an absolute pathname, anyway:

```javascript
var fs = require('fs');
var path = require('path');

fs.realpath(__dirname+'/'+'data.txt', function(err, pathname) {
  var p = {
    'dirname': path.dirname(pathname),
    'basename': path.basename(pathname),
    'extension': path.extname(pathname).substring(1),
    'filename': path.basename(pathname, path.extname(pathname))
  };

  console.log('The dirname is '+p['dirname']);
  console.log('The basename is '+p['basename']);
  console.log('The extension is '+p['extension']);
  console.log('The filename is '+p['filename']);
});
```

For convenience, the second parameter to the callback function, normally named `re solvedPath`, has been renamed to `pathname`. The initialization code for the Node.js `p` variable demonstrates how to construct a Node.js object with the same name/value pairs as the PHP array that is returned from the PHP `pathinfo()` API function.

The following find-and-replace action converts the PHP `pathinfo()` API function to Node.js. But first, add a Node.js `require()` API function call to the top of the file to import the `path` built-in module:

```
Operation: "Find/Replace" in Eclipse PDT
Find: pathinfo(
Replace:
Options: None
Action: Find, then Replace/Find
```

At each occurrence, replace the PHP `pathinfo()` API function call with the following Node.js object, which generates a Node.js object that contains the same values. Replace the `arg1` variable in the Node.js code here with the argument that was passed to the PHP `pathinfo()` API function call:

```
{
  'dirname': path.dirname(arg1),
  'basename': path.basename(arg1),
  'extension': path.extname(arg1).substring(1),
  'filename': path.basename(arg1, path.extname(arg1))
};
```

Until now, this chapter has always used a forward slash (/) to create pathnames. Since many operating systems, including Windows, Macintosh, and Linux, support the forward slash (/) in path names, there is no reason not to do this. However, there is a `DIRECTORY_SEPARATOR` constant in PHP that can be used in place of the forward slash (/), and if it is already being used in the PHP, it can be converted to Node.js. The PHP `DIRECTORY_SEPARATOR` constant converts to the Node.js `path.sep` constant from the `path` built-in module.

The following find-and-replace action converts the PHP `DIRECTORY_SEPARATOR` into the Node.js `path.sep` constant. Add a Node.js `require()` API function call to the top of the file to import the `path` built-in module:

```
Operation: "Find/Replace" in Eclipse PDT
Find: DIRECTORY_SEPARATOR
Replace: path.sep
Options: None
Action: Replace All
```

The find-and-replace action can be executed globally without visiting each occurrence.

Temporary filenames and files are occasionally needed in PHP. The PHP `tempname()` API function creates a unique filename to be used as a temporary file. The PHP `tmpfile()` API function creates a new temporary file for reading and writing and returns a handle to that file. The PHP `sys_get_temp_dir()` API function, introduced in PHP 5.2.1, retrieves the operating system temporary directory.

Node.js does not have any built-in support for temporary filenames and files, or retrieving the operating system temporary directory. However, there is a `temp` npm package that can be downloaded and installed to create temporary filenames, files, and directories. Please refer to the documentation for the Node.js `temp` npm package for more information.

Finally, PHP provides support for file permissions, file ownership, and ownership groups for some operating systems, such as Linux. The PHP chmod(), chown(), and chgrp() API functions modify these properties for a file.

The Node.js fs.chmod() API function corresponds to the PHP chmod() API function although the Node.js fs.chmod() API function is asynchronous and uses a callback.

The PHP chmod() API function takes an octal number; for example, "0640" means "first zero indicates an octal number, read and write for owner, read only for group, no access for everybody else." The Node.js chmod() API function also takes an octal number. Octal numbers in PHP and Node.js are specified in the exact same way and need no conversion. The Node.js chmod() API function also accepts a string, which contains an octal number but without the preceding zero (0). For example, the string "640" would be passed as the argument.

The following PHP code changes the permissions on the *data.txt* file:

```
chmod('data.txt', 0640);
```

The following Node.js code changes the permissions on the *data.txt* file twice to demonstrate using both the octal number argument and the string argument:

```
var fs = require('fs');

fs.chmod(__dirname+'/'+'data.txt', 0640, function() {
  fs.chmod(__dirname+'/'+'data.txt', '640', function() {
  });
});
```

The following find-and-replace action converts the PHP chmod() API function to Node.js. A Node.js require() API function call to the fs built-in module is needed:

```
Operation: "Find/Replace" in Eclipse PDT
Find: chmod(
Replace: fs.chmod(
Options: None
Action: Find, then Replace/Find
```

At each occurrence, apply the linearity concepts from previous chapters to correctly implement the Node.js callback function. Also, insert the __dirname constant before the first Node.js argument, if required.

The PHP chown() and chgrp() API functions are converted to the Node.js fs.chown() API function. The PHP API functions accept both names or numbers while the Node.js fs.chown() API function only accepts numbers. Currently, there is no standard way in Node.js to convert an owner or group name into an owner or group number.

The following PHP code demonstrates how to use the PHP chown() and chgrp() API functions in both its forms:

```
chown('data.txt', 10);
chgrp('data.txt', 12);
chown('data.txt', 'sysadmin');
chgrp('data.txt', 'admins');
```

Here's the corresponding Node.js code:

```
fs.chown(__dirname+'/'+'data.txt', 10, 12, function() {
  // no standard way to do fs.chown() with "sysadmin" argument
  // no standard way to do fs.chown() with "admins" argument
});
```

The following find-and-replace action converts the PHP `chown()` API function to Node.js. A Node.js `require()` API function call to the `fs` built-in module is needed:

```
Operation: "Find/Replace" in Eclipse PDT
Find: chown(
Replace: fs.chown(
Options: None
Action: Find, then Replace/Find
```

At each occurrence, apply the linearity concepts from previous chapters to correctly implement the Node.js callback function. If required, insert the `__dirname` constant before the first Node.js argument. If a PHP `chgrp()` API function call is nearby, incorporate it into the Node.js `fs.chown()` API function call.

This chapter has covered the gamut of converting PHP file handling API functions into Node.js. In both languages, operating system files are one way to store and retrieve permanent and semi-permanent data. In the next chapter, databases, specifically the popular MySQL database, will be covered. A database is an alternative for storing and retrieving permanent and semi-permanent data.

CHAPTER 10

MySQL Access

One way to store and retrieve data is by reading and writing files directly to the filesystem of the computer that either PHP or Node.js is running on.

An alternative to reading and writing files is to read and write rows and columns of data into a database. Database servers can be accessed remotely so PHP or Node.js code can access a database even if it is running on a different computer than the web server. Data in a database is also divided up into rows and columns, which can make it easier to organize and store some data, like usernames, and harder to organize and store other data, like image files.

Some web hosting services duplicate an application across multiple web servers for faster response and more reliability. But each web server still has its own filesystem, so writing a file will only write to one web server, not all web servers. But since a database is accessed remotely, multiple web servers will still access the same database. A database can be viewed as a sort of remote shared filesystem that provides special data organization features. This can be a significant advantage and a convenience, even a necessity.

Files and databases both have their uses. Reading and writing files in PHP and how to convert PHP file handling code to Node.js was covered in the previous chapter. This chapter will cover using MySQL databases in PHP and how to convert PHP code that uses MySQL databases into Node.js.

MySQL is arguably the most popular database. Nearly all web hosting services, even the cheapest ones, offer both PHP and MySQL database services to clients. Many PHP applications are designed with that in mind and use a MySQL database to store most data.

To use and create a MySQL database, a MySQL server must be installed and set up. Web hosting services might already have MySQL databases installed and ready for use or they may provide a custom web page as part of a user account for installing and configuring MySQL databases. Refer to the web hosting provider documentation and support for how to set up a MySQL database with a particular web hosting service. If you are running your own computer hardware, you will have to set up a MySQL server yourself. Use Google to find detailed explanations on how to install a MySQL server for your particular operating system. In both cases, MySQL database installation and setup is beyond the scope of this book.

Once a MySQL database is installed and working, the PHP or Node.js server must be altered to enable access to MySQL databases.

In PHP, a PHP-to-MySQL extension must be added to the web server installation. The way to install and configure this module will vary depending on the web server and the operating system.

For the Apache2 web server running on Linux, the `php5-mysql` extension needs to be installed. Naturally, if PHP 4 or PHP 6 is being used, the `php4-mysql` or `php6-mysql` extension (not available at the time of this writing) will need to be installed, respectively.

For the Apache2 web server running on Windows, the PHP-to-MySQL extension can be installed during the Apache2 web server installation.

In PHP 4 and below, there was only one set of PHP MySQL API functions, referred to as the PHP `mysql` API functions. Different PHP extensions (`php4-mysql`, `php5-mysql`, and `php6-mysql`) implemented the same set of PHP MySQL API functions for the corresponding PHP version. But in PHP 5, the PHP `mysqli` API functions were introduced as a second set of PHP MySQL API functions. Then, in PHP 5.1, the PHP `PDO` API functions were added as a third set of PHP API functions for accessing a MySQL database, which required the use of a PHP `PDO_MySQL` PDO driver.

These other PHP MySQL API functions are relatively new and the majority of PHP code still uses the first set of PHP MySQL API functions. For the purposes of converting PHP code to Node.js code, this book will focus on the first set of PHP MySQL API functions and mention the other two sets only in passing with the hope that converting PHP code using one of the other two sets can be figured out given specific details on how to convert the first set from PHP to Node.js.

Database Approaches

In Node.js, there are a number of different modules for accessing a MySQL database. None of the modules are Node.js built-in modules; they are all npm packages that need to be installed. The Node.js npm packages use a variety of approaches.

One very easy and convenient approach is a Node.js npm package that implements the MySQL socket protocol entirely in Node.js. The Node.js npm package uses the built-in `net` module to open a simple network socket to the MySQL server and then exchanges packets with the MySQL server according to the format that the MySQL server expects. The Node.js npm package impersonates and emulates other MySQL drivers, written in the C language, that are distributed with the MySQL server and the MySQL server never realizes that it is communicating with a MySQL driver built in Node.js instead of C.

The primary benefit is that a Node.js npm package does not depend on the C language, and as a result, is cross-platform and does not rely on the native operating system, such as Windows or Linux. The primary drawbacks are that the Node.js implementation may be significantly slower than C language implementations, may "choke" on large amounts of data, and will probably not support the alternative nonsocket methods of accessing a MySQL server, such as pipes.

The most popular Node.js implementation of the MySQL protocol is the node-mysql Node.js npm package, which can be found on GitHub (*http://github.com/felixge/node-mysql*). Another Node.js implementation of the MySQL protocol is the mysql-native Node.js npm package, which can also be found on GitHub (*http://github.com/sidorares/nodejs-mysql-native*).

An alternative to a pure Node.js implementation is a Node.js npm package that provides a Node.js "wrapper" around the MySQL library, written in the C language, that is distributed with the MySQL server. The Node.js npm package uses the *v8.h* and *node.h* include files for the C language from the Node.js source code to link to the MySQL library and also create a Node.js npm package. The *v8.h* and *node.h* include files are used to create a Node.js npm package that can be loaded by Node.js code just like any other Node.js npm package, but the npm package itself is written in the C language instead of Node.js.

The source code in the C language for Node.js is stored on GitHub (*http://github.com/joyent/node*). The *v8.h* and *node.h* include files are inside the Node.js source code on GitHub here (*http://github.com/joyent/node/blob/master/src/node.h*) and here (*http://github.com/joyent/node/blob/master/deps/v8/include/v8.h*).

The technique for writing Node.js npm packages in the C language may vary from Node.js version to Node.js version. The *v8.h* and *node.h* include files are specific to Node.js v0.8.4, which is the latest Node.js version at the time of this writing.

The benefits and drawbacks of using the MySQL driver and the C language are the opposite of the pure Node.js implementation. The primary benefits of the C language implementation are that it's well-tested and provide fast MySQL access, which can handle large volumes of data and support all methods, both socket and nonsocket, of accessing a MySQL server. The primary drawback is that a different Node.js npm package will be needed for each operating system, such as Windows or Linux. Different MySQL libraries are needed for different platforms; the MySQL libraries are not cross-platform.

The mysql-libmysqlclient Node.js npm package is a straightforward implementation of a Node.js "wrapper" around the MySQL library. This package requires the MySQL library to be separately installed on the operating system before the Node.js npm package will work. More information about the mysql-libmysqlclient Node.js npm package can be found here (*http://github.com/Sannis/node-mysql-libmysqlclient*).

There are other databases besides MySQL—Microsoft SQL Server, IBM DB2, and Oracle are at the head of a very long list. There has been a decades-long effort to provide libraries in various languages and through various means that will allow a single library with a single set of API functions to access multiple different kinds of databases.

Continuing this effort, there are various Node.js npm packages that not only provide a Node.js "wrapper" around the MySQL library but also provide "wrappers" around other database libraries, as well as provide a common set of Node.js API functions to access each supported database with minimal changes to the Node.js database calling code.

The node-db Node.js npm package supports both MySQL and Drizzle databases, providing a set of common API functions to access both. More information about the node-db Node.js npm package can be found here (*http://nodejsdb.org/*).

While the node-db Node.js npm package is implemented by calling the individual database libraries directly, there are already C language libraries that provide a common set of API functions to access many different kinds of databases. Node.js npm packages can be implemented to call these C language libraries and gain access to many different kinds of databases without writing custom C language code to interface with the individual database libraries directly.

ODBC (Open Database Connectivity) is a C language library that provides a set of common API functions to access many different kinds of databases. In ODBC terminology, the C language library with a common set of API functions is called an ODBC driver manager. Additionally, each supported database is distributed with an ODBC driver, which is installed and allows the ODBC driver manager to communicate with the specific database. Nearly all databases are distributed with an ODBC driver.

The node-odbc Node.js npm package is implemented similarly to the mysql-libmysqlclient Node.js npm package, except that the node-odbc Node.js npm package is linked with the ODBC driver manager instead of directly with the MySQL library. To access a MySQL server with the node-odbc Node.js npm package, both ODBC and the MySQL ODBC driver need to be installed and configured on the computer where the Node.js server is running. Of course, the node-odbc Node.js npm package also needs to be installed, too. More information on the node-odbc Node.js npm package can be found on GitHub (*http://github.com/w1nk/node-odbc*).

To read and write data from and to a database, including a MySQL database, the SQL language is used. The SQL language consists of common commands such as SELECT, UPDATE, INSERT, and DELETE along with dozens of other SQL commands. A brief explanation is provided for these common commands later in this chapter. But for now, it is sufficient to say that the SQL language was designed to read and write data in the context of database columns and rows, which is a substantially different organizational approach than the Node.js approach, which stores data as properties on a Node.js object.

Object-relational mapping (ORM), which is also sometimes abbreviated as O/R mapping, is a set of strategies for reading and writing objects, such as Node.js objects, to an SQL database, such as a MySQL database. The word "relational" refers to databases that organize data as a set of columns, rows, and values—essentially, an SQL database.

ORM is implemented on top of other database access approaches. So, a Node.js ORM npm package could use any of the other Node.js npm packages that have been mentioned so far, including the `node-mysql`, `mysql-native`, `node-db`, or `node-odbc` Node.js npm packages, to actually read and write from and to a database. Invariably, ORM npm packages use SQL statements in their implementation but provide a more convenient and logical set of API functions to read and write Node.js objects from and to a database.

The `persistencejs` Node.js npm module provides object-relational mapping for Node.js. More information on the `persistencejs` Node.js ORM npm package can be found here (*http://www.persistencejs.org/*).

The `sequelize` Node.js npm module is another object-relational mapping module for Node.js. More information on the `sequelize` Node.js ORM npm package can be found here (*http://www.sequelizejs.com/*).

In certain situations, an object-relational mapping layer can make Node.js code simpler, more straightforward, convenient, and understandable.

Beyond MySQL databases and object-relational mapping, Node.js supports a number of other databases, including the Postgres database via the `node-postgres` Node.js npm package, the SQLite database via the `node-sqlite` Node.js npm package, and the NoSQL MongoDB database via the `node-mongodb-native` Node.js npm package. A search engine, such as Google, will reveal Node.js support for a wide variety of databases and database approaches.

node-mysql

Now, let us look in detail how to use the `node-mysql` Node.js npm package, which is arguably the most popular way to access a MySQL database using Node.js.

To use the `node-mysql` Node.js npm package, it must first be installed. The `node-mysql` Node.js npm package is installed by running the following command:

```
npm install mysql
```

Once the node-mysql Node.js npm package is installed, the Node.js require() API function is used to make the Node.js module available for use. The following Node.js code creates a mysql variable for accessing the node-mysql Node.js module:

```
var mysql = require('mysql');
```

In both PHP and Node.js, a database must be connected to before it can be read or written.

As you recall, there are three sets of PHP APIs that may be used to access a MySQL database: the PHP mysql, mysqli, and PDO API functions using the PDO_MySQL driver. Below, the PHP mysql API functions will be used to demonstrate how to convert PHP MySQL code to Node.js MySQL code.

In PHP, using the PHP mysql API functions, the PHP mysql_connect() API function connects to a database. It takes three important arguments. The first argument is the database server, as an IP address (e.g., '192.168.2.20') or a DNS name (e.g., 'db.ex ample.com'), to connect to. The second argument is the database username to connect with, such as the 'admin' user. The third argument is the password of the database user, such as the 'passw0rd' text:

```
$sql_host = '192.168.2.20';
$sql_user = 'admin';
$sql_pass = 'passw0rd';
$link = mysql_connect($sql_host, $sql_user, $sql_pass);
```

The PHP $link variable contains the database connection.

With the node-mysql Node.js npm package, the Node.js createClient() API function works the same way. But instead of accepting three parameters, the Node.js create Client() API function takes a Node.js object with three properties—the host property, the user property, and the password property:

```
var sql_host = '192.168.2.20';
var sql_user = 'admin';
var sql_pass = 'passw0rd';
var sql_conn = {host: sql_host, user: sql_user, password: sql_pass};
var link = mysql.createClient(sql_conn);
```

Of course, the last two statements can be rewritten into one statement to more closely parallel the PHP mysql_connect() API function:

```
var sql_host = '192.168.2.20';
var sql_user = 'admin';
var sql_pass = 'passw0rd';
var link = mysql.createClient({host: sql_host, user: sql_user, password: sql_pass});
```

To convert the PHP mysql_connect() API function into Node.js, first insert a Node.js require() API function call near the top of the .njs file to load the mysql Node.js npm package:

```
var mysql = require('mysql');
```

Execute the following find-and-replace action to convert the PHP `mysql_connect()` API function calls into Node.js `mysql.createClient()` API function calls:

```
Operation: "Find/Replace" in Eclipse PDT
Find: mysql_connect(
Replace: mysql.createClient({host:
Options: None
Action: Find, then Replace/Find
```

At each occurrence, add the `user` property name and the `password` property name as well as colons (:) in the proper places with a right curly bracket (}) before the right parenthesis ( )) to close the Node.js object.

For both the PHP `$link` variable and the Node.js `link` variable, a "truthful" value will be assigned if the MySQL server can be connected to, and a "falseful" value will be assigned if the connection attempt is rejected. In many cases, no extra changes need to be made to convert MySQL error checking code from PHP to Node.js.

Later, when the database is no longer needed, it should be disconnected from, also known as closed.

In PHP, a MySQL connection variable, such as the PHP `$link` variable, is closed using the PHP `mysql_close()` API function:

```
$closed = mysql_close($link);
```

The PHP `mysql_close()` API function returns a boolean variable to indicate success or failure. Usually, the return value is ignored because it is not clear what should be done if a database cannot be closed.

In Node.js, the `destroy()` method on the `link` object closes the database connection:

```
link.destroy();
```

The following find-and-replace action converts PHP `mysql_close()` API function calls into Node.js `link.destroy()` API function calls:

```
Operation: "Find/Replace" in Eclipse PDT
Find: mysql_close(
Replace: link.destroy();
Options: None
Action: Find, then Replace/Find
```

At each occurrence, replace the hardcoded `link` variable of the Replace field with the first argument to the PHP `mysql_close()` API function call.

Once the database is connected to, the specific MySQL database on the MySQL server needs to be selected. The PHP `mysql_select_db()` API function chooses a single database to use from all the databases stored on the MySQL server. The return value, stored in the PHP $selected variable in the following PHP code, is a boolean that indicates whether the function call succeeded or failed. In the following PHP example, the 'myapp' database is selected as the specific database to use:

```
$sql_db = 'myapp';
$selected = mysql_select_db($sql_db, $link);
```

In PHP, the second argument, the PHP $link variable, is optional. The PHP engine infers and uses the most recently opened MySQL connection for the PHP mysql_select_db() API function call. In the most common case, only one MySQL server and only one MySQL database is ever used. The PHP $link variable is not just optional for the PHP mysql_select_db() API function but it is optional for all PHP mysql API functions.

Node.js, however, does not support this feature. The Node.js link variable must be available and explicitly used. For the purposes of converting PHP code to Node.js code, the PHP code should be refactored to explicitly pass the PHP $link variable to all PHP mysql API functions and avoid relying on the PHP engine to infer it so it can be more easily converted to Node.js.

Once a database is selected using the PHP mysql_select_db() API function, the PHP mysql_query() API function can be used to retrieve data from the database.

In Node.js, the MySQL query function is used to both select and retrieve a database. The Node.js query() method is a property of the Node.js link object. In both PHP and Node.js, the first argument to the PHP mysql_query() API function and the Node.js query() method is a string value that contains an SQL statement.

To select a database, the SQL USE command is used. The following SQL statement selects the 'myapp' database on the MySQL server for use. The semicolon (;) is optional for single SQL statements, but for multiple SQL statements, it is used to separate the SQL statements from each other:

```
USE myapp;
```

In Node.js, the USE myapp SQL command must be sent explicitly using the Node.js query() method. The following Node.js code selects the 'myapp' database from the MySQL server that is available via the Node.js link variable:

```
var sql_db = 'myapp';
var sql_db_stmt = 'USE '+sql_db;
link.query(sql_db_stmt, function(err) {
  if (!err) {
    // the MySQL database was selected
  } else {
    // the MySQL database selection error
  }
});
```

The Node.js `sql_db_stmt` variable can be substituted into the Node.js `query()` method call:

```
var sql_db = 'myapp';
link.query('USE '+sql_db, function(err) {
  if (!err) {
    // the MySQL database was selected
  } else {
    // the MySQL database selection error
  }
});
```

To convert the PHP `mysql_select_db()` API function calls to Node.js, execute the following find-and-replace action:

```
Operation: "Find/Replace" in Eclipse PDT
Find: mysql_select_db(
Replace: link.query('USE '+
Options: None
Action: Find, then Replace/Find
```

At each occurrence, copy the first argument to the PHP `mysql_select_db()` API function call after the plus sign (+) in the Node.js `link.query()` call. Replace the hardcoded `link` variable of the Replace field with the second argument to the PHP `mysql_select_db()` API function call. Finally, apply the linearity concepts from previous chapters to correctly implement the Node.js callback function that replaces the PHP return value.

After connecting to a MySQL server and selecting a MySQL database stored on that server, the data inside the database can be read and written using SQL commands. The six most common SQL commands are: `CREATE TABLE`, `DROP TABLE`, `SELECT`, `UPDATE`, `INSERT`, and `DELETE`.

SQL databases, including MySQL databases, are organized into columns and rows of data, like a spreadsheet. The columns specify fields, like a full name or a zip code, and the rows contain a value for each of the fields for a particular item, like Bob's full name or Bob's zip code. Rather than having one gigantic set of rows and columns for everything, the rows and columns can be stored in separate tables. Each table is like a separate spreadsheet with its own rows and columns. Unlike a spreadsheet, though, an SQL database is relatively inflexible when it comes to empty columns and rows. It is best to have a neatly organized database of tables, columns, and rows with each "cell" (i.e., value) holding a specific piece of data.

A SQL `CREATE TABLE` statement creates a table.

In PHP, an SQL `CREATE TABLE` statement is executed by using the PHP `mysql_query()` API function. The following PHP code executes the `CREATE TABLE myapp_users (id int AUTO_INCREMENT KEY, user text)` SQL statement:

```
$sql_pre = 'myapp_';
$sql_stmt =
  'CREATE TABLE `'.$sql_pre.'users` (`id` int AUTO_INCREMENT KEY, `user` text)';
$created = mysql_query($sql_stmt, $link);
```

This SQL CREATE TABLE statement creates a table with two columns: an id column and a user column. The id column, which is an integer, has the SQL AUTO_INCREMENT option and the SQL KEY option. Together, those SQL options specify that the MySQL server should set a unique value for each row in the id column; the caller cannot set the value directly. The user column, which is a string (e.g., "text"), will be set to whatever value the caller indicates when a new row is inserted into the MySQL database.

The return value is a boolean, indicating whether the SQL statement succeeded or failed. The PHP $sql_pre variable (which might also be $sql_prefix) is a widespread practice to organize the tables of an application by giving them a common prefix.

In Node.js, the query() method is used:

```
var sql_pre = 'myapp_';
var sql_stmt =
  'CREATE TABLE `'+sql_pre+'users` (`id` int AUTO_INCREMENT KEY, `user` text)';
var created = false;
link.query(sql_stmt, function(e, rows, f) {
  if (!e) {
    created = true;
  }
});
```

The Node.js e parameter in the callback function of the query() method indicates whether there was an error or not. If there is an error, the Node.js e variable will have a number property that indicates the MySQL error number.

A SQL DROP TABLE statement deletes a table.

In PHP, an SQL DROP TABLE statement is executed just like an SQL CREATE TABLE statement:

```
$sql_pre = 'myapp_';
$sql_stmt = 'DROP TABLE `'.$sql_pre.'users`';
$dropped = mysql_query($sql_stmt, $link);
```

It is also converted to Node.js in the same way:

```
var sql_pre = 'myapp_';
var sql_stmt = 'DROP TABLE `'+sql_pre+'users`';
var dropped = false;
link.query(sql_stmt, function(e, rows, f) {
  if (!e) {
    dropped = true;
  }
});
```

A SQL SELECT statement reads data from a table.

In PHP, the PHP `mysql_query()` API function executes the statement and returns an opaque result object, stored in the PHP `$sql_result` variable. To access the actual data, the PHP `mysql_fetch_assoc()` API function is called repeatedly to retrieve the data, one row at a time:

```
$sql_pre = 'myapp_';
$sql_stmt = 'SELECT user FROM `'.$sql_pre.'users`';
$sql_result = mysql_query($sql_stmt, $link);
while ($row = mysql_fetch_assoc($sql_result)) {
  $user = $row['user'];
  print $user;
}
```

It is a good practice to extract the PHP `$row` variable into a nonarray variable like the `$user` variable above. Not only does it make the PHP code clearer, but it eliminates confusion when converting the PHP code to Node.js.

In Node.js, the Node.js `query()` method executes the statement and returns the data as arguments to the callback function passed as the second argument. The `rows` parameter to the callback function contains a two-dimensional array of data—an indexed array of rows with an associative array of values for each row:

```
var sql_pre = 'myapp_';
var sql_stmt = 'SELECT user FROM `'.$sql_pre.'users`';
link.query(sql_stmt, function(e, rows, f) {
  if (!e) {
    for (var r=0; r < rows.length; ++r) {
      var row = rows[r];
      var user = row['user'];
      console.log(user);
    }
  }
});
```

The Node.js `user` variable could also be defined as `rows[r]['user']` to more clearly show that the Node.js `rows` variable is a two-dimensional array.

The f parameter to the callback function is a Node.js object with field names as property names with a variety of data describing the field as its property value. In this case, the array would contain only one property: the `user` property.

For brevity, both in this book and in code, the Node.js callback function has been defined with the parameters named `e`, `rows`, and `f` to make the function prototype be `func tion(e, rows, f)`. However, if you look at other Node.js `node-mysql` npm package code examples, you may see that the parameters are named `err`, `rows`, and `fields` to make the function prototype be `function(err, rows, fields)`. The names of the parameters may be changed without affecting the operation of the code as long as the code inside the callback function is changed as well.

An SQL UPDATE statement changes data in a table.

In PHP, an SQL UPDATE statement is executed by using the PHP mysql_query() API function:

```
$sql_pre = 'myapp_';
$sql_stmt =
  'UPDATE `'.$sql_pre.'users` SET `user`="jsmith" WHERE `user`="dhoward"';
$updated = mysql_query($sql_stmt, $link);
if ($updated) {
  $rows_updated = mysql_affected_rows($link);
  print 'Changed '.$rows_updated.' rows.';
}
```

The PHP mysql_affected_rows() API function returns the number of rows changed by the SQL UPDATE statement.

In Node.js, the same SQL UPDATE statement is used. The affectedRows property of the rows object contains the same value that is returned from the PHP mysql_affec ted_rows() API function in PHP:

```
var sql_pre = 'myapp_';
var sql_stmt =
  'UPDATE `'+sql_pre+'users` SET `user`="jsmith" WHERE `user`="dhoward"';
link.query(sql_stmt, function(e, rows, f) {
  if (!e) {
    var rows_updated = rows.affectedRows;
    console.log('Changed '+rows_updated+' rows.');
  }
});
```

A SQL INSERT statement adds a row of data to a table.

In PHP, an SQL INSERT statement is executed by using the PHP mysql_query() API function:

```
$sql_pre = 'myapp_';
$sql_stmt =
  'INSERT INTO `'.$sql_pre.'users` (`id`, `user`) VALUES (0, "dhoward")';
$inserted = mysql_query($sql_stmt, $link);
if ($inserted) {
  $inserted_id = mysql_insert_id($link);
  print 'Inserted row with id='.$inserted_id.'.';
}
```

The PHP mysql_insert_id() API function returns the value that the id column for the newly inserted row was set to. A table can only have one column that is set automatically by the MySQL database.

In Node.js, the same SQL INSERT statement is used. The insertId property of the rows object contains the same value that is returned from the PHP mysql_insert_id() API function in PHP:

```
var sql_pre = 'myapp_';
var sql_stmt =
```

```
    'INSERT INTO `'+sql_pre+'users` (`id`, `user`) VALUES (0, "dhoward")';
link.query(sql_stmt, function(e, rows, f) {
  if (!e) {
    var inserted_id = rows.insertId;
    console.log(''Inserted row with id='+inserted_id+'.');
  }
});
```

A SQL DELETE statement deletes one or more rows of data from a table.

As with the previous five SQL commands, an SQL DELETE statement is executed by using the PHP mysql_query() API function:

```
$sql_pre = 'myapp_';
$sql_stmt = 'DELETE FROM `'.$sql_pre.'users` WHERE `user`="dhoward"';
$deleted = mysql_query($sql_stmt, $link);
if ($deleted) {
  $rows_deleted = mysql_affected_rows($link);
  print 'Deleted '.$rows_deleted.' rows.';
}
```

The PHP mysql_affected_rows() API function returns the number of rows deleted by the SQL DELETE statement.

In Node.js, the same SQL DELETE statement is used. The affectedRows property of the rows object contains the same value that is returned from the PHP mysql_affec ted_rows() API function in PHP:

```
var sql_pre = 'myapp_';
var sql_stmt = 'DELETE FROM `'+sql_pre+'users` WHERE `user`="dhoward"';
link.query(sql_stmt, function(e, rows, f) {
  if (!e) {
    var rows_deleted = rows.affectedRows;
    console.log('Deleted '+rows_deleted +' rows.');
  }
});
```

CREATE TABLE, DROP TABLE, SELECT, UPDATE, INSERT, and DELETE are the six fundamental SQL commands needed for manipulating a MySQL database. In PHP, all six can be executed using the PHP mysql_query() API function. PHP mysql_query() API function calls are converted to the Node.js query() method on the connection object for all six.

Execute the following find-and-replace action to convert the PHP mysql_query() API function calls to Node.js query() method calls:

```
Operation: "Find/Replace" in Eclipse PDT
Find: mysql_query(
Replace: link.query(
Options: None
Action: Find, then Replace/Find
```

At each occurrence, replace the hardcoded `link` variable of the Replace field with the second argument to the PHP `mysql_query()` API function call. The first argument remains the same for both languages. Next, apply the linearity concepts from previous chapters to correctly implement the Node.js callback function that replaces the PHP return value. Finally, implement any error handling in the Node.js callback function using the `e` or `err` argument, which is passed as the first parameter to the Node.js callback function.

For SQL `SELECT` statements, refactor the PHP code that uses the PHP `mysql_fetch_as soc()` API function to extract the data into a PHP `$row` variable. To convert this PHP code to Node.js, create a `for` statement inside the Node.js `query()` method callback function and extract the data into a Node.js `row` variable.

Once the SQL queries are converted, the PHP `mysql_affected_rows()` API function calls can be converted to use the Node.js `affectedRows` property on the `rows` object. Execute the following find-and-replace action to perform that conversion:

```
Operation: "Find/Replace" in Eclipse PDT
Find: mysql_affected_rows\((.*)\)
Replace: rows.affectedRows
Options: Regular expressions, Wrap search
Action: Find, then Replace/Find
```

Assuming that the Node.js code always uses the name `rows` for the callback function passed as the second parameter to the Node.js `query()` method, no extra steps are needed at each occurrence. However, if the name `rows` has been changed to something else, such as `result`, replace the hardcoded `rows` variable with the renamed variable (e.g., "result").

Finally, the PHP `mysql_insert_id()` API function calls can be converted to use the Node.js `insertId` property on the `rows` object. Execute the following find-and-replace action to perform that conversion:

```
Operation: "Find/Replace" in Eclipse PDT
Find: mysql_insert_id\((.*)\)
Replace: rows.insertId
Options: Regular expressions, Wrap search
Action: Find, then Replace/Find
```

Assuming that the Node.js code always uses the name `rows` for the callback function passed as the second parameter to the Node.js `query()` method, no extra steps are needed at each occurrence. However, if the name `rows` has been changed to something else, such as `result`, replace the hardcoded `rows` variable with the renamed variable (e.g., "result").

Occasionally, only one row will be expected with a particular SQL SELECT statement. Instead of using a PHP while statement, a PHP if statement will be used in conjunction with the PHP mysql_num_rows() API function. The following PHP code expects only one row from the SQL SELECT statement, and if more than one row is returned, executes the error handling code:

```
$sql_pre = 'myapp_';
$sql_stmt = 'SELECT id FROM `'.$sql_pre.'users` WHERE `user`="dhoward"';
$sql_result = mysql_query($sql_stmt, $link);
if ((mysql_num_rows($sql_result) === 1)
    && ($row = mysql_fetch_assoc($sql_result))) {
  $id = $row['id'];
  print $id;
} else {
  // an error occurred
}
```

In Node.js, the length property of the Node.js rows indexed array can be checked to confirm that there is a single row. The returned row is then extracted from index #0:

```
var sql_pre = 'myapp_';
var sql_stmt = 'SELECT id FROM `'+sql_pre+'users` WHERE `user`="dhoward"';
link.query(sql_stmt, function(e, rows, f) {
  if (!e && (rows.length === 1)) {
    var row = rows[0];
    var id= row['id'];
    console.log(id);
  } else {
    // an error occurred
  }
});
```

The following find-and-replace action will convert PHP mysql_num_rows() API function calls into the Node.js rows.length property:

```
Operation: "Find/Replace" in Eclipse PDT
Find: mysql_num_rows\((.*)\)
Replace: rows.length
Options: Regular expressions, Wrap search
Action: Find, then Replace/Find
```

Assuming that the Node.js code always uses the name rows for the callback function passed as the second parameter to the Node.js query() method, no extra steps are needed at each occurrence. However, if the name rows has been changed to something else, such as result, replace the hardcoded rows variable with the renamed variable (e.g., "result").

Although it is rarely used, the f parameter of the callback function passed to the Node.js query() method of the connection object (e.g., the Node.js link variable) may contain field names as property names with an object as its property value. If an SQL SELECT statement is executed similar to the previous examples, the f argument might contain the user property and the id property. For other cases, such as an SQL INSERT statement, the f parameter would be undefined.

For an SQL SELECT statement, the following is an example of what property names and property values for a column in the Node.js f argument might contain:

```
length: 54
received: 54
number: 2
type: 4
catalog: 'def'
db: 'test'
table: 'myapp_users'
originalTable: 'myapp_users'
name: 'id'
originalName: 'id'
charsetNumber: 63
fieldLength: 11
fieldType: 3
flags: 16899
decimals: 0
```

Since these properties are rather arcane, this book will not describe each field.

The following Node.js code displays the attributes and values of all columns in the f argument:

```
var columns = Object.keys(f);
for (var c=0; c < columns.length; ++c) {
  console.log(columns[c]);
  var attributes = Object.keys(f[columns[c]]);
  for (var a=0; a < attributes.length; ++a) {
    console.log('  '+attributes[a]+': '+f[columns[c]][attributes[a]]);
  }
}
```

PHP provides a set of information that partially overlaps and is partially disjointed from the Node.js f argument via the PHP mysql_fetch_field() API function. The PHP mysql_fetch_field() API function returns a PHP object. The PHP object can be converted into a PHP associative array, which is accessed in the same way as the Node.js f parameter by executing the following PHP code:

```
$f = array();
$f_num = mysql_num_fields($sql_result);
for ($fi=0; $fi < $f_num; ++$fi) {
  $field = mysql_fetch_field($sql_result, $fi);
  $f[$field->name] = array();
  $f[$field->name]['name'] = $field->name;
  $f[$field->name]['table'] = $field->table;
  $f[$field->name]['max_length'] = $field->max_length;
```

```
    $f[$field->name]['not_null'] = $field->not_null;
    $f[$field->name]['primary_key'] = $field->primary_key;
    $f[$field->name]['unique_key'] = $field->unique_key;
    $f[$field->name]['multiple_key'] = $field->multiple_key;
    $f[$field->name]['numeric'] = $field->numeric;
    $f[$field->name]['blob'] = $field->blob;
    $f[$field->name]['type'] = $field->type;
    $f[$field->name]['unsigned'] = $field->unsigned;
    $f[$field->name]['zerofill'] = $field->zerofill;
}
```

For an SQL SELECT statement, the following is an example of what property names and property values the PHP $f argument might contain:

```
name: id
table: myapp2_users
max_length: 1
not_null: 1
primary_key: 1
unique_key: 0
multiple_key: 0
numeric: 1
blob: 0
type: int
unsigned: 0
zerofill: 0
```

The following PHP code displays the attributes and values of all columns in the PHP $f variable:

```
foreach ($f as $field => $attributes) {
  print $field;
  foreach ($attributes as $attribute => $value) {
    print '  '.$attribute.': '.$value;
  }
}
```

The PHP mysql_fetch_field() API function can be converted in the Node.js f argument manually as the need arises. No PHP to Node.js conversion recipe is provided here.

Of course, there are additional SQL commands besides these six, some of which are common to all SQL databases and some of which are specific to MySQL. There are also a large set of keywords, clauses, attributes, and types. To learn more about the SQL language and about the MySQL database in particular, search using a search engine such as Google.

Nearly all SQL statements can be executed using the PHP mysql_query() API function, which can be converted in the Node.js query() method on the MySQL connection object (e.g., the Node.js link variable). The meaning of the Node.js parameters to the callback function will vary depending on the SQL statement. The following Node.js code uses Node.js for…in statements to discover the properties and their types for each of the parameters, e, rows, and f:

```
console.log('the "e" argument contains:');
console.log('  variable itself is of type "'+typeof(e)+'"');
for (var ep in e) {
  console.log('  "'+ep+'" property of type "'+typeof(e[ep])+'"');
}
console.log('the "rows" argument contains:');
console.log('  variable itself is of type "'+typeof(rows)+'"');
for (var rowsp in rows) {
  console.log('  "'+rowsp+'" property of type "'+typeof(rows[rowsp])+'"');
}
console.log('the "f" argument contains:');
console.log('  variable itself is of type "'+typeof(f)+'"');
for (var fp in f) {
  console.log('  "'+fp+'" property of type "'+typeof(f[fp])+'"');
}
```

The following output is an example of what will be shown for an SQL SELECT statement:

```
the "e" argument contains:
  variable itself is of type "object"
the "rows" argument contains:
  variable itself is of type "object"
  "0" property of type "object"
the "f" argument contains:
  variable itself is of type "object"
  "id" property of type "object"
  "user" property of type "object"
```

For comparison, the following output is an example of what will be shown for an SQL INSERT statement:

```
the "e" argument contains:
  variable itself is of type "object"
the "rows" argument contains:
  variable itself is of type "object"
  "affectedRows" property of type "number"
  "insertId" property of type "number"
  "serverStatus" property of type "number"
  "warningCount" property of type "number"
  "message" property of type "string"
  "setMaxListeners" property of type "function"
  "emit" property of type "function"
  "addListener" property of type "function"
  "on" property of type "function"
  "once" property of type "function"
  "removeListener" property of type "function"
```

```
  "removeAllListeners" property of type "function"
  "listeners" property of type "function"
the "f" argument contains:
  variable itself is of type "undefined"
```

The properties and types of the parameters will help to convert PHP code correctly to Node.js.

In PHP, MySQL errors are returned by calling the PHP `mysql_errno()` and `mysql_error()` API functions. The PHP `mysql_errno()` API function returns the MySQL error number, such as `1050`, and the PHP `mysql_error()` API function returns the MySQL error message, such as `Table 'myapp_users' already exists`.

The following PHP code prints out the MySQL error number and MySQL error message after a MySQL error occurs:

```
print mysql_errno($link);
print mysql_error($link);
```

In Node.js, the `e` parameter to the callback function of the Node.js `query()` method of the connection object (e.g., the Node.js `link` variable) will contain a `number` property and a `message` property. These properties will contain the same number and the same message as the PHP `mysql_errno()` and `mysql_error()` API functions would return.

The following Node.js code prints out the MySQL error number and MySQL error message after a MySQL error occurs:

```
console.log(e.number);
console.log(e.message);
```

The following find-and-replace action will convert PHP `mysql_errno()` API function calls into the Node.js `e.number` property:

```
Operation: "Find/Replace" in Eclipse PDT
Find: mysql_errno\((.*)\)
Replace: e.number
Options: Regular expressions, Wrap search
Action: Find, then Replace/Find
```

Assuming that the Node.js code always uses the name e for the callback function passed as the first parameter to the Node.js `query()` method, no extra steps are needed at each occurrence. However, if the name e has been changed to something else, such as `err`, replace the hardcoded e variable with the renamed variable (e.g., "err").

Similarly, the following find-and-replace action will convert PHP `mysql_error()` API function calls into the Node.js `e.message` property:

```
Operation: "Find/Replace" in Eclipse PDT
Find: mysql_error\((.*)\)
Replace: e.message
Options: Regular expressions, Wrap search
Action: Find, then Replace/Find
```

Assuming that the Node.js code always uses the name e for the callback function passed as the first parameter to the Node.js query() method, no extra steps are needed at each occurrence. However, if the name e has been changed to something else, such as err, replace the hardcoded e variable with the renamed variable (e.g., "err").

One final issue remains. Sometimes, careless or inexperienced developers will write PHP code to loop over MySQL query code. For example, the following PHP code uses a PHP for statement to run multiple queries:

```
for ($u=0; $u < count($users); ++$u) {
  $sql_stmt = 'SELECT id FROM `'.$sql_pre.'users` WHERE `user`="'.$users[$u].'"';
  $sql_result = mysql_query($sql_stmt, $link);
}
```

This is the "nested callbacks" conversion issue as seen in previous chapters. For database code, the generic solution works just as well.

If possible, the code that will be converted to use callbacks, that is, the PHP mysql_query() API function calls that will be converted to Node.js query() method calls with callback functions, should be removed from the for statement. In this case, the SQL IN keyword can be used to construct a single SQL statement that achieved the same effect as multiple SQL statements:

```
$sql_clause = '';
for ($u=0; $u < count($users); ++$u) {
  if ($u > 0) {
    $sql_clause .= ', ';
  }
  $sql_clause .= '"'.$users[$u].'"';
}
$sql_stmt = 'SELECT id FROM `'.$sql_pre.'users` WHERE `user` IN('.$sql_clause.')';
$sql_result = mysql_query($sql_stmt, $link);
```

If it is not possible to remove the SQL statement from the for statement, the more general solution from previous chapters of using anonymous functions, either simulated or actual, can be used.

With databases and file handling, as presented in this chapter and the previous one, two of the most common ways of reading and writing data in PHP have been converted to Node.js. The next chapter will delve into the formats of the data itself, including the JSON format, which may be needed to complete the conversion of a PHP application into Node.js.

CHAPTER 11

Plain Text, JSON, and XML

By now, nearly all the important aspects of converting PHP code to Node.js code have been covered. This chapter covers one remaining topic of relatively minor importance: data formats.

To communicate, a client, such as a web browser, passes data to the PHP code or Node.js on the server as an HTTP GET or an HTTP POST and the PHP code or Node.js server passes data back to the client in an HTTP response. A client passes data either by submitting an HTML form or making an Ajax (Asynchronous JavaScript and XML) call. A server only has a single way to respond, though: by returning data in an HTTP response body.

If a client uses an HTTP GET to pass data, the data is sent as URL parameters, which on most web browsers are shown in the address bar after the question mark (?). If there is no question mark (?), there is no data sent; the fact that an HTTP GET was made to a certain URL is the only piece of data. If there is a question mark (?) and URL parameters, the parameters are in the "URL-encoded" format. For example, the following shows some URL-encoded data:

```
action=save&data=This%20is%20some%20data
```

URL-encoded data is name/value pairs separated by ampersands (&). Special characters, such as spaces ( ), are encoded using percent signs (%) followed by a specific two-digit hexadecimal number.

An HTTP GET request concatenates the URL-encoded data to the end of the URL in the first line in the HTTP header. The following shows an HTTP GET request that sends some URL-encoded data:

```
GET /myapp/page.html?action=save&data=This%20is%20some%20data HTTP/1.1
...
```

If a client uses an HTTP POST to pass data, the data can be sent in several different formats, but the two most common data formats are URL-encoded and multipart. When an HTML form is submitted using a web browser, the web browser passes the data to the PHP code or Node.js server according to the `enctype` HTML form attribute.

URL-encoded data for an HTTP POST is the same as URL-encoded data for an HTTP GET, but instead of being concatenated to the URL in the HTTP header, the URL-encoded data is stored in the HTTP request body. The following shows an HTTP POST request that sends some URL-encoded data:

```
POST /myapp/page.html HTTP/1.1
...

action=save&data=This%20is%20some%20data
```

Multipart data for an HTTP POST is much, much less commonly used. The data is formatted using a unique separator string called a "boundary," which is defined in the HTTP POST header and then used in the HTTP request body. Each part of the multipart request has a header and body, similar to an HTTP request.

The following shows an HTTP POST request that sends some multipart data:

```
POST /myapp/page.html HTTP/1.1
...
Content-Type: multipart/form-data; boundary=----------------------48829594378
...

----------------------------48829594378
Content-Disposition: form-data; name="title"

My image
----------------------------48829594378
Content-Disposition: form-data; name="an_image"; filename="page.png"
Content-Type: image/png

...
----------------------------48829594378
Content-Disposition: form-data; name="submit"

Submit
----------------------------48829594378--
```

An HTTP request from an HTML form almost always uses one of these three ways: URL-encoded data in an HTTP GET request, URL-encoded data in an HTTP POST request, or multipart data in an HTTP POST request.

An Ajax call from client-side JavaScript often uses the second approach: URL-encoded data in an HTTP POST request.

No matter what format the HTTP request is sent from the client to the server, the client may use different, more flexible, and more convenient data formats for smaller pieces of data within the format of the data to be sent to the server.

For example, a simple array data format could be defined so [x, y, z] would mean an array with the values x, y, and z in it. The simple array data format could then be URL-encoded so that it could be sent in an HTTP GET request or an HTTP POST request. When URL-encoded, the [x,y,z] data would become the %5bx%2cy%2cz%5d string because %5b, %2c, and %5d are how the left square bracket ([ ), a comma (,), and a right square bracket ( ]) are URL-encoded, respectively. The simple array data format is encoded "inside" the URL-encoding data format.

The following URL-encoded data has an action name/value pair and an array name/value pair. The action name/value pair has the value select, apparently in a "plain text" format. The array name/value pair has the value [4,8,12] in our example simple array data format:

```
action=select&array=%5b4%2c8%2c12%2c%5d
```

In this way, a client can send data to the server in whatever data format is most convenient for the client and the server.

Sending data from the server to the client via an HTTP response is simpler. Unlike HTTP requests, HTTP responses do not restrict or prefer certain data formats. The server always sends data to the client in the HTTP response body and can use whatever format is most convenient for both the client and the server, be it URL-encoded, plain text, HTML, binary, or something else.

In both directions, from client-to-server and server-to-client, any data format can ultimately be used. The data format could be a text format, similar to the example simple array data format, or even a binary format. It is up to the developer to choose what data format the server will use and, hopefully, consistently use the chosen data format whenever sensible.

Over time, three data formats have become popular: plain text, JSON, and XML.

Plain Text

The plain text data format consists of lines and words. It is not really a data format, per se, but is just the simplest way to create a document. The concept was quickly repurposed for communication between a client and a server. By definition, the plain text format is a text format, not a binary format.

To separate lines, the ASCII 13 character, also known as the carriage return or CR character, is used. It is URL-encoded as %0d. To separate words, the ASCII 32 character, the "space" character ( ), is used. A space ( ) is URL-encoded as %20.

The following example data is in the plain text format:

```
The first name is John.
The last name is Smith.
The zip code is 80001.
```

This example data could be URL-encoded and sent to the server using an HTTP GET or an HTTP POST:

```
customer=The%20first%20name%20is%20John.%0dThe%20last%20name%20is%20Smith.
%0dThe%20zip%20code%20is%2080001.
```

The example data could be returned from the server in the HTTP response body just as it is:

```
The first name is John.
The last name is Smith.
The zip code is 80001.
```

The HTTP response header could even specify the "text/plain" value for the `Content-type` HTTP response header, just to be clear.

The benefit of the plain text format is that it is very readable. It is plain English.

The drawback is that it is too flexible. To separate the important data, such as the `John`, `Smith`, and `80001` values, from the surrounding text is a nuisance to the code that is receiving the data. The plain text format is more convenient for a single document than it is for multiple small pieces of data that need to be used by client-side JavaScript, PHP, or Node.js code.

To use the plain text format, inevitably, some smaller ad hoc formats need to be agreed upon. For example, the strings "the last name is Smith" and "the last name is set to Smith" might mean approximately the same thing, but for easy communication using the plain text format, the client and the server would agree that both would always use "is" and never use "is set to."

Even more inconvenient, differentiating between arrays, objects, strings, and numbers in the plain text format is a common requirement and the only way to handle the specifics of each of those is with more ad hoc formats.

For example, a client may wish to tell the server to create an object with certain attributes, such as the first name, last name, and zip code, or the server may wish to return an object that the client requested. If the client and server are communicating using the plain text format, they would need to communicate the following object properties in each communication:

```
the 'first name' property has the string, 'John'
the 'last name' property has the string, 'Smith'
the 'zip code' property has the string, '80001'
```

Of course, an ad hoc format could be invented to convey this specific object inside the plain text format. But instead, it is a better idea to select one of the other formats, such as the JSON data format or the XML data format, that is specifically designed to work in this style.

Many web applications still communicate using the plain text as their data format.

If PHP code is using this data format, it uses the PHP dot operator (.) to create the data. To convert this PHP code to Node.js, the PHP dot operator (.) is converted to the Node.js plus (+) operator as shown in Chapter 6.

If PHP code needs to parse data and extract it from the plain text format, it usually uses the PHP string position API functions, such as the PHP `strpos()` API function, and PHP substring API functions, such as the PHP `substr()` API function, to separate the values from the surrounding text. To convert this PHP code to Node.js, the PHP API functions can be implemented in Node.js using the information from the next chapter.

As a replacement for the plain text format and the complication of the ad hoc formats that it leads to, the JSON format has been gaining popularity in recent years.

JSON

The JSON data format uses a JavaScript object declaration as its model. JSON stands for JavaScript Object Notation. JSON is a text format, not a binary format. The original concept was that the JavaScript `eval()` API function could be called with the JSON data and the object would be instantiated in JavaScript. At this point, though, there are specific functions for encoding (i.e., creating) and decoding (i.e., parsing) JSON data for many languages, including client-side JavaScript, PHP, and Node.js.

JSON data is a JavaScript object declaration using curly braces ({ and }). One or more properties are created in the object declaration. The property values can be strings, numbers, booleans, or other fundamental (JavaScript) data types, or they can be objects or arrays. Declaring values in JSON follows the same syntax as declaring values in JavaScript or Node.js.

The following example data is in the JSON format:

```
{"first name": "John",
 "last name": "Smith",
 "zip code": "80001"
}
```

This example data could be URL-encoded and sent to the server using an HTTP GET or an HTTP POST:

```
customer=%7b%22first%20name%22%3a%20%22John%22%2c%20%22last%20name%22%3a%20
%22Smith%22%2c%20%22zip%20code%22%3a%20%2280001%22%7d
```

The example data could be returned from the server in the HTTP response body just as it is, specifying the `application/json` value for the `Content-type` HTTP response header:

```
{"first name": "John",
 "last name": "Smith",
 "zip code": "80001"
 }
```

In PHP 5.2.0, JSON support was built into the PHP language. The PHP `json_en code()` API function creates a string in the JSON format from a PHP variable. The PHP `json_decode()` API function parses a string in the JSON format and returns a PHP value.

The following PHP 5.2.0 code shows how the PHP `json_encode()` API function is used to create JSON data in a PHP string from a nested PHP array:

```
$data = array('first name'=>'John',
  'last name'=>'Smith',
  'address'=>array('zip code'=>'80001'));
$json = json_encode($data);
```

The following PHP 5.2.0 code shows how the PHP `json_decode()` API function is used to create a nested PHP array from JSON data stored in a PHP string:

```
$data = json_decode($json);
```

In PHP 4 and other versions previous to PHP 5.2.0, a separate PHP library or PHP code needed to use read and write JSON data in PHP.

PEAR (*http://pear.php.net/*), the PHP Extension and Application Repository, provides the `Services_JSON` PEAR package that supports creating and parsing JSON data for PHP 4 and above. Specific information about the `Services_JSON` PEAR package can be found here (*http://pear.php.net/package/Services_JSON*).

The entire PHP source code for the `Services_JSON` PHP implementation is contained in a *JSON.php* file (*http://svn.php.net/viewvc/pear/packages/Services_JSON/trunk/JSON.php?view=markup*) that can be added directly to a PHP application.

The `Services_JSON` PEAR package provides a `Services_JSON` PHP class, which has several methods including a PHP `encode()` and `decode()` method. To access these methods, a `Services_JSON` PHP object must first be created.

The following PHP 4 code shows how the PHP `encode()` method is used to create JSON data in a PHP string from a nested PHP array:

```
$data = array('first name'=>'John',
  'last name'=>'Smith',
  'address'=>array('zip code'=>'80001'));
$json_obj = new Services_JSON();
$json = $json_obj->encode($data);
```

The following PHP 4 code shows how the PHP `decode()` method is used to create a nested PHP array from JSON data stored in a PHP string:

```
$json_obj = new Services_JSON();
$data - $json_obj->decode($json);
```

In Node.js, the global JSON object provides support for the JSON format. The JSON has several methods including a Node.js `stringify()` method and a Node.js `parse()` method.

The Node.js `stringify()` method corresponds to the PHP 5.2.0 `json_encode()` API function. The Node.js `stringify()` method accepts a Node.js object as its first argument and returns a Node.js string containing the corresponding JSON data.

The following Node.js code uses the Node.js `stringify()` method to create a `json` string variable from the `data` Node.js object:

```
var data = {
  "first name": "John",
  "last name": "Smith",
  "zip code": "80001"
}
var json = JSON.stringify(data);
```

The Node.js `parse()` method corresponds to the PHP 5.2.0 `json_decode()` API function. The Node.js `parse()` method accepts JSON data in a Node.js string as its first argument and returns a Node.js object that instantiates the data:

```
var data = JSON.stringify(json);
```

To convert PHP code for handling JSON data to Node.js, it is recommended that the PHP code be refactored to create two global functions: a PHP `json_stringify()` function and a PHP `json_parse()` function.

For PHP 5.2.0 and above, the PHP `json_stringify()` and `json_parse()` functions can be implemented to turn around and call the PHP `json_encode()` and `json_decode()` API functions directly:

```
function json_stringify($o) {
  return json_encode($o);
}

function json_parse($s) {
  return json_decode($s);
}
```

For PHP 4, a global `Services_JSON` PHP object can be created and the PHP `json_stringify()` and `json_parse()` functions can be implemented to turn around and call the PHP `encode()` method and the PHP `decode()` API method on the global `Services_JSON` PHP object:

```
$json_global_obj = new Services_JSON();

function json_stringify($o) {
  return $json_global_obj->encode($o);
}

function json_parse($s) {
  return $json_global_obj->decode($s);
}
```

By refactoring such that all PHP code, regardless of PHP version, has access to the PHP `json_stringify()` and `json_parse()` functions, two goals are accomplished: (1) a single conversion recipe can convert JSON PHP functions to Node.js, and (2) all PHP and Node.js versions can use the much clearer "stringify" and "parse" verbs in their code instead of less consistent and less understandable "encode" and "decode" verbs.

To convert the PHP `json_stringify()` function into the Node.js `JSON.stringify()` method, execute the following find-and-replace action:

```
Operation: "Find/Replace" in Eclipse PDT
Find: json_stringify(
Replace: JSON.stringify(
Options: None
Action: Replace All
```

After executing the find-and-replace action, delete the PHP `json_stringify()` function implementation and, if needed, the PHP `$json_global_obj` global variable declaration.

To convert the PHP `json_parse()` function into the Node.js `JSON.parse()` method, execute the following find-and-replace action:

```
Operation: "Find/Replace" in Eclipse PDT
Find: json_parse(
Replace: JSON.parse(
Options: None
Action: Replace All
```

After executing the find-and-replace action, delete the PHP `json_parse()` function implementation, and if needed, the PHP `$json_global_obj` global variable declaration.

XML

XML (eXtensible Markup Language) is an alternative to the JSON format. XML is a tag-based format, like HTML. The original idea was to have a data format that was similar to HTML such that data in the XML data format could be created, parsed, and handled using existing tools that performed the same operations on HTML.

XML data uses open and close tags, which are defined using a less-than sign (<) and a greater-than sign (>). An open tag looks like <customer> whereas a close tag uses a forward slash (/) before the name, like </customer>. An open tag may have name/value pairs defined as part of it; these are called *XML attributes.*

The following XML data demonstrates how customer data might be represented in XML. The first line is called an *XML version declaration,* which indicates the XML version that will be used for subsequent XML:

```
<?xml version="1.0"?>
<customer firstname="John" lastname="Smith" zipcode="80001">
</customer>
```

Additional tags may be inserted between the open tag and the close tag. These tags can be described as child tags and the tags that they are inserted in are described as parent tags. If no additional child tags are inserted, an open tag and a close tag can be combined into a single tag with a forward slash (/) inserted before the greater-than sign (>). The following XML contains a single customer XML parent tag with three child tags inserted into it. The three child tags combine their open tags and close tags into a single tag for brevity:

```
<?xml version="1.0"?>
<customer>
  <firstname value="John" />
  <lastname value="Smith" />
  <zipcode value="80001" />
</customer>
```

As you can see, there is a good deal of flexibility in deciding how to represent a single set of data as XML data. One set of data might predominantly describe itself using XML attributes or it might prefer XML tags inserted into a parent tag.

This example data could be URL-encoded and sent to the server using an HTTP GET or an HTTP POST:

```
customer=%3C%3Fxml%20version%3D%221.0%22%3F%3E%3Ccustomer%3E%20%20%3Cfirstname%20
value%3D%22John%22%20%2F%3E%20%20%3Clastname%20value%3D%22Smith%22%20%2F%3E%20
%20%3Czipcode%20value%3D%2280001%22%20%20%2F%3E%3C%2Fcustomer%3E
```

PHP 5.1.0 introduced XML support to the PHP language. It introduced several different XML PHP API sets: SimpleXML, DOM API, XML Parser, XMLReader, and XMLWriter.

To generate an XML string in PHP, PHP code may simply use the dot operator (.) to concatenate strings together. The following PHP code creates a string with customer data encoded in XML:

```
$xml = '';
$xml .= '<?xml version="1.0"?>'."\n";
$xml .= '<customer>'."\n";
$xml .= '  <firstname value="John" />'."\n";
```

```
$xml .= '  <lastname value="Smith" />'."\n";
$xml .= '  <zipcode value="80001" />'."\n";
$xml .= '</customer>'."\n";
print $xml;
```

The same concatenation technique works in Node.js. Converting this PHP code to Node.js does not require any special handling; Chapter 6 described how to convert basic PHP syntax to Node.js:

```
var xml = '';
xml += '<?xml version="1.0"?>'+"\n";
xml += '<customer>'+"\n";
xml += '  <firstname value="John" />'+"\n";
xml += '  <lastname value="Smith" />'+"\n";
xml += '  <zipcode value="80001" />'+"\n";
xml += '</customer>'+"\n";
console.log(xml);
```

A more sophisticated way to create XML data in PHP is to use the XMLWriter PHP class. The XMLWriter PHP class was introduced in PHP 5.1.2. The following PHP 5.1.2 code generates the same XML data, although the whitespace may differ:

```
$xml_writer = new XMLWriter();
$xml_writer->openMemory();
$xml_writer->setIndent(2);
$xml_writer->startDocument('1.0');
$xml_writer->startElement('customer');
$xml_writer->startElement('firstname');
$xml_writer->writeAttribute('value', 'John');
$xml_writer->endElement();
$xml_writer->startElement('lastname');
$xml_writer->writeAttribute('value', 'Smith');
$xml_writer->endElement();
$xml_writer->startElement('zipcode');
$xml_writer->writeAttribute('value', '80001');
$xml_writer->endElement();
$xml_writer->endElement();
$xml_writer->endDocument();
$xml = $xml_writer->outputMemory();
print $xml;
```

In Node.js, the node-xml-writer npm package provides a very similar API to the PHP XMLWriter class. The node-xml-writer Node.js npm package is found on GitHub (*http://github.com/lindory-project/node-xml-writer*).

To use the node-xml-writer Node.js npm package, it must first be installed. The node-xml-writer Node.js npm package is installed by running the following command:

```
npm install xml-writer
```

As you can see, the Node.js XMLWriter example code is very similar to the PHP XMLWriter code. In both languages, the startDocument(), startElement(), write Attribute(), endElement(), and endDocument() methods take the same parameters:

```
var XMLWriter = require('xml-writer');

var xml_writer = new XMLWriter();
xml_writer.startDocument('1.0');
xml_writer.startElement('customer');
xml_writer.startElement('firstname');
xml_writer.writeAttribute('value', 'John');
xml_writer.endElement();
xml_writer.startElement('lastname');
xml_writer.writeAttribute('value', 'Smith');
xml_writer.endElement();
xml_writer.startElement('zipcode');
xml_writer.writeAttribute('value', '80001');
xml_writer.endElement();
xml_writer.endElement();
xml_writer.endDocument();
var xml = writer.toString();
console.log(xml);
```

The only difference is that the Node.js version does not support or need the PHP openMemory() or setIndent() method. Also, the PHP outputMemory() method converts to the Node.js toString() method.

To convert the XMLWriter objects in PHP into Node.js, first insert a Node.js require() API function call near the top of the *.njs* file to load the xml-writer Node.js npm package:

```
var XMLWriter = require('xml-writer');
```

Then, execute the following find-and-replace action to delete the PHP openMemory() method calls in Node.js:

```
Operation: "Find/Replace" in Eclipse PDT
Find: openMemory(
Replace:
Options: None
Action: Find, then Replace/Find
```

At each occurrence, delete the PHP openMemory() method call. Confirm that the PHP setIndent() method call is being used on a PHP XMLWriter object.

Next, execute the following find-and-replace action to delete the PHP setIndent() method calls in Node.js:

```
Operation: "Find/Replace" in Eclipse PDT
Find: setIndent(
Replace:
Options: None
Action: Find, then Replace/Find
```

At each occurrence, delete the PHP setIndent() method call. Confirm that the PHP setIndent() method call is being used on a PHP XMLWriter object.

Finally, use the following find-and-replace action to convert PHP outputMemory() method calls into Node.js toString() method calls:

```
Operation: "Find/Replace" in Eclipse PDT
Find: .outputMemory()
Replace: .toString()
Options: None
Action: Replace All
```

The find-and-replace action can be executed without visiting each occurrence because the PHP XMLWriter class is the only PHP class or Node.js object that has an output Memory() method.

Concatenation and the XMLWriter class are two primary ways to generate XML data in both PHP and Node.js.

To read or parse XML data, PHP provides the SimpleXML, DOM API, XML Parser, and XMLReader API sets.

To use the PHP SimpleXML API functions, a PHP SimpleXMLElement object is created from the PHP string that contains the XML data:

```
$xml_simple = new SimpleXMLElement($xml);
```

The newly created PHP SimpleXMLElement object parses the XML data and creates a complex PHP variable that corresponds to the XML layout and data. A PHP Simple XMLElement object is created for each XML tag. A parent XML tag assigns PHP SimpleXMLElement objects that represent its child XML tags as data members or properties of the PHP object. PHP SimpleXMLElement objects can also be accessed as associative arrays using the square brackets ([and]) notation, which represent the XML attributes of the XML tag.

From earlier in this chapter, you will recall the following XML data:

```
<?xml version="1.0"?>
<customer>
  <firstname value="John" />
  <lastname value="Smith" />
  <zipcode value="80001" />
</customer>
```

For this XML data, the PHP $xml_simple variable represents the customer XML tag.

The firstname child XML tag is stored in the firstname data member of the PHP $xmlnode variable so it is accessed using the pointer operator (->). So, $xml_simple->firstname contains the PHP SimpleXMLElement object that represents the first name child XML tag.

The value XML attribute is accessed using the square brackets ([and]) notation on a PHP SimpleXMLElement object.

The following PHP code prints the value XML attribute of all three XML child tags of the customer XML tag:

```
$xml_simple = new SimpleXMLElement($xml);
print $xml_simple->firstname['value'];
print $xml_simple->lastname['value'];
print $xml_simple->zipcode['value'];
```

Additional PHP properties, methods, and idioms allow the selection of XML tags that meet specific criteria and that iterate over groups of XML tags. A full description of the PHP SimpleXMLElement API set is beyond the scope of this book, but you can find more information on the Web.

Unfortunately, there is not any Node.js module or npm package that provides a similar API set to the PHP SimpleXML API functions. It is recommended that any PHP code that uses the PHP SimpleXML API functions be converted to use the PHP DOM API or the PHP XML Parser. The PHP DOM API and the PHP XML Parser do have corresponding Node.js API sets and it is not worth trying to convert PHP SimpleXML API functions directly to Node.js. In the future, perhaps a Node.js npm module will be created that will mimic the PHP SimpleXML API functions.

The PHP DOM API is an XML parser that is based on the W3C (World Wide Web Consortium) standard.

To use the PHP DOM API functions, a PHP DOMDocument object is created and the PHP $xml string variable is loaded and parsed into it:

```
$xml_dom = new DOMDocument();
$xml_dom->loadXML($xml);
```

Next, PHP foreach statements are used to process the PHP childNodes properties descending from the root PHP DOMDocument object. The PHP childNodes property of each object can be interrogated to find the children, grandchildren, great grandchildren, and so on of the root PHP DOMDocument object. Each object can be tested to see what kind of XML node that it is:

```
foreach ($xml_dom->childNodes as $customer) {
  foreach ($customer->childNodes as $tag) {
    if ($tag->nodeType != XML_TEXT_NODE) {
      print $tag->nodeName;
```

```
      ...
    }
  }
}
```

Finally, if XML attributes are needed, the PHP hasAttributes() method and the PHP attributes property along with a PHP foreach statement can be used to extract the attribute names and values for a specific XML tag:

```
if ($tag->hasAttributes()) {
  foreach ($tag->attributes as $attr) {
    print 'attribute '.$attr->name.' = '.$attr->value;
  }
}
```

The following PHP code shows a simple but common use of the PHP DOM API functions:

```
$xml_dom = new DOMDocument();
$xml_dom->loadXML($xml);
foreach ($xml_dom->childNodes as $customer) {
  foreach ($customer->childNodes as $tag) {
    if ($tag->nodeType != XML_TEXT_NODE) {
      print $tag->nodeName;
      if ($tag->hasAttributes()) {
        foreach ($tag->attributes as $attr) {
          print 'attribute '.$attr->name.' = '.$attr->value;
        }
      }
    }
  }
}
```

In Node.js, the xmldom Node.js npm package implements a very similar API set to the PHP DOM API set. The xmldom Node.js npm package is found on GitHub (*http://github.com/jindw/xmldom*).

To use the xmldom Node.js npm package, it must first be installed. The xmldom Node.js npm package is installed by running the following command:

```
npm install xmldom
```

A Node.js require() API function call must be added to the top of the Node.js *.njs* file. For convenience, the Node.js DOMParser constructor function is extracted immediately from the xmldom Node.js npm package and assigned to the Node.js DOMParser variable:

```
var DOMParser = require('xmldom').DOMParser;
```

As you will recall, with the PHP DOM API functions, a PHP DOMDocument object is created and the PHP loadXML() method changes the PHP DOMDocument object to contain the XML objects that represent the XML data in the PHP $xml variable:

```
$xml_dom = new DOMDocument();
$xml_dom->loadXML($xml);
```

In Node.js, it is not quite the same. First, a Node.js DOMParser object is created, not a DOMDocument object, and then the Node.js DOMDocument object is returned from a call to the Node.js parseFromString() method, instead of changing the empty DOM Document to contain the corresponding XML objects:

```
var xml_domparser = new DOMParser();
var xml_dom = xml_domparser.parseFromString(xml,'text/xml');
```

After the DOMDocument object is created, regardless of the language, the childNodes property of the DOMDocument object can be iterated on, as well as the childNodes properties of those child nodes.

In PHP, the PHP foreach statement is used to iterate over the PHP childNodes property:

```
foreach ($xml_dom->childNodes as $customer) {
  foreach ($customer->childNodes as $tag) {
    if ($tag->nodeType != XML_TEXT_NODE) {
      print $tag->nodeName;
      ...
    }
  }
}
```

In Node.js, the childNodes property is a Node.js indexed array. The Node.js for statement is used to create indexes and these indexes are used to access the Node.js DOM object for each XML child tag. In most cases, the properties of a Node.js DOM object must be tested for existence and determined to have the correct name to confirm that the correct Node.js DOM object has been found:

```
for (var cc=0; xml_dom.childNodes && (cc < xml_dom.childNodes.length); ++cc) {
  var customer = xml_dom.childNodes[cc];
  if (customer.tagName && (customer.tagName == 'customer')) {
    for (var c=0; c < customer.childNodes.length; ++c) {
      var tag = customer.childNodes[c];
      if (tag.tagName) {
        console.log(tag.tagName);
        ...
      }
    }
  }
}
```

In PHP, XML attributes are accessed by testing whether they exist or not, and if they exist, using a PHP foreach statement to extract each attribute of a particular XML tag. Each XML attribute object has a PHP name and value property that describes the XML attribute name/value pair:

```
if ($tag->hasAttributes()) {
  foreach ($tag->attributes as $attr) {
    print 'attribute '.$attr->name.' = '.$attr->value;
  }
}
```

In Node.js, XML attributes are accessed in nearly the same way. XML attributes are tested to see if they exist or not and, if they exist, they are extracted using a Node.js for statement to loop over the Node.js indexed array of XML attributes of a particular XML tag. Each XML attribute object has a Node.js `name` and `value` property that describes the XML attribute name/value pair.

Put together, here's the entire Node.js code that uses the `xmldom` Node.js npm package:

```
var xml_domparser = new DOMParser();
var xml_dom = xml_domparser.parseFromString(xml,'text/xml');
for (var cc=0; xml_dom.childNodes && (cc < xml_dom.childNodes.length); ++cc) {
  var customer = xml_dom.childNodes[cc];
  if (customer.tagName && (customer.tagName == 'customer')) {
    for (var c=0; c < customer.childNodes.length; ++c) {
      var tag = customer.childNodes[c];
      if (tag.tagName) {
        console.log(tag.tagName);
        if (tag.attributes) {
          for (var a=0; a < tag.attributes.length; ++a) {
            console.log('attribute '+tag.attributes[a].name+' = '
              +tag.attributes[a].value);
          }
        }
      }
    }
  }
}
```

To convert PHP code that uses the PHP DOM API functions, first insert a Node.js `require()` API function call at the top of the *.njs* file to access the Node.js `DOMParser` constructor function:

```
var DOMParser = require('xmldom').DOMParser;
```

Next, execute the following find-and-replace action to find PHP `DOMDocument` objects:

```
Operation: "Find/Replace" in Eclipse PDT
Find: DOMDocument(
Replace:
Options: None
Action: Find, then Replace/Find
```

At each occurrence, convert the PHP `DOMDocument` code to use a Node.js `DOMParser` object. Add Node.js code to use the Node.js `DOMParser` object to parse the XML data.

After that, execute the following find-and-replace action to identify uses of the PHP `childNodes` property and convert them to Node.js:

```
Operation: "Find/Replace" in Eclipse PDT
Find: .childNodes
Replace:
Options: None
Action: Find, then Replace/Find
```

At each occurrence, rewrite PHP code around the area where the PHP `childNodes` property is used to use the Node.js `childNodes` property.

Since the PHP DOM API and the `xmldom` Node.js npm package are both expansive, this book cannot give a complete conversion recipe to convert any arbitrary PHP DOM API code into Node.js. However, since both are based on W3C standard, the PHP DOM API and the `xmldom` Node.js npm package will share a large number of properties and methods that will ease conversion. If necessary, the PHP code that uses the PHP DOM API should be refactored so it is limited to a specific PHP function or method and can be easily tested. Then, that specific PHP function or method can be converted to Node.js. The converted Node.js code should be testable in a similar way to the PHP code to confirm that the conversion was successful.

The PHP SimpleXML API, PHP DOM API, and the `xmldom` Node.js npm package all read the entire XML data first, then build a PHP or Node.js object structure to represent it, and finally return the possibly large object structure to the calling code. These object-based XML parsers are called DOM-style XML parsers.

However, there are other APIs that read the XML data one tag at a time and fire "events" (i.e., call functions) for each XML tag or other XML structure. Event-based XML parsers, as opposed to DOM-style XML parsers, are called SAX-style parsers. For these XML parsers, the calling code processes the XML data while the XML parser parses it, rather than waiting for an object structure to be returned when parsing is complete. The PHP XML Parser API is one such event-based XML parser.

With the PHP XML Parser, the PHP calling code creates functions that handle XML events, such as a `startElement` and `endElement` event. The PHP `startElement` event will be sent when an XML open tag is parsed. The PHP `endElement` event will be sent when an XML close tag is parsed.

The following PHP code defines a PHP `myStartElement` and `myEndElement` function suitable for use with the PHP XML Parser API functions:

```php
function myStartElement($parser, $tag, $attrs) {
  print 'open tag '.$tag;
  foreach ($attrs as $name => $value) {
    print 'attribute '.$name.' = '.$value;
  }
}

function myEndElement($parser, $tag) {
  print 'close tag '.$tag;
}
```

The PHP `myStartElement()` function will be called when the XML parser parses an open tag. The XML tag name and the XML tag attributes, both attribute names and attribute values, will be passed as arguments. The PHP `myEndElement()` function will be called when the XML parser parses a close tag with the XML tag name passed to the function as its second argument.

To actually parse the XML data, a PHP `XML Parser` object is created using the PHP `xml_parser_create()` API function:

```
$xml_parser = xml_parser_create();
```

XML element (tag) event handlers are added using the PHP `xml_set_element_handler()` API function. The following PHP code adds the PHP `myStartElement` and `myEndElement` functions as event handlers:

```
xml_set_element_handler($xml_parser, 'myStartElement', 'myEndElement');
// set additional PHP XML Parser API event handlers here
```

Additional PHP XML Parser API event handlers or general parsing parameters are added by calling PHP `XML Parser` API functions where the comment is.

Next, when the PHP `xml_parse()` API function is called, the PHP `XML Parser` object starts parsing the XML data. The XML data is passed as the second parameter to the PHP `xml_parse()` API function. In the following PHP code, the PHP `$xml` variable is a PHP string that contains the XML data and is passed as the second argument to the PHP `xml_parse()` API function call:

```
xml_parse($xml_parser, $xml, true);
```

As the PHP `xml_parse()` API function call executes, the PHP `myStartElement()` and `myEndElement()` functions will be called for each XML tag before the PHP `xml_parse()` API function call returns. Every XML tag will be processed, but unlike the PHP SimpleXML API, PHP DOM API, and the `xmldom` Node.js npm package, event handling functions will be called instead of an object created for each XML tag.

Once the XML data is completely parsed, the PHP `xml_parser_free()` API function is called to dispose of the PHP `XML Parser` object:

```
xml_parser_free($xml_parser);
```

The PHP `XML Parser` is a basic SAX-style XML parser. Node.js also has a basic SAX-style XML parser: the `sax-js` Node.js npm package. The `sax-js` Node.js npm package is hosted on GitHub (*http://github.com/isaacs/sax-js*).

To install the `sax-js` Node.js npm package, the following command must be executed:

```
npm install sax
```

As usual, a Node.js `require()` API function call must be inserted at the beginning of the *.npm* file to access the `sax-js` Node.js npm package:

```
var sax = require('sax');
```

In PHP, the event handling functions, such as the PHP myStartElement() function, are standalone functions that were defined beforehand. However, with the sax-js Node.js npm package, the Node.js parser object is created first by calling the Node.js parser() method:

```
var sax_parser = sax.parser();
```

This corresponds to the PHP xml_parser_create() API function call:

```
$xml_parser = xml_parser_create();
```

Next, for the sax-js Node.js npm package, the event handling functions are created and assigned to the onopentag and onclosetag properties of the Node.js parser object.

Instead of taking three parameters, like the PHP myStartElement function, the function assigned to the onopentag property only takes one parameter. Instead of the PHP $parser parameter, the Node.js this object can be used to access the parser object. For Node.js, the PHP $tag parameter and $attrs have been combined into the single Node.js node parameter. The Node.js node parameter is an object with the name property containing the XML tag name and the attributes property containing the XML tag attributes:

```
sax_parser.onopentag = function(node) {
  console.log('open tag '+node.name);
  for (var name in node.attributes) {
    console.log('attribute '+name+' = '+node.attributes[name]);
  }
};
```

The Node.js onclosetag() method takes a single parameter, like the PHP myEnd Element function, and the parameter serves the exact same purpose; it is the XML tag name:

```
sax_parser.onclosetag = function(name) {
  console.log('close tag '+name);
};
```

Of course, the Node.js code does not need to define and assign Node.js anonymous functions directly to the onopentag and onclosetag properties if named functions already exist elsewhere.

For example, if the Node.js myStartElement() and myEndElement() functions exist elsewhere in the Node.js code, the following Node.js code could assign those functions to the onopentag and onclosetag properties:

```
sax_parser.onopentag = myStartElement;
sax_parser.onclosetag = myEndElement;
```

In PHP, standalone event-handling functions must be defined elsewhere. The names of the PHP functions are passed as string arguments to the PHP `xml_set_element_handler()` API function:

```
xml_set_element_handler($xml_parser, 'myStartElement', 'myEndElement');
```

Once event handlers have been assigned, the Node.js `write()` method call actually parses the XML data and calls the appropriate event handling methods. The Node.js `xml` variable contains the XML data as a Node.js string:

```
sax_parser.write(xml);
```

The PHP `xml_parse()` API function performs the same function in PHP, parsing the XML data and calls the event handling functions. The PHP `$xml` variable contains the XML data as a PHP string:

```
xml_parse($xml_parser, $xml, true);
```

Finally, when parsing is complete, the Node.js `close()` method is called:

```
sax_parser.close();
```

Similarly, the PHP `xml_parser_free()` API function "closes" the PHP parser object:

```
xml_parser_free($xml_parser);
```

To convert PHP code that uses the XML Parser API functions to Node.js, first insert a Node.js `require()` API function call at the top of the *.njs* file to access the `sax` Node.js npm package:

```
var sax = require('sax');
```

Next, execute the following find-and-replace action to convert PHP `xml_parser_create()` API function calls into Node.js `parser()` method calls:

```
Operation: "Find/Replace" in Eclipse PDT
Find: xml_parser_create()
Replace: sax.parser()
Options: None
Action: Replace All
```

The variable type and name that the return values of both the PHP `xml_parser_create()` API function call and the Node.js `sax.parser()` method call are assigned to is irrelevant and does not need specific conversion.

Then, convert PHP `xml_set_element_handler()` API function calls to assign Node.js functions to the `onopentag` and `onclosetag` properties of the Node.js parser object:

```
Operation: "Find/Replace" in Eclipse PDT
Find: xml_set_element_handler(
Replace:
Options: None
Action: Find, then Replace/Find
```

At each occurrence, convert the PHP string arguments into assignments to the appropriate Node.js properties.

For example, the following PHP xml_set_element_handler() API function call takes the values, myStartElement and myEndElement, for the second and third parameters:

```
xml_set_element_handler($parser, 'myStartElement', 'myEndElement');
```

The PHP xml_set_element_handler() API function call would be transformed into the following Node.js code:

```
parser.onopentag = myStartElement;
parser.onclosetag = myEndElement;
```

Now, convert the PHP xml_parse() API function call into the Node.js write() method call:

```
Operation: "Find/Replace" in Eclipse PDT
Find: xml_parse\((.*),\s*(.*),\s*(.*)\)
Replace: $1.write($2)
Options: Regular expressions, Wrap search
Action: Replace All
```

Finally, convert the PHP xml_parser_free() API function call into the Node.js close() method call:

```
Operation: "Find/Replace" in Eclipse PDT
Find: xml_parser_free\((.*)\)
Replace: $1.close()
Options: Regular expressions, Wrap search
Action: Replace All
```

As you can see, the PHP XML Parser can straightforwardly and mechanically be converted into Node.js code using the sax-js Node.js npm package.

PHP supports one final XML parser that has no corresponding Node.js npm package. The PHP XMLReader API reads XML data in a way similar to a SAX-style XML parser, which is reminiscent of how PHP file-handling APIs read files.

To use the PHP XMLReader API, an XML reader object is created:

```
$xml_reader = new XMLReader();
```

Then, the XML data is attached to the XML reader object using the PHP XML() method:

```
$xml_reader->XML($xml);
```

The PHP read() method is called to retrieve the next "node" of the XML data to be processed. An XML node might be an open tag, a close tag, a text node, or some other XML node. A PHP while statement continuously retrieves XML nodes until all the XML nodes have been retrieved:

```
while ($xml_reader->read()) {
  ...
}
```

As each XML node is retrieved, its type can be examined using the PHP `nodeType` property. The following PHP code uses a PHP `switch` statement to separate out each node type and execute the appropriate PHP code:

```
switch ($xml_reader->nodeType) {
  case XMLReader::ELEMENT:
    ...
    break;
  case XMLReader::END_ELEMENT:
    ...
    break;
  default:
    break;
}
```

This PHP code shows a complete but simple example using the PHP XMLReader API:

```
$xml_reader = new XMLReader();
while ($xml_reader->read()) {
  switch ($xml_reader->nodeType) {
    case XMLReader::ELEMENT:
      $tag = $xml_reader->name;
      $hasChildTags = !$xml_reader->isEmptyElement;
      print 'open tag '.$tag;
      if ($xml_reader->hasAttributes) {
        while ($xml_reader->moveToNextAttribute()) {
          print 'attribute '.$xml_reader->name.' = '.$xml_reader->value;
        }
      }
      if (!$hasChildTags) {
        print 'close tag '.$tag;
      }
      break;
    case XMLReader::END_ELEMENT:
      print 'close tag '.$xml_reader->name;
    default:
      break;
  }
}
```

Since there is no corresponding Node.js npm package, it is recommended that PHP code that uses the PHP XMLReader API be refactored to use the PHP XML Parser API or the PHP DOM API and then converted to Node.js. In the future, perhaps a Node.js npm module will be created that will mimic the PHP XMLReader API functions, but for now, none exists.

Whichever data format you use, either plain text, JSON, or XML, it is important to consistently use it. Consistent use will allow PHP code to be easily ported to Node.js.

CHAPTER 12

Miscellaneous Functions

Throughout the book, a common quick-and-dirty solution to porting certain PHP code to Node.js has been to implement PHP API functions as Node.js standalone functions. Since function calls in PHP and Node.js use the same syntax, no changes need to be made to the PHP calling code to call the new Node.js function; the previous PHP function call now becomes a Node.js function call simply by copying and pasting some Node.js code into the source file. While additional PHP to Node.js conversion will be needed, implementing PHP API functions as Node.js standalone functions can speed along PHP to Node.js conversion by resolving a large group of Node.js errors temporarily and leaving the developer to focus on the much fewer, remaining conversion issues.

It is astonishing how heavily the PHP language relies on PHP API functions, even though this is a long-running tradition that dates back to the C language. In contrast, Node.js relies heavily on object properties. Converting from PHP to Node.js is a much easier task than converting Node.js to PHP (if that was ever desirable) because emulating a Node.js property or method in PHP is a much more involved task than simply creating a Node.js function to emulate a PHP function. One way that PHP is superior to Node.js is how easily the underlying foundation of PHP API functions can be moved to a different language with much fewer changes needed to the PHP code itself.

For example, the following PHP code calls the PHP `strlen()` API function to retrieve the length of a string:

```
$s = 'this string may be too long';
$len = strlen($s);
```

In Node.js, the `length` property of a Node.js string is used to retrieve a string's length:

```
var s = 'this string may be too long';
var len = s.length;
```

Rather than search all the PHP code and replace PHP `strlen()` API function calls with Node.js `String` property accesses, the following Node.js function could be copied and pasted into the code as a quick-and-dirty solution to make `strlen()` function calls, even in Node.js, work:

```
function strlen(s) {
    return s.length;
}
```

By adding this Node.js `strlen()` function to the source code, the `strlen()` function call can remain unchanged. The developer has quickly disposed of dozens of PHP to Node.js conversion issues:

```
var s = 'this string may be too long';
var len = strlen(s);
```

As luck would have it, the php.js open source project has already implemented a large number of PHP API functions in JavaScript. Although the php.js implementations are not guaranteed compatible with Node.js, it is still a valuable resource for use in conjunction with this chapter of the book.

Where portions of the php.js open source project have been used for the implementation of a certain PHP API function, it is noted in the surrounding text of the Node.js implementation.

The remainder of this chapter will present Node.js functions that can be used in the same way. Each function is introduced by a brief commentary. In some cases, rarely used optional parameters and certain rarely used PHP idioms are not supported to keep the Node.js implementation simple and brief.

Array

The PHP `count()` API function returns the length of both indexed and associative arrays. In Node.js, these are implemented as Node.js arrays and Node.js objects, respectively, so this divergence must be compensated for. The following is an implementation of a Node.js `count()` function:

```
function count(a) {
  var c = 0;
  if (a instanceof Array) {
    c = a.length;
  } else {
    c = Object.keys(a).length;
  }
  return c;
}
```

The PHP in_array() API function returns if a value exists in an array or not. The following is an implementation of a Node.js in_array() function. The third parameter, the $strict parameter, has been removed for brevity:

```
function in_array(needle, haystack) {
  if (haystack instanceof Array) {
    for (var i=0; i < haystack.length; ++i) {
      if (haystack[i] == needle) {
        return true;
      }
    }
  } else {
    for (var p in haystack) {
      if (haystack[p] === needle) {
        return true;
      }
    }
  }
  return false;
}
```

The PHP array_key_exists() API function returns if an array has a certain key or not. The following is an implementation of a Node.js array_key_exists() function:

```
function array_key_exists(key, a) {
  if (a instanceof Array) {
    return (key < a.length) && ((typeof a[key]) != 'undefined');
  }
  return a.hasOwnProperty(key);
}
```

The PHP array_merge() API function returns a concatenation of two indexed arrays or a union of two associative arrays. The following is an implementation of a Node.js array_merge() function. Additional array parameters are not supported for brevity:

```
function array_merge(a, a2) {
  if (a instanceof Array) {
    return a.concat(a2);
  } else {
    var p, r = {};
    for (p in a) {
      r[p] = a[p];
    }
    for (p in a2) {
      r[p] = a2[p];
    }
    return r;
  }
}
```

The PHP `array_map()` API function calls a function on every element of an array and returns the resulting array. The following is an implementation of a Node.js `array_map()` function. The first parameter does not support a string value for simplicity. If possible, it is recommended that PHP `array_map()` API function calls be refactored into PHP code that does not use callbacks:

```
function array_map(f, a) {
  if (a instanceof Array) {
    var r = [];
    for (var i=0; i < a.length; ++i) {
      r[i] = f(a);
    }
    return r;
  } else {
    var r = {};
    for (p in a) {
      r[p] = f(a[p]);
    }
    return r;
  }
}
```

The PHP `array_slice()` API function returns a subset of an indexed array. The following is an implementation of a Node.js `array_slice()` function. The third parameter, the `$preserve_keys` parameter, has been removed for brevity:

```
function array_slice(a, offset, length) {
  length = length || (a.length - offset);
  return a.slice(offset, offset + length);
}
```

The PHP `array_splice()` API function modifies an indexed array by deleting and/or adding values. The following is an implementation of a Node.js `array_splice()` function:

```
function array_splice(a, offset, length, replacement) {
  length = length || 0;
  a.splice(offset, length);
  if ((typeof replacement) != 'undefined') {
    for (var r=0; r < replacement.length; ++r) {
      a.splice(offset+r, 0, replacement[r]);
    }
  }
  return a;
}
```

The PHP `array_values()` API function converts an associative array into an indexed array. The following is an implementation of a Node.js `array_values()` function:

```
function array_values(a) {
  var r = [];
  for (var p in a) {
```

```
      r.push(a[p]);
    }
    return r;
  }
```

The PHP `array_unique()` API function returns an array that does not have any duplicate values. For indexed arrays, it will usually return a sparse array. Refer back to Chapter 7 for more information on sparse arrays. The following is an implementation of a Node.js `array_unique()` function. The second parameter, `$sort_values`, has been removed for brevity:

```
function array_unique(a) {
  var r;
  if (a instanceof Array) {
    r = [];
    for (var i=0; i < a.length; ++i) {
      r[i] = a[i];
      for (var j=0; j < i; ++j) {
        if ((a[i]+'') == (a[j]+'')) {
          r[i] = undefined;
        }
      }
    }
  } else {
    r = {};
    var i=0, ia = [];
    for (var p in a) {
      ia[i++] = p;
    }
    ia.sort();
    for (var i=0; i < ia.length; ++i) {
      var found = false;
      for (var j=0; j < i; ++j) {
        if ((a[ia[i]]+'') == (a[ia[j]]+'')) {
          found = true;
        }
      }
      if (!found) {
        r[ia[i]] = a[ia[i]];
      }
    }
  }
  return r;
}
```

The PHP `sort()` API function sorts an array. The following is an implementation of a Node.js `sort()` function:

```
function sort(a) {
  a.sort();
  return true;
}
```

Time and Date

The PHP `time()` API function returns the number of seconds since January 1, 1970, whereas the Node.js `getTime()` method returns the number of milliseconds since January 1, 1970. The following is an implementation of a Node.js `time()` function:

```
function time() {
    return new Date().getTime() / 1000;
}
```

The PHP `getdate()` API function returns an associative array with a variety of data information. The following is an implementation of a Node.js `getdate()` function. The Node.js implementation incorporates portions of the php.js open source project:

```
function getdate(timestamp) {
  var _w = ['Sunday', 'Monday', 'Tuesday', 'Wednesday', 'Thursday',
    'Friday', 'Saturday'];
  var _m = ['January', 'February', 'March', 'April', 'May', 'June', 'July',
    'August', 'September', 'October', 'November', 'December'];
  var d = new Date();
  if ((typeof timestamp) == 'object') {
    d = new Date(timestamp);
  } else if ((typeof timestamp) != 'undefined') {
    d = new Date(timestamp * 1000);
  }
  var w = d.getDay();
  var m = d.getMonth();
  var y = d.getFullYear();
  var r = {};
  r.seconds = d.getSeconds();
  r.minutes = d.getMinutes();
  r.hours = d.getHours();
  r.mday = d.getDate();
  r.wday = w;
  r.mon = m + 1;
  r.year = y;
  r.yday = Math.floor((d - (new Date(y, 0, 1))) / 86400000);
  r.weekday = _w[w];
  r.month = _m[m];
  r['0'] = parseInt(d.getTime() / 1000, 10);
  return r;
}
```

The PHP `basename()` API function extracts the filename from a path. The following is an implementation of a Node.js `basename()` function:

```
var path = require('path');

function basename(f, ext) {
  return path.basename(f, ext);
}
```

File

The PHP `dirname()` API function extracts the directory name from a path. The following is an implementation of a Node.js `dirname()` function:

```
var path = require('path');

function dirname(f, ext) {
  return path.dirname(f);
}
```

The PHP `file_exists()` API function determines if a path exists or not. The following is an implementation of a Node.js `file_exists()` function. The "sync" version of the Node.js `exists()` API function is a quick-and-dirty solution until the calling code can be addressed directly:

```
var fs = require('fs');

function file_exists(f) {
  return fs.existsSync(f);
}
```

The PHP `file_get_contents()` API function reads a text file and returns it as a string. The following is an implementation of a Node.js `file_get_contents()` function. The optional parameters have been removed for brevity. The "sync" version of the Node.js `readFile()` API function is a quick-and-dirty solution until the calling code can be addressed directly:

```
var fs = require('fs');

function file_get_contents(f) {
  return fs.readFileSync(f, 'utf8');
}
```

The PHP `realpath()` API function gets the full absolute pathname for a relative path. The following is an implementation of a Node.js `realpath()` function. The "sync" version of the Node.js `realPath()` API function is a quick-and-dirty solution until the calling code can be addressed directly:

```
var fs = require('fs');

function realpath(path) {
  return fs.realPathSync(path);
}
```

JSON

The PHP `json_encode()` API function returns the JSON string representing an object. The following is an implementation of a Node.js `json_encode()` function:

```
function json_encode(obj) {
  return JSON.stringify(obj);
}
```

The PHP `json_decode()` API function returns an object created from a JSON string. The following is an implementation of a Node.js `json_decode()` function:

```
function json_decode(s) {
  return JSON.parse(s);
}
```

Math

The PHP `abs()` API function returns the absolute value of a number. The following is an implementation of a Node.js `abs()` function:

```
function abs(n) {
  return Math.abs(n);
}
```

The PHP `ceil()` API function returns a floating-point value rounded up to the next integer. The following is an implementation of a Node.js `ceil()` function:

```
function ceil(n) {
  return Math.ceil(n);
}
```

The PHP `floor()` API function returns a floating-point value rounded down to the previous integer. The following is an implementation of a Node.js `floor()` function:

```
function floor(n) {
  return Math.floor(n);
}
```

The PHP `max()` API function returns the highest of two values. The following is an implementation of a Node.js `max()` function. Additional parameters and unusual idioms are not supported for brevity:

```
function max(n, n2) {
  return (n > n2)? n: n2;
}
```

The PHP `min()` API function returns the lowest of two values. The following is an implementation of a Node.js `min()` function. Additional parameters and unusual idioms are not supported for brevity:

```
function min(n, n2) {
  return (n < n2)? n: n2;
}
```

The PHP `round()` API function returns a floating-point value rounded to the nearest integer. The following is an implementation of a Node.js `round()` function. The two optional parameters, `$precision` and `$mode`, have been removed for brevity:

```
function round(n) {
  return Math.round(n);
}
```

The PHP `rand()` API function generates a random integer between two integers. The Node.js `Math.random()` API function generates a random floating-point number between 0 and 1. The following is an implementation of a Node.js `rand()` function:

```
function rand(min, max) {
  return Math.floor(Math.random()*(max-min+1))+ min;
}
```

The PHP `mt_rand()` API function works the same as the PHP `rand()` API function for Node.js purposes. The following is an implementation of a Node.js `mt_rand()` function:

```
function mt_rand(min, max) {
  return Math.floor(Math.random()*(max-min+1))+ min;
}
```

String

The PHP `explode()` API function splits a string into an array of strings. The following is an implementation of a Node.js `explode()` function. The optional parameter, `$limit`, has been removed for brevity:

```
function explode(delimiter, s) {
  return s.split(delimiter);
}
```

The PHP `implode()` API function creates a string from an array of strings. The following is an implementation of a Node.js `implode()` function:

```
function implode(glue, a) {
  return ((typeof a) == 'undefined')? glue.join(''): a.join(glue);
}
```

The PHP `join()` API function creates a string from an array of strings. It is the same as the PHP `implode()` API function. The following is an implementation of a Node.js `join()` function:

```
function join(glue, a) {
  return ((typeof a) == 'undefined')? glue.join(''): a.join(glue);
}
```

The PHP `strcmp()` API function compares two strings and returns 0, 1, or −1. The greater-than operator (>) and the less-than operator (<) work for Node.js strings as well as Node.js numbers. The following is an implementation of a Node.js `strcmp()` function:

```
function strcmp(s, s2) {
  if (s == s2) return 0;
  return (s > s2)? 1 : -1;
}
```

The PHP `strcasecmp()` API function compares two strings, ignoring case, and returns 0, 1, or −1. The following is an implementation of a Node.js `strcasecmp()` function:

```
function strcasecmp(s, s2) {
  s = s.toLowerCase();
  s2 = s2.toLowerCase();
  if (s == s2) return 0;
  return (s > s2)? 1 : -1;
}
```

The PHP `strpos()` API function returns the position of a substring inside a longer string. The following is an implementation of a Node.js `strpos()` function:

```
function strpos(s, needle, offset) {
  return s.indexOf(needle, offset);
}
```

The PHP `substr()` API function returns a substring inside a longer string. The following is an implementation of a Node.js `substr()` function:

```
function substr(s, start, length) {
  return ((typeof length) == 'undefined')?
    s.substring(start): s.substring(start, start+length);
}
```

The PHP `str_replace()` API function replaces a substring with another substring. The following is an implementation of a Node.js `str_replace()` function:

```
function str_replace(search, replace, subject) {
  var ret = '';
  var p = 0;
  var n = subject.indexOf(search, p);
  while (n != -1) {
    ret += subject.substring(p, n) + replace;
    p = n + search.length;
    n = subject.indexOf(search, p);
  }
  return ret + subject.substring(p);
}
```

The PHP `strip_tags()` API function removes HTML and PHP tags from a string. The following is an implementation of a Node.js `strip_tags()` function. The Node.js implementation incorporates portions of the php.js open source project:

```
function strip_tags (input, allowable_tags) {
  allowable_tags = (((allowable_tags || '') + '').toLowerCase()
    .match(/<[a-z][a-z0-9]*>/g) || []).join('');
  var tags = /<\/?([a-z][a-z0-9]*)\b[^>]*>/gi,
    commentsAndPhpTags = /<!--[\s\S]*?-->|<\?(?:php)?[\s\S]*?\?>/gi;
```

```
    return input.replace(commentsAndPhpTags, '')
      .replace(tags, function ($0, $1) {
        return allowable_tags.indexOf('<' + $1.toLowerCase() + '>') > -1 ? $0 : '';
    });
}
```

The PHP trim() API function removes whitespace from the beginning and the end of a string. The following is an implementation of a Node.js trim() function. The optional parameter, $charlist, has been removed for brevity. The Node.js implementation incorporates portions of the php.js open source project:

```
function trim(s) {
  var ws = ' \t\n\r\0\x0B';
  var p = 0, n = s.length;
  while ((p < n) && (ws.indexOf(s.charAt(p)) != -1)) {
    ++p;
  }
  while ((n > p) && (ws.indexOf(s.charAt(n-1)) != -1)) {
    --n;
  }
  return s.substring(p, n);
}
```

The PHP ltrim() API function removes whitespace from the beginning of a string. The following is an implementation of a Node.js ltrim() function. The optional parameter, $charlist, has been removed for brevity. The Node.js implementation incorporates portions of the php.js open source project:

```
function ltrim(s) {
  var ws = ' \t\n\r\0\x0B';
  var p = 0, n = s.length;
  while ((p < n) && (ws.indexOf(s.charAt(p)) != -1)) {
    ++p;
  }
  return s.substring(p, n);
}
```

The PHP rtrim() API function removes whitespace from the end of a string. The following is an implementation of a Node.js rtrim() function. The optional parameter, $charlist, has been removed for brevity. The Node.js implementation incorporates portions of the php.js open source project:

```
function rtrim(s) {
  var ws = ' \t\n\r\0\x0B';
  var p = 0, n = s.length;
  while ((n > p) && (ws.indexOf(s.charAt(n-1)) != -1)) {
    --n;
  }
  return s.substring(p, n);
}
```

The PHP `strtolower()` API function returns the string in all lowercase. The following is an implementation of a Node.js `strtolower()` function:

```
function strtolower(s) {
  return s.toLowerCase();
}
```

The PHP `strtoupper()` API function returns the string in all uppercase. The following is an implementation of a Node.js `strtoupper()` function:

```
function strtoupper(s) {
  return s.toUpperCase();
}
```

The PHP `chr()` API function returns a one-character string from the ASCII value. The following is an implementation of a Node.js `chr()` function:

```
function chr(n) {
  return String.fromCharCode(n);
}
```

The PHP `ord()` API function returns the ASCII value from a one-character string. The following is an implementation of a Node.js `ord()` function:

```
function ord(ch) {
  return ch.charCodeAt(0);
}
```

The PHP `preg_match()` API function matches a PHP regular expression pattern. The following is an implementation of a Node.js `preg_match()` function. The optional third parameter, $matches, requires the argument to be a Node.js array and requires the following Node.js code to follow each Node.js `preg_match()` API function:

```
matches = matches[0];
```

Here's the implementation of the Node.js `preg_match()` function, which handles PHP regular expression pattern strings for the most part:

```
function preg_match(pattern, s, matches) {
  var mod = '';
  if ((pattern.charAt(0) == '/') || (pattern.charAt(0) == '@')) {
    var n = pattern.lastIndexOf(pattern.charAt(0));
    if (n != 0) {
      pattern = pattern.substring(1, n);
      mod = pattern.substring(n+1);
    }
  }
  var rx = new RegExp(pattern, mod);
  if (!(matches instanceof Array)) {
    matches = [];
  }
  matches[0] = rx.exec(s);
  return (matches[0] === null)? 0: 1;
}
```

Type

The PHP `is_array()` API function returns if a variable is an array, either indexed or associative, or not. The following is an implementation of a Node.js `is_array()` function. It usually can differentiate between a Node.js object acting as an associative array and a true Node.js object:

```
function is_array(a) {
  return (a instanceof Array)
    || ((a !== null) && ((typeof a) == 'object')
    && (a.constructor.name === 'Object'));
}
```

Th PHP `is_bool()` API function returns if a variable is a boolean or not. The following is an implementation of a Node.js `is_bool()` function:

```
function is_bool(b) {
  return (typeof b) == 'boolean';
}
```

The PHP `is_float()` API function returns if a variable is a floating-point number or not. The following is an implementation of a Node.js `is_float()` function:

```
function is_float(f) {
  return ((typeof f) == 'number') && (Math.round(f) !== f);
}
```

The PHP `is_int()` API function returns if a variable is an integer number or not. The following is an implementation of a Node.js `is_int()` function:

```
function is_int(i) {
  return ((typeof i) == 'number') && ((i %1) === 0);
}
```

The PHP `is_object()` API function returns if a variable is an object or not. The following is an implementation of a Node.js `is_object()` function. It usually can differentiate between a Node.js object acting as an associative array and a true Node.js object:

```
function is_object(n) {
  return (!(a instanceof Array))
    && (a !== null) && ((typeof a) == 'object')
    && (a.constructor.name !== 'Object');
}
```

The PHP `is_null()` API function returns if a variable is a string or not. The following is an implementation of a Node.js `is_null()` function:

```
function is_null(n) {
  return n === null;
}
```

The PHP `is_string()` API function returns if a variable is a string or not. The following is an implementation of a Node.js `is_string()` function:

```
function is_string(s) {
  return (typeof s) == 'string';
}
```

The PHP `gettype()` API function returns the type of the variable. The following is an implementation of a Node.js `gettype()` function. It does not support the PHP resource type; it never returns the "resource" string:

```
function gettype(v) {
  if (v === null) {
    return 'NULL';
  } else if ((typeof v) == 'boolean') {
    return 'boolean';
  } else if (((typeof v) == 'number') && ((v % 1) === 0)) {
    return 'integer';
  } else if (((typeof v) == 'number') && (Math.round(v) !== v)) {
    return 'double';
  } else if ((typeof v) == 'string') {
    return 'string';
  } else if (v instanceof Array) {
    return 'array';  // indexed array
  } else if (((typeof v) == 'object') && (v.constructor.name === 'Object')) {
    return 'array';  // associative array
  } else if ((typeof v) == 'object') {
    return 'object';
  }
  return 'unknown type';
}
```

Text

The PHP `md5()` API function creates an MD5 digest as a 32-character hexadecimal number. The following is an implementation of a Node.js `md5()` function. The `crypto` Node.js built-in module is required for the Node.js implementation:

```
var crypto = require('crypto');

function md5(text) {
  return crypto.createHash('md5').update(text).digest('hex');
}
```

The PHP `sha1()` API function creates a SHA1 digest as a 40-character hexadecimal number. The following is an implementation of a Node.js `sha1()` function. The `crypto` Node.js built-in module is required for the Node.js implementation:

```
var crypto = require('crypto');

function sha1(text) {
  return crypto.createHash('sha1').update(text).digest('hex');
}
```

The PHP md5_file() API function creates an MD5 digest as a 32-character hexadecimal number from the contents of a file. The following is an implementation of a Node.js md5_file() function. Both the fs Node.js built-in module and the crypto Node.js built-in module is required for the Node.js implementation:

```
var fs = require('fs');
var crypto = require('crypto');

function md5_file(f) {
  var contents = fs.readFileSync(f, 'utf8');
  return crypto.createHash('md5').update(contents).digest('hex');
}
```

The PHP rawurldecode() API function decodes a string that has been made safe to be passed in the query string of a URL. The following is an implementation of a Node.js rawurldecode() function. The Node.js implementation incorporates portions of the php.js open source project:

```
function rawurldecode(s) {
  return decodeURIComponent(s + '');
}
```

The PHP urldecode() API function needs to modify the Node.js decodeURI Component() API function to account for spaces ( ). The PHP urldecode() API function is meant for legacy use only. The following is an implementation of a Node.js urlde code() function. The Node.js implementation incorporates portions of the php.js open source project:

```
function urldecode(s) {
  return decodeURIComponent((s + '')
    .replace(/\+/g, '%20'));
}
```

The PHP rawurlencode() API function encodes a string so it is safe to be passed in the query string of a URL. It needs to modify the Node.js encodeURIComponent() API function to account for exclamation points (!), single quotes ('), parentheses ((and)), asterisks (*), and tildes (~). The following is an implementation of a Node.js rawurl encode() function. The Node.js implementation incorporates portions of the php.js open source project:

```
function rawurlencode(s) {
  return encodeURIComponent(s + '')
    .replace(/!/g, '%21')
    .replace(/'/g, '%27')
    .replace(/\(/g, '%28')
    .replace(/\)/g, '%29')
    .replace(/\*/g, '%2A')
    .replace(/~/g, '%7E');
}
```

The PHP `urlencode()` API function needs to modify the Node.js `encodeURI` `Component()` API function to account for exclamation points (!), single quotes ('), parentheses ((and)), asterisks (*), and spaces ( ). The following is an implementation of a Node.js `urlencode()` function. The PHP `urlencode()` API function is meant for legacy use only. The Node.js implementation incorporates portions of the php.js open source project:

```
function urlencode(s) {
  return encodeURIComponent(s + '')
    .replace(/!/g, '%21')
    .replace(/'/g, '%27')
    .replace(/\(/g, '%28')
    .replace(/\)/g, '%29')
    .replace(/\*/g, '%2A')
    .replace(/%20/g, '+');
}
```

The PHP `mail()` API function sends email. Node.js does not have any built-in modules to support sending email but the `Nodemailer` Node.js npm package is very popular. The following command installs the `Nodemailer` Node.js npm package:

```
npm install nodemailer
```

The PHP `mail()` API function implementation hardcodes the mail server configuration. In PHP, the PHP configuration contains the mail configuration. The following is an implementation of a Node.js `mail()` function:

```
var email = require('nodemailer');

function mail(to, subject, message) {
  var server = email.createTransport('SMTP', {
    service: 'Gmail',
    auth: {
      user: 'gmail.user@gmail.com',
      pass: 'passw0rd'
    }
  });
  var letter = {
    from: 'Sender <sender@example.com>',
    to: to,
    subject: subject,
    text: message
  }
  server.sendMail(letter, function(e, resp) {
    if (e) {
      console.log(e);
    } else {
      console.log('Message sent to '+to);
    }
```

```
    server.close();
  });
  return true;
}
```

MySQL

The PHP `mysql_real_escape_string()` API function adds a backslash (\) to certain character sequences so they will be interpreted as SQL data instead of an SQL statement. The following is an implementation of a Node.js `mysql_real_escape_string()` function:

```
function mysql_real_escape_string(s) {
  return (s + '')
    .replace(/\0/g, '\\x00')
    .replace(/\n/g, '\\n')
    .replace(/\r/g, '\\r')
    .replace(/\\/g, '\\\\')
    .replace(/'/g, '\\\'')
    .replace(/"/g, '\\"')
    .replace(/\x1a/g, '\\\x1a');
}
```

The PHP `mysql_num_rows()` API function returns the number of rows returned from a MySQL database query. The following is an implementation of a Node.js `mysql_num_rows()` function. The `rows` parameter takes the `rows` argument from the callback function instead of the return value from the `query()` method call:

```
function mysql_num_rows(rows) {
  return rows.length;
}
```

Variable

The PHP `empty()` API function returns if a variable is considered empty or not. The following is an implementation of a Node.js `empty()` function:

```
function empty(v) {
  return !v;
}
```

The PHP `isset()` API function determines if a variable is defined or not. The following is an implementation of a Node.js `isset()` function. In Node.js, a variable that has the undefined type is a close approximation but not an exact match to an undefined variable in PHP. As a result, the following Node.js `isset()` function may not work for certain uses of the PHP `isset()` API function:

```
function isset(v) {
  return (typeof v) != 'undefined';
}
```

By implementing these PHP API functions in Node.js, a PHP to Node.js conversion can be sped up and more important conversion issues addressed. Later, these implementations can be revisited and implemented in truly native and more effective Node.js code. It is also instructive to take note of how PHP implementations differ from their Node.js cousins, especially in some of the more arcane corners of both languages.

php.js License

The php.js (*http://phpjs.org/*) open source project license is shown below.

This is version: 3.26

php.js is copyright 2011 Kevin van Zonneveld.

Portions copyright Brett Zamir, Kevin van Zonneveld, Onno Marsman, Theriault, Michael White, Waldo Malqui Silva, Paulo Freitas, Jack, Jonas Raoni Soares Silva, Philip Peterson, Legaev Andrey, Ates Goral, Alex, Ratheous, Martijn Wieringa, Rafał Kukawski, lmeyrick, Nate, Philippe Baumann, Enrique Gonzalez, Webtoolkit.info, Carlos R. L. Rodrigues, Ash Searle, Jani Hartikainen, travc, Ole Vrijenhoek, Erkekjetter, Michael Grier, Johnny Mast, T.Wild, d3x, stag019, pilus, WebDevHobo, marrtins, GeekFG, Andrea Giammarchi, Arpad Ray, gorthaur, Paul Smith, Tim de Koning, Joris, Oleg Eremeev, Steve Hilder, majak, gettimeofday, KELAN, Josh Fraser, Marc Palau, Kevin van Zonneveld, Martin, Breaking Par Consulting Inc., Chris, Mirek Slugen, saulius, Alfonso Jimenez, Diplom@t, felix, Mailfaker, Tyler Akins, Caio Ariede, Robin, Kankrelune, Karol Kowalski, Imgen Tata, mdsjack, Dreamer, Felix Geisendoerfer, Lars Fischer, AJ, David, Aman Gupta, Michael White, Public Domain, Steven Levithan, Sakimori, Pellentesque Malesuada, Thunder.m, Dj, Steve Clay, David James, Francois, class_exists, nobbler, T. Wild, Itsacon, date, Ole Vrijenhoek, Fox, Raphael (Ao RUDLER), Marco, noname, Mateusz "loonquawl" Zalega, Frank Forte, Arno, ger, mktime, john, Nick Kolosov, marc andreu, Scott Cariss, Douglas Crockford, madipta, Slawomir Kaniecki, ReverseSyntax, Nathan, Alex Wilson, kenneth, Bayron Guevara, Adam Wallner, paulo kuong, jmweb, Lincoln Ramsay, djmix, Pyerre, Jon Hohle, Thiago Mata, lmeyrick, Linuxworld, duncan, Gilbert, Sanjoy Roy, Shingo, sankai, Oskar Larsson Högfeldt, Denny Wardhana, 0m3r, Everlasto, Subhasis Deb, josh, jd, Pier Paolo Ramon, P, merabi, Soren Hansen, Eugene Bulkin, Der Simon, echo is bad, Ozh, XoraX, EdorFaus, JB, J A R, Marc Jansen, Francesco, LH, Stoyan Kyosev, nord_ua, omid, Brad Touesnard, MeEtc, Peter-Paul Koch, Olivier Louvignes, T0bsn, Tim Wiel, Bryan Elliott, Jalal Berrami, Martin, JT, David Randall, Thomas Beaucourt, taith, vlado houba, Pierre-Luc Paour, Kristof Coomans (SCK-CEN Belgian Nucleair Research Centre), Martin Pool, Kirk Strobeck, Rick Waldron, Brant Messenger, Devan Penner-Woelk, Saulo Vallory, Wagner B. Soares, Artur Tchernychev, Valentina De Rosa, Jason Wong, Christoph, Daniel Esteban, strftime, Mick@el, rezna, Simon Willison, Anton Ongson, Gabriel Paderni, Marco van Oort, penutbutterjelly, Philipp Lenssen, Bjorn Roesbeke, Bug?, Eric Nagel, Tomasz Wesolowski, Evertjan Garretsen, Bobby Drake, Blues, Luke Godfrey, Pul, uestla, Alan C, Ulrich,

Yves Sucaet, sowberry, Norman "zEh" Fuchs, hitwork, Zahlii, johnrembo, Nick Callen, Steven Levithan, ejsanders, Scott Baker, Brian Tafoya, Philippe Jausions, Aidan Lister, Rob, e-mike, HKM, ChaosNo1, metjay, strcasecmp, strcmp, Taras Bogach, jpfle, Alexander Ermolaev, DxGx, kilops, Orlando, dptr1988, Le Torbi, James, Pedro Tainha, James, Arnout Kazemier, Chris McMacken, gabriel paderni, Yannoo, FGFEmperor, baris ozdil, Tod Gentille, Greg Frazier, jakes, 3D-GRAF, Allan Jensen, Howard Yeend, Benjamin Lupton, davook, daniel airton wermann, Atli Þór, Maximusya, Ryan W Tenney, Alexander M Beedie, fearphage, Nathan Sepulveda, Victor, Matteo, Billy, stensi, Cord, Manish, T.J. Leahy, Riddler, FremyCompany, Matt Bradley, Tim de Koning, Luis Salazar, Diogo Resende, Rival, Andrej Pavlovic, Garagoth, Le Torbi, Dino, Josep Sanz, rem, Russell Walker, Jamie Beck, setcookie, Michael, YUI Library, Blues, Ben, DtTvB, Andreas, William, meo, incidence, Cagri Ekin, Amirouche, Amir Habibi, Luke Smith, Kheang Hok Chin, Jay Klehr, Lorenzo Pisani, Tony, Yen-Wei Liu, Greenseed, mk.keck, Leslie Hoare, dude, booeyOH, Ben Bryan

Index

Symbols

& (ampersand)
    separating query arguments, 29
    in URL-encoded data, 219
* (asterisk), multiplication operator, 108
\ (backward slash), path separator, 178
: (colon)
    in inline conditional, 109, 118
    in object literals, 130
{} (curly brackets)
    enclosing code blocks, v, 108
    enclosing JSON data, 223
    in alternative if statement syntax, 117
    object initialization, 6, 15, 130
$ (dollar sign), preceding PHP variables, 108, 125
. (dot operator)
    for object properties, 131, 139, 165
    string concatenation operator, 111
" (double quotes), enclosing string literals, 109
= (equal sign), in query arguments, 29
== (equal sign, double), equals operator, 108
=> (equal sign, right angle bracket), pair operator in PHP, 129
!= (exclamation point, equals), does not equal operator, 108
/ (forward slash)
    path separator, 178, 196

    in XML tags, 227
-> (hyphen, right angle bracket), pointer operator, 165
< (left angle bracket)
    less than operator, 108
    in XML tags, 227
<= (left angle bracket, equals), less than or equals operator, 108
- (minus sign), subtraction operator, 108
-- (minus sign, double), decrement operator, 108
( ) (parentheses), defining precedence, 108
% (percent sign)
    remainder operator, 108
    in URL-encoded data, 219
+ (plus sign)
    addition operator, 107, 108
    array union operator, 112
    double (++), increment operator, 108
    string concatenation operator, 110
? (question mark)
    in inline conditional, 109, 118
    preceding query arguments, 29
    in URL-encoded data, 219
> (right angle bracket)
    greater than operator, 108
    in XML tags, 227
>= (right angle bracket, equals), greater than or equals operator, 108

We'd like to hear your suggestions for improving our indexes. Send email to index@oreilly.com.

static variables in, 175–176
variables in, 158–159
close() function, fs module, 50, 51, 53, 187, 188, 190
closures, 66–69
in PHP 5.3, 69–73
simulating in PHP 4, 74–87
code examples, permission to use, xii
colon (:)
in inline conditional, 109, 118
in object literals, 130
conditional operators, 108
conditional statements (see for statements; if statements; while statements)
configurable attribute, 165
console module, log() function, 25
constructor function, 22, 158
constructor property, 163
contact information for this book, xiii
conventions used in this book, xii
$_COOKIE PHP variable, 34–35
cookies, 34–35
count() function, arrays, 133, 134, 136–137, 139–141, 242
cPanel website hosting services, v
CREATE TABLE SQL statement, 207–208
create() function, objects, 164
createClient() function, 204
createReadStream() function, fs module, 180–181, 189
createServer() function, http module, 3, 22–24, 26–28
curly brackets ({})
enclosing code blocks, v, 108
enclosing JSON data, 223
in alternative if statement syntax, 117
object initialization, 6, 15, 130

D

Dahl, Ryan (developer of Node.js), 48
data formats, 219–221
JSON, 223–226, 247
plain text, 221–223
XML, 226–240
DOM functions, 231–235
node-xml-writer package, 228–230
sax-js package, 236–239
SimpleXML functions, 230–231
XML Parser functions, 235–239

xmldom package, 232–235
XMLReader functions, 239–240
XMLWriter class, 228–230
databases, 199, 207
MySQL (see MySQL database)
ORM for, 203
SQL language for (see SQL language)
supported by Node.js, 200, 203
date and time functions, 246–246
decode() method, 225
delete keyword, 145
DELETE SQL statement, 211–211
derived class, 166, 168
destroy() method, 205
diff viewer, 12–15
directories
of current .njs file, 178
existence of, determining, 192–193
of specified path or file, 194, 247
DIRECTORY_SEPARATOR constant, 196
__dirname variable, 178
dirname() function, PHP and path module, 194, 247
do...while statement (see while statements)
dollar sign ($), preceding PHP variables, 108, 125
DOM functions, 231–235
dot operator (.)
for object properties, 131, 139, 165
string concatenation operator, 111
double quotes ("), enclosing string literals, 109
double type, 126, 127
DROP TABLE SQL statement, 208

E

echo keyword, 92
Eclipse PDT (PHP Development Tools), 9–19
alternatives to, 19
diff viewer, 12–15
Find/Replace, 16–18
installing, 10–11
Java required for, 10
.njs files recognized by, 11–12
editors (see Eclipse PDT; text editors)
Eich, Brendan (developer of JavaScript), 48
else keyword, 28
(see also if statements)
empty() function, 257
encapsulation, 157–165

encode() method, 224

end() function, response object, 26, 91, 94–96, 102, 103

endDocument() method, 229

endElement() method, 229

enumerable attribute, 164

eocp() function, 95, 102

EOL constant, 182

equal sign (=), in query arguments, 29

equal sign, double (==), equals operator, 108

equal sign, right angle bracket (=>), pair operator in PHP, 129

events

    HTTP POST request using, 32

    JavaScript using, 48

exclamation point, equals (!=), does not equal operator, 108

exists() function, fs module, 191

explode() function, 249

extends keyword, 168–172

extname() function, path module, 194

F

fclose() function, 143, 186

feof() function, 187

fflush() function, 190

fgets() function, 188

fgetss() function, 188

file handling, 49–57

file serving objects, 22–22

    listen() function, 24

    serve() function, 22–24

file() function, 183–186

files

    absolute and relative paths for, 193–196

    closing, 186, 188, 190

    end of file, testing for, 187

    existence of, determining, 191–193

    flushing data to, 190

    functions for, implemented in Node.js, 247–247

    information about, determining, 192

    opening, 186–186, 189

    permissions for, 197–198

    reading into a variable, 177–181, 186–188

    reading into an array, 183–186

    reading line by line, 188

    temporary, 196

    writing, 181–182, 189–191

file_exists() function, 191, 247

file_get_contents() function, 94, 177–180, 247

file_put_contents() function, 181–182

Find/Replace, Eclipse PDT, 16–18

float type, 253

floor() function, 248

flush() function, 92

fopen() function, 143, 186, 189

for statements, 36

    alternative syntax for, 120–121

    differences between, 113–117

    linear, criteria for, 56

    MySQL queries in, 218

    nonlinear, refactoring to be linear, 58, 63–64, 65, 66–69

    similarities of, 108

forward slash (/)

    path separator, 178, 196

    in XML tags, 227

fputs() function, 189

fread() function, 143, 186

fs module, 50

    chmod() function, 197

    chown() function, 197

    close() function, 50, 51, 53, 187, 188, 190

    createReadStream() function, 180, 189

    exists() function, 191

    open() function, 50, 51, 53, 186

    read() function, 187

    readFile() function, 178, 179

    readFileSync() function, 177

    realpath() function, 193, 247

    stat() function, 192

    write() function, 50, 51, 53, 58

    writeFile() function, 182

    writeFileSync() function, 182

function arguments

    default values for, 155–156

    passing by reference, 151, 152–155

    passing by value, 151, 152

function calls, 109

function keyword, v, 14, 109, 158

function scope, 151–156

function type, 127, 144

fwrite() function, 143

G

get attribute, 165

$_GET PHP variable, 29–32

O

object literals
    converting PHP associative arrays to, 129–131
    creating objects using, 163–164
object type, 126, 127, 128
object-relational mapping (ORM), 203
objects (see classes)
ODBC (Open Database Connectivity), 202
on() function, 32
open() function, fs module, 50, 51, 53, 186
openMemory() method, 229, 229
operators
    array union operator, 112
    conditional operators, 108
    dot operator (.), 111, 131, 139, 165
    math operators, 108
    pair operator (=>), 129
    pointer operator (->), 165
    similarities of, 108
    string concatenation operators, 110
ord() function, 252
ORM (object-relational mapping), 203
os module, 182
outputMemory() method, 229, 230

P

packages, 3
    (see also specific packages)
page() function, 31–31, 42–45
pair operator (=>), 129
parent keyword, 173–175
parentheses (( )), defining precedence, 108
parse() JSON method, 225
parseFromString() method, 233
passing arguments
    by reference, 151, 152–155
    by value, 151, 152
path module
    basename() function, 194, 246
    dirname() function, 194, 247
    extname() function, 194
    sep constant, 196
pathinfo() function, 194–196
PDO_MySQL functions, 200, 204
PEAR (PHP Extension and Application Repository), 224

percent sign (%)
    remainder operator, 108
    in URL-encoded data, 219
permissions for files, 197–198
persistencejs package, 203
PHP
    compared to Node.js, v, 47, 49
    converting to Node.js, vi–ix, 5–7, 25–28, 42–45, 52–57, 241–242
    global variables
        $_COOKIE variable, 34–35
        $_GET variable, 29–32
        implementing in Node.js, 29–41
        $_POST variable, 32–34
        $_REQUEST variable, 35–37
        $_SESSION variable, 37–41
    history of, 47
    learning, vi
    MySQL access from, 200
    version 4
        file() function, 183
        file_get_contents() function, 177
        libraries for JSON data, 224
        mysql functions, 200
        reasons to support, 73
        refactoring to be like Node.js, 73–87
    version 5
        exceptions, 179
        file_put_contents() function, 181
        mysqli functions, 200
    version 5.1
        PDO functions, 200
        XML support, 227
    version 5.2
        JSON support, 224
    version 5.3
        callback variables, 144
        refactoring to be like Node.js, 69–73
    versions of, vii
PHP Extension and Application Repository (PEAR), 224
<?php tag, 92
php.js license, 258
PHP_EOL constant, 182
plain text data format, 221–223
plus sign (+)
    addition operator, 107, 108
    array union operator, 112
    double (++), increment operator, 108

string concatenation operator, 110
pointer operator (->), 165
$_POST PHP variable, 32–34
Postgres database, 203
preg_match() function, 252
print keyword, 92
__proto__ property, 163, 171
prototype object, 159
prototype property, 163, 171
prototype-based object system, 157
push() method, arrays, 133

Q

query arguments, for HTTP GET requests, 29
query() method, 206–207, 208, 211, 215
question mark (?)
    in inline conditional, 109, 118
    preceding query arguments, 29
    in URL-encoded data, 219

R

rand() function, 249
rawurldecode() function, 255
rawurlencode() function, 255
read() function, fs module, 187
readFile() function, fs module, 94, 178, 179
readFileSync() function, fs module, 177–179
realpath() function, PHP and fs module, 193, 247
regular expressions
    in Find/Replace, 17
    functions for, 252
request object (see HTTP request object)
$_REQUEST PHP variable, 35–37
$_REQUEST variable, 99
require() function, 3, 21, 22
resource type, 126, 143
response object (see HTTP response object)
right angle bracket (>)
    greater than operator, 108
    in XML tags, 227
right angle bracket, equals (>=), greater than or equal operator, 108
round() function, 249
rtrim() function, 251

S

sax-js package, 236–239
scope of variables, 126, 148–156
    class scope, 151
    function scope, 151–156
    global scope, 148–149
    local scope, 149
    static scope, 150–151
search command, npm, 4
SELECT SQL statement, 208–209, 212–215
semicolon (;)
    ending statements, vii, 108
    separating SQL statements, 206
sep constant, path module, 196
sequelize package, 203
serve() function, file serving object, 22–24, 25, 28, 96, 102
Server() function, node-static module, 22
Services_JSON PEAR package, 224
$_SESSION PHP variable, 37–41
set attribute, 165
setIndent() method, 229, 229
sha1() function, 254
SimpleXML functions, 230–231
single quotes('), enclosing string literals, 109
slash (/), division operator, 108
sort() function, 245
sparse arrays, 133–135
splice() method, arrays, 138
SQL language, 202
    (see also MySQL database)
    CREATE TABLE statement, 207–208
    DELETE statement, 211–211
    DROP TABLE statement, 208
    INSERT statement, 210, 216
    SELECT statement, 208–209, 212–215
    UPDATE statement, 209–210
    USE statement, 206
SQLite database, 203
square brackets ([]), for array and object indexes, 108, 129, 130, 139
stack traces, analyzing, 7–9
startDocument() method, 229
startElement() method, 229
stat() function, PHP and fs module, 192
static keyword, 175–176
static scope, 150–151
stats variable, 192
strcasecmp() function, 250

strcmp() function, 249
string concatenation operators, 110
string functions, 249–252, 253
string literals, 109–112
string type, 126, 127, 128, 253
stringify() JSON method, 225
strip_tags() function, 250
strpos() function, 250
strtolower() function, 252
strtoupper() function, 252
str_replace() function, 250
substr() function, 250
switch statement, alternative syntax for, 122–123

T

temporary files, 196
text (plain) data format, 221–223
text editors, 9, 10
text functions, 254–256
    (see also string functions)
that variable, 162–162
this variable, 161–162
time and date functions, 246–246
time() function, 246
toString() method, 229, 230
trim() function, 251
typeof operator, 127, 146, 147, 155
types (see variables: types of)

U

undefined type, 127, 144–148
unknown type, 126, 127, 144
unset() function, 144–146
UPDATE SQL statement, 209–210
URL-encoded data, 219
urldecode() function, 255
urlencode() function, 256
USE SQL statement, 206
user-defined functions, nonlinear, 59–62
util module, inspect() function, 31

V

v8.h include file, 201
var statement, 126, 126
variables
    array variables (see arrays)

declaring, 126, 126
functions for, implemented for Node.js, 257
in classes, 158–159, 175–176
naming conventions for, 125
scope of, 126, 148–156
types of, 126–127, 143–144, 253–254

W

web server
    converting PHP files to Node.js for, 25–28
    creating, 21–25
    Node.js as, 21
    starting, 2
    for static content (see node-static module)
while statements
    alternative syntax for, 121–122
    linear, criteria for, 56
    similarities of, 108
writable attribute, 164
write() function
    fs module, 50, 51, 53, 58
    response object, 91, 93, 98, 100, 102
writeAttribute() method, 229
writeFile() function, fs module, 182
writeFileSync() function, fs module, 182
writeHead() function, response object, 90, 101, 103

X

XML data format, 226–240
    DOM functions, 231–235
    node-xml-writer package, 228–230
    sax-js package, 236–239
    SimpleXML functions, 230–231
    XML Parser functions, 235–239
    xmldom package, 232–235
    XMLReader functions, 239–240
    XMLWriter class, 228–230
XML Parser functions, 235–239
xmldom package, 232–235
XMLReader functions, 239–240
XMLWriter class, 228–230

Z

Zend Server Community Edition (CE), 10

About the Author

Daniel Howard has worked as a software developer for over 20 years. He has worked at startups, Fortune 500 companies, and a range of companies in between. Currently, he is a Senior Principal Engineer at Ricoh Americas Corporation where he has worked for the past 10 years.

He is also the founder and maintainer of the ajaximrpg open source project and a maintainer of the Ajax IM open source project. Both projects use PHP and Node.js and use techniques directly from this book.

He believes that everybody can benefit from understanding a range of technologies, both old and new.

Colophon

The animal on the cover of *Node.js for PHP Developers* is the Wallachian or Cretan sheep, which is found in Crete, Wallachia, Hungary, and Western Asia. Their horns are exceedingly large and twisted and their bodies are very strong—they are said to be extremely vicious and unruly. Their fleece is composed of a mix of wool and hair, which makes it long and silky, like that of a spaniel, and of great length, falling almost to the ground.

They are large animals with long, deep trunks. Their tails are long (60–65 centimeters), broad, and fat at the base, gradually narrowing toward the end. They are used for the production of wool, meat, and milk.

Their horns are their most striking feature. The first spiral turn is always the largest, and the horns are not precisely the same in every specimen. In the ram, they usually spring perpendicularly from the ridge of the frontal bone, and then take a spiral form. In the female, they protrude nearly at right angles from the head, and then become twisted in a singular way.

The cover image is from *Shaw's Zoology*. The cover font is Adobe ITC Garamond. The text font is Adobe Minion Pro; the heading font is Adobe Myriad Condensed; and the code font is Dalton Maag's Ubuntu Mono.

Have it your way.

Get even more for your money.

Join the O'Reilly Community, and register the O'Reilly books you own. It's free, and you'll get:

- $4.99 ebook upgrade offer
- 40% upgrade offer on O'Reilly print books
- Membership discounts on books and events
- Free lifetime updates to ebooks and videos
- Multiple ebook formats, DRM FREE
- Participation in the O'Reilly community
- Newsletters
- Account management
- 100% Satisfaction Guarantee

Signing up is easy:

1. Go to: oreilly.com/go/register
2. Create an O'Reilly login.
3. Provide your address.
4. Register your books.

Note: English-language books only

To order books online:
oreilly.com/store

For questions about products or an order:
orders@oreilly.com

To sign up to get topic-specific email announcements and/or news about upcoming books, conferences, special offers, and new technologies:
elists@oreilly.com

For technical questions about book content:
booktech@oreilly.com

To submit new book proposals to our editors:
proposals@oreilly.com

O'Reilly books are available in multiple DRM-free ebook formats. For more information:
oreilly.com/ebooks

Spreading the knowledge of innovators   oreilly.com

CPSIA information can be obtained at www.ICGtesting.com
Printed in the USA
BVOW061153041212

307217BV00001B/1/P

9 781449 333607